Jacob V. Brower

The Missouri River and its Utmost Source

curtailed narration of geologic, primitive and geographic distinctions descriptive of

the evolution and discovery of the River and its headwaters

Jacob V. Brower

The Missouri River and its Utmost Source
*curtailed narration of geologic, primitive and geographic distinctions descriptive of the
evolution and discovery of the River and its headwaters*

ISBN/EAN: 9783337302276

Printed in Europe, USA, Canada, Australia, Japan

Cover: Foto ©Andreas Hilbeck / pixelio.de

More available books at **www.hansebooks.com**

THE MISSOURI RIVER

AND

ITS UTMOST SOURCE

———

CURTAILED NARRATION OF GEOLOGIC PRIMITIVE AND GEOGRAPHIC
DISTINCTIONS DESCRIPTIVE OF THE EVOLUTION AND DIS-
COVERY OF THE RIVER AND ITS HEADWATERS

———

CONTAINING AN
ARCHÆLOGICAL ADDENDUM NARRATING DESCRIPTION OF EXAMINATIONS

FIRST: AT THE HEADWATERS OF THE MISSOURI.
SECOND: FORT FLAT MOUTH.
THIRD: QUIVIRA; THE ELLIOTT INDIAN VILLAGE SITE.

WITH AN APPENDIX

———

BY HON. J. V. BROWER
AUTHOR OF
THE MISSISSIPPI RIVER AND ITS SOURCE
PREHISTORIC MAN AT THE HEADWATERS OF THE MISSISSIPPI, ETC

———

PROFUSELY ILLUSTRATED

———

St. Paul, Minnesota, U. S. A
1897

To CUSHMAN K. DAVIS,

A SENATOR OF THE UNITED STATES:

For the sentiments expressed in your "Modern Feudalism," every prediction of which has been foreshadowed, and for the intense Americanism of your course in the Senate, permit me to dedicate to the remembrance of your faithful efforts the pages of this address.

JACOB V. BROWER.

SECOND EDITION.

FIVE HUNDRED COPIES, NUMBERED CONSECUTIVELY FROM
THREE HUNDRED AND ONE TO EIGHT HUNDRED,
BOTH INCLUSIVE.

To the HISTORICAL SOCIETY OF THE STATE OF MON-
TANA,

AND,

To the MANCHESTER GEOGRAPHICAL SOCIETY OF
ENGLAND,

the contents of this volume are respectfully addressed by the
author.

INTRODUCTORY COMMENTS.

Extant contemporaneous historic and scientific literature, alike in Europe and America, incidentally deplore the unnatural designation by several distinct names of the longest surface channel of water of the globe, perennially flowing from the summit of the Rocky Mountains, in a continuous and unbroken channel, to the seaboard at the delta of the Mississippi. The modern nomenclature of this channel which has been periodically attached is firmly entrenched in the pages of an unalterable historic record covering a period of about three hundred years. From a Mystic Basin among extinct volcanic craters in the Rocky Mountains, at the continental divide between Montana and Idaho, to the southern limit of the Alaska Basin, this channel up to this time bears no name. From the Alaska Basin down through the Centennial Valley to a point below the immediate vicinity of a picturesque and rocky red butte, this channel of water is known as Red Rock river; thence to the mouth of the Big Hole river, whence it has flowed past Beaver Head Rock, it is known as Beaver Head river; thence to the mouth of the Madison river it is known as the Jefferson Fork; thence to the channel of the Mississippi river it is known as the Missouri river; and thence to the Gulf of Mexico it is known as the Lower Mississippi river.

The excusable reason for this is found in the fact, that the march of civilized if not primitive life has spanned the continent to the westward from the East, discovering the central but shorter channel first; thence at the end of long intervals, other and further discoveries of the upper waters have been made and new names to the same channel selected, in honor of a band of Indians, a chief magistrate, or following some topographic or geologic feature. Had the discovery of this principal and chief river channel proceeded from the West toward the East, there would have been but one name for its entire course from the continental divide to the Gulf of Mexico, and the mouth of the Mississippi would be where is now the mouth of the Missouri.

These considerations do not necessarily conflict with the opinions and conclusions expressed in vol. vii. of the Minnesota State Historical Collections, as prepared under the immediate personal supervision of the writer, minutely describing the ultimate basin of the Mississippi. A regret may be expressed, however, that the fault of terminology, the westward march of discovery and civilization, and apparently, a primordial element in hydrography, have combined in forcing the selection of the shorter channel as the main river.

These papers have been gathered into this form for preservation and dissemination, preliminary to a final consummation of researches and explorations resulting from a desire to complete certain self-imposed geographic labors in the basin of the Mississippi, and if they throw any new light upon unsettled questions before the scientific world, that fact alone will compensate for efforts expended.

The very able gentlemen who have generously contributed toward a desired success of this labor, and without whose assistance a greater accuracy would be endangered, are entitled to the broadest recognition and acknowledgment, and the limited information possessed by the writer of these pages shall not be unduly enhanced by the results of the researches of others, and therefore to the fullest extent the remarkably unselfish aid extended to me by abler writers will be fully recognized and credited in the preparation of the text, incidentally collaborated herewith and made the most interesting portion of the same, in addition to specific endorsement.

J. V. B.

St. Paul, Minn., May 1, 1896.

UTMOST BRANCH OF THE MISSOURI.
Above Upper Red Rock Lake, Montana.
Alaska Basin in the distance.

PREFACE TO SECOND EDITION.

The first edition of this publication, consecutively numbered from one to three hundred, both inclusive, while apparently complete, contained no detailed chart, and the most important topographic features at the utmost limit of the Missouri Basin remained unexamined.

During the year 1896 surveys and explorations at and above the Red Rock lakes, Montana, were continued, preparatory to a more comprehensive description of an interesting mountainous region scarcely known and meagerly understood by geographic students and historians.

Other and miscellaneous examinations were carried forward, incident to the principal labor, and all the work of the past year is included in this edition, numbered three hundred and one to eight hundred, octavo volumes, with a reprint of an official report, in the appendix, particularly describing the utmost basin of the Mississippi, deemed desirable, since the two principal rivers of North America are closely united in one system. No preponderating hydrographic or topographic feature of the headwater basin of either of the two rivers has escaped thorough exploration, and to that extent the result of my work must stand or fall on the merits of each record.

No misleading purpose or personal end has been permitted to intervene, derogatory to the truth of geographic history, or the honor due the memory of the earliest discoverers.

No original discovery by legitimate explorers has received at my hands other than a commendatory recognition, but irresponsible adventurers, found falsifying the record, have been exposed, and the correctness of their statements challenged.

The present opportunity is available to refer to and describe the scope of the work, intended to be at least partially accomplished, when the determination was reached to explore the country lying between Lake Superior and the crest of the Rocky Mountains, which encompasses the headwater region of the Mississippi, and of the Missouri; thereby perfecting some studies in geographic nomenclature and other conditions, and obtaining a more comprehensive knowledge of the early advance by prehistoric man, and his descendants and successors in the Northwest.

The first principle that suggested itself was the cause which precipitated the water to the hemispheres, if such ex-

2

isted, previous to the appearance of any form of life. Evolution thence made possible river channelling, and the spontaneity of the emergence of man naturally followed the preparations of nature for his appearance and reception.

That at once presents a suppositious force resulting in the original formation of our planet—the earth—from the elements extant in space in mechanical combination and chemical unity.

Such a tremendous energy, in its physical volume, must necessarily have been electric. If that be true, the formation of electricity is as simple as it is forcible, and, as applied to the original precipitation by the natural energies, of earth, of water, of air, a combination resulting in spontaneous production, presented the opportunity for the appearance of life, changeable in form by the lapse of time, the modification of climate, and the happening of events.

The electric energy may come from a sensitized vapor, for incidental experiments in analytical and technical chemistry, by the analysis of various substances pertaining to the electric current, indicate beyond any reasonable doubt that electricity is a complex compound of oxygen, carbon and hydrogen, produced by friction or oxidation. In all batteries it is necessary to have a negative and positive element, hence the negative and positive poles. The rule holds good for the different kinds of electric currents, and the ultimate cause of the different currents produced is due to the incidental arrangement of the electric molecule, and the same rule applies to the electric current generated by the dynamo. No element can result or escape from such oxidation or friction, except oxygen, carbon and hydrogen. If this be true, at a time when the elements pervaded the universe, a complex mixture would certainly have generated such a tremendous electric energy in the recesses of all space, that forcible tribute to the precipitation of planets resulted, and the earth, as a molten mass of magma, was formulated, and the beginning of the encrustment of the cooling surface made possible the saturation which superinduced evaporation, rainfall, the earliest existence of life beginning in the sea, the coal measures, river channelling, mountain building, the intermediate forms of vertebrata, and finally, the appearance of man in at least two zones of temperature, one with the existence of pigment in the cuticle, and one without it; the former, black, and the latter, white.

The foregoing considerations brought about a desire to more fully understand the exact status of the man of the North and the man of the South. Coincident therewith, painstaking efforts were usual in connection with a desire to secure a preserved investment or epidermis in contact with copper, from some characteristic prehistoric interment, that the color of the Mound-Builder might be physically demonstrated, in proof of the usually accepted theory that they were, in fact, the ancestry of a portion of the numerous tribes of the North American Indians of the Columbian period.

Such a belief is strengthened and sustained by the widespread distribution of the tumuli existing from the Lake of the Woods to the Gulf of Mexico and from the Atlantic seaboard to the Rocky Mountains. A numerous people would not wholly disappear, under ordinary circumstances, from the localities of such a widespread distribution, and be succeeded by an entirely different tribal occupancy, without some authenticated legendary information concerning their existence, their departure or disappearance, and some description of the advent of a succeeding occupancy. To that extent my views have been slightly modified, that they may conform to certain ascertained facts in connection with incidental explorations in the West and Northwest.

Arduous preparations have constantly been under way for the formulation of a detailed chart, covering the entire field of my explorations, and the adjacent localities identical in hydrographic importance.

The prehistoric Northwest in its archæologic significance has received such careful attention, that explorations have been extended to partially cover the territory from the headwaters of the Mississippi to the utmost limit of the basin of the Missouri.

Manuscripts, maps, photographs, field notes, and a miscellaneous collection of material for a history of the Sibley expedition against the Sioux Indians, in 1863, with which I served as a volunteer cavalryman, had been accumulated, until all necessary material was available and ready for immediate use.

A discovery of the position of the Province of Quivira, and its village sites, in Kansas, between 39° and 40° north latitude, has probably been effected, after 356 years since the Spaniards, under Coronado, strangled "The Turk" and looted the locality.

From May, 1860, when I became a resident of the Ojibway country in Northern Minnesota, until December, 1897, a valuable accumulation of historic, geographic, hydrographic and archæologic data had been collected for preservation.

The archæologic collection of stone implements and ornaments came from every state and territory in the United States, including 650 Quiviran flint knives, tomahawks, spears and points, from Kansas, the Itasca lake collection, and the Montana obsidian implements.

On the 19th day of December, 1896, at St. Paul, Minn., the *entire* accumulation was destroyed by fire.

This volume was in press, and thereby preserved.

Certain fossiliferous blocks from the summit of the Rocky Mountains, indicating the age of the Carboniferous, were also preserved, and an illustration, accompanied by an opposite page description, was available, and is included within subsequent pages.

A description of the excavation of a large mound near the mouth of Blue river, Kansas, by Mr. C. P. Blachley, and the late Prof. B. F. Mudge, was received too late for use in connection with the article relating to the Elliott Indian Village site, and the discovery of Quivira, if such it be.

Two important documents, one from the pen of Hon. Granville Stuart, of South America, defining the true meaning of the name Tozabe-Shock-up, as applied to Montana, meaning, "The Country of the Mountains," and one from the Kanza Indians, declaring that they do not know the meaning of the word "Kaw" or Kanza," both procured for publication herewith, were destroyed.

During 1896 numerous friends and advisers have extended very valuable aid, many of whom are unmentioned under the head of personal acknowledgments, and there is no data from which to express a merited gratitude to them, except by the recollection of occurrences or the printed text. Memories are defective, but the force of events is a reminder of some obligations that cannot justly be ignored, and I therefore beg the following gentlemen to accept the expressions of my most respectful esteem:

Mr. James Blair, of Magdalen, Montana.

Prof. Thomas A. Edison, of Orange, New Jersey.

Mr. J. A. Coulter, of Dawson, North Dakota.

Mr. L. R. Elliott, of Manhattan, Kansas.

Mr. W. J. Griffing, of Manhattan, Kansas.

Mr. Henry Hackett, of Magdalen, Montana.

Mr. W. J. Whitefield, of Sauk Center, Minnesota.

To Prof. N. Lehnen, Ph. D., a graduate of the University of Göttingen, I am indebted for numerous and exhaustive personal discussions on the question of the electric forces in nature.

To Mr. Cyrus C. Adams, and Mr. George C. Hurlbut, of the American Geographical Society, is extended the declaration that I appreciate the comprehensiveness of their views upon geographical questions.

A learned physician of New York favored me immeasurably on the question of pigment. The papers were burned with the name and address, and to my sorrow, no credit is extended.

J. V. B.

St. Paul, Jan. 1, 1897.

VIEWS ON THE UTMOST BRANCH OF THE MISSOURI RIVER.

In the Rocky Mountains, State of Montana.

Obverse.

Reverse.

A MEDAL COIN-RELIC OF THE PAST, FOUND IN MONTANA.

From a Photo by F. Jay Haynes, the owner.

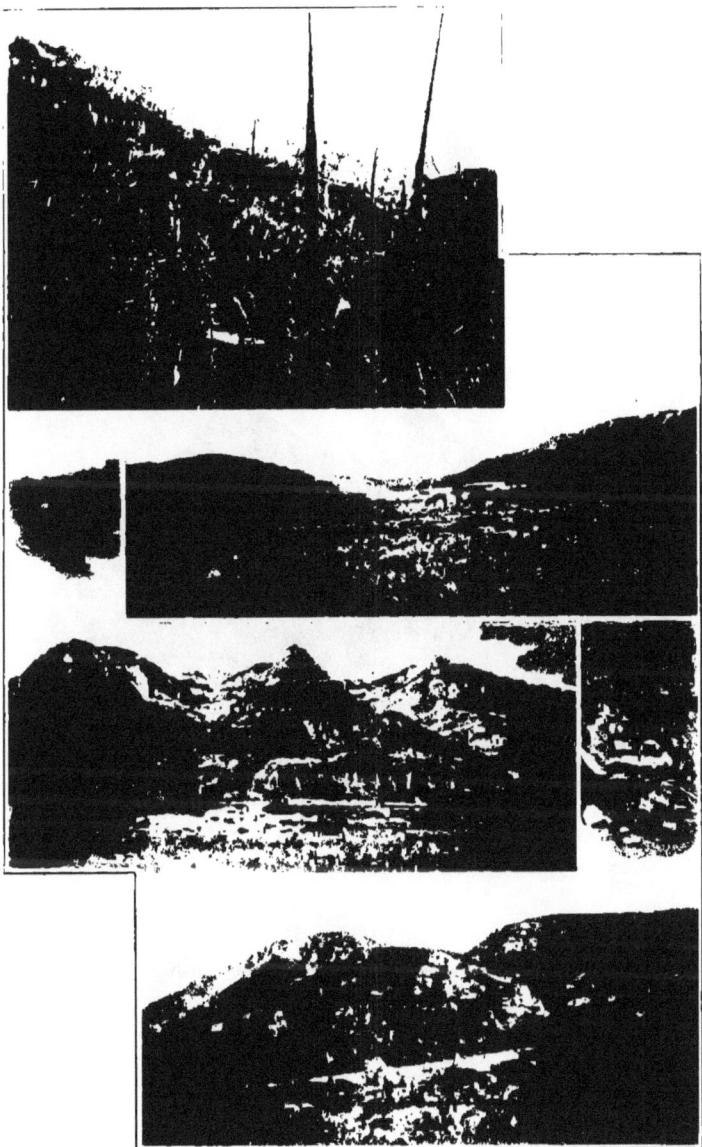

ON THE MISSOURI, SUMMIT OF THE MOUNTAINS.
                    VIEW NEAR UPPER RED ROCK LAKE.
SNOW-CAPPED RANGE, CENTENNIAL VALLEY.
                    BASE OF THE ROCKY MOUNTAINS

MONTANA MOUNTAIN VIEWS.

MR. D. F. BARRY.
The accomplished photographer of many of the wildest Indians of the Upper
Missouri.

PI-ZI. (Chief Gall.)

The noted Sioux warrior who led the Indian forces at the Custer massacre.

DR. A. C. PEALE,
Leader of the Exploratory Examination at Upper Red Rock Lake, Montana, 1872.

THE MARQUIS DE NADAILLAC.

Comprehensive Author of *Prehistoric America.*

(TRANSLATED BY N. D'ANVERS.)

(EDITED BY W. H. DALL.)

GEN. BENJAMIN L. E. BONNEVILLE.
By courteous permission of Nathaniel Pitt Langford.

GEN. BENJAMIN L. E. BONNEVILLE.

"Bvt. Brig. Gen. Benjamin L. E. Bonneville, the last survivor of the West Point class of 1815, died June 12, 1878, at Fort Smith, Ark., at the advanced age of eighty-five. He was born in France during the Reign of Terror, in the eventful year 1793, when Louis XVI. and Marie Antoinette were beheaded; in which Marat was assassinated and Danton guillotined; when the Revolutionary Tribunal was established and the Girondists fell; in which war was declared against England, Spain, and Holland, and insurrection triumphed in La Vendeé; when royal tombs were desecrated, the Sabbath abolished, and the Goddess of Reason worshiped; and in which, throughout the new republic, horrors on horrors accumulated.

"Bonneville's father, a man of classic culture, was a member of the National Convention and the intimate friend of Condorcet, Lafayette, and Thomas Paine. By nature earnest and excitable, he dared years later to denounce, in the 'Bien Informé,' which he edited, the rising Bonaparte as the Cromwell of France, for which his journal was suppressed and himself and family forced to emigrate to America. Taking up his abode in New York City, he mingled little with the money-making world, preferring his elysium in the pages of Voltaire, Corneille, Racine, or Shakespeare. Almost on any summer's day he was to be seen, book in hand, under one of the Battery trees, or in the shadow of St. Paul's church, little heeding, in his poetic dreams, the passing throng or the passing hour.

"The son, inheriting the ardent temperament of his father, decided to follow the stirring and adventurous career of a soldier."—"Biographical Register," U. S. Mil. Academy, 1891, vol. i., p. 146.

The record that follows is a remarkable one:

Appointed to West Point from New York, April 14, 1813. Graduated and appointed brevet second lieutenant, Dec. 11, 1815. On leave, secretary to Lafayette, voyage to France, 1825. Returned to military service in the West, 1826. Granted leave of absence, Aug. 3, 1831, until October, 1833, "on condition, that, without any expense to the government, Bonneville was to provide himself with maps, instruments, and a complete outfit to explore the country to the Pacific; ascertain the nature, character, and mode of warfare of the Indian tribes; the agricultural and mineral resources of the Great West," etc.

Left Fort Osage on the Missouri with 120 men and twenty ox and mule teams for the Rocky Mountains May 1, 1832. Up the Sweetwater, through the Black Hills July 20, 1832. Crossed Rocky Mountains and reached Salmon river Sept. 19, 1832, to cantonment. Starvation drove the party back to Snake river, in sight of the Three Tetons, Jan. 13, 1833. Returned to Salmon river with terrible suffering, March 11, 1833. Sent expedition to Basin of Great Salt Lake, 1833. To a winter encampment near Portneuf river close of 1833. Left with three companions for Columbia river, Dec. 25, 1833. With terrible suffering, sixty-six days' travel brought them to the Columbia river at Fort Walla Walla, March 4, 1834. Returned to Portneuf, through much suffering, May 18, 1834. Reached Little Snake river June 13, 1834. Expedition sent to Great Salt Lake now returned. One detachment sent to St. Louis and one to Black Hills. Bonneville and twenty-three men commenced a return to the Columbia Blue Mountains, Oct. 1, 1834, and back to Snake river Oct. 20, 1834. Cantonment on Bear river, November, 1834 to April 1, 1835. At Wind River Mountains, June 10, 1835. "Tatterdemallion band" reached the frontier, Nebraska, Aug. 22, 1835. Absent without leave, the secretary of war had dropped his name from the army rolls. Restoration refused. President Jackson ordered his restoration. Served under General Scott in Mexican War. Retired with rank of Colonel, Sept. 9, 1861. Brevetted brigadier general, for long and faithful service, March 13, 1865. Died June 12, 1878, at Fort Smith, Ark., aged eighty-five years.

Adjutant General's Office,
Washington, 31 May, 1834.

Order No. 42.

Captain Bonneville of the 7th Regiment of Infantry, having been absent without leave since October, 1833, is this day, by order of the President of the United States, dropped from the rolls of the army.

By order of Major General Macomb.

R. JONES, Adjt. Genl.

Adjutant General's Office,
Washington, April 22, 1836.

General Order No. 25.

I. Captain B. L. E. Bonneville is reinstated in the army, and by the President, by and with the advice and consent of the Senate, is restored to his former rank and regiment, as captain in the 7th Infantry, to rank as such, from the 4th of October, 1825.

II. Captain Bonneville will immediately proceed to Fort Gibson, report for duty and join his company.

[L. S.]

By order:
R. JONES, A. G.

MR. WILLIAM N. CULVER.
Resident near Culver's Cañon, Montana.

Lillian Hackett Culver

MRS. MARY J. BLAKE,
Collector of Archæologic Material,
Red Rock Lakes, Montana.

MRS. CLARA SHANGLE.

Lady tourist to Missourian *Caldera*, 1896, after whom Shangle Peak was named.

MR. R. W. ROCK.

Expert Hunter in the Rocky Mountains. Game preserve at Lake Henry, Idaho.

MRS. R. W. ROCK.

VIEW AT THE SOURCE OF THE MISSOURI RIVER.

VIEW AT CULVER'S CAÑON. MONTANA.

EXPLORATION OF CULVER'S CAÑON.

August, 1895.

VIEW ABOVE HANSON MOUNTAIN.
(From the bed of the stream.)

VIEW ABOVE HANSON MOUNTAIN.
(Looking down the stream.)

OBSIDIAN CHIPPED IMPLEMENTS.
From the Centennial Valley, Montana.

FOSSILIFEROUS SPECIMEN FOUND ON THE SOUTHERN SLOPE OF
BROWER PEAK.

Main Range of the Rocky Mountains.

(See opposite page explanatory note.)

THE BROWER PEAK FOSSIL DEPOSIT.

The opposite page illustrates one of a large number of fossiliferous blocks discovered on the southern slope of Brower Peak, near the crest. From Burnside Mountain to the Missourian *caldera*, quantities of fossiliferous rocks were discovered and collected. From the center of a fractured rock a trilobite, in a perfect state of fossilized preservation, was removed. ,

The deposit at Brower Peak appears to have been sedimentary, and was compact, until broken and upheaved.

A quantity of the specimens collected was submitted for scientific examination, to Professor N. H. Winchell, geologist in charge of the Minnesota survey.

The conclusion arrived at is embodied in the following communication:

GEOLOGICAL AND NATURAL HISTORY SURVEY OF MINNESOTA.

N. H. WINCHELL,
  State Geologist.
U. S. GRANT,
  Assistant Geologist.   MINNEAPOLIS, MINN., Dec. 19th, 1896.

Hon. J. V. Brower, St. Paul, Minn.,

DEAR SIR: The specimens of fossiliferous limestone which you brought from a point on the southern slope of Brower Peak, near Henry lake, found in north latitude 44° 35', west longitude 111° 38', contain many fossils, among which the following are identifiable with tolerable certainty :

Phillipsia tuberculata   Meek and Worthen.
Spirifera camerata   Morton.
Productus cora   D'Orbigny.
The following are more doubtful:
Spiriferina kentuckensis   Shumard.
Athyris argentea   Shepard.
The following genera are also identified:
Straparollus, Setopora or *Fenestella*, and probably *Streptelasma*, with many crinoidal remains.

The group of fossils indicates the age of the Carboniferous, probably the horizon of the coal measures.

Very truly,

N. H. WINCHELL.

The specimens examined by Professor Winchell will be found on deposit with the Minnesota State Historical Society.

TREETOPS PROTRUDING THROUGH THE SNOW.   IN A DRIFT.
            BLAIR MOUNTAIN.   AT THE CRATER WALLS.

SNOW SCENES; CREST OF THE ROCKY MOUNTAINS.

June, 1896.

STONE MONUMENTS.

Erected by Messrs. Brower and Blair on the state boundary between Montana and Idaho. Missourian *Caldera*.

MR. L. R. ELLIOTT.
Of Manhattan, Kansas

Sketch of the
ELLIOTT INDIAN VILLAGE SITE
Situated upon
Section 1, Township 12. S. Range 7 E.
Geary County, Kansas
North Latitude 39° West Longitude 96°35'.

Drawn by
J.V. Brower
1897

Distance from the Kansas River, South, seven miles.
2000 stone knives, axes, hammers, cells, spears and arrow-
points have been found at the site of this Indian Village.

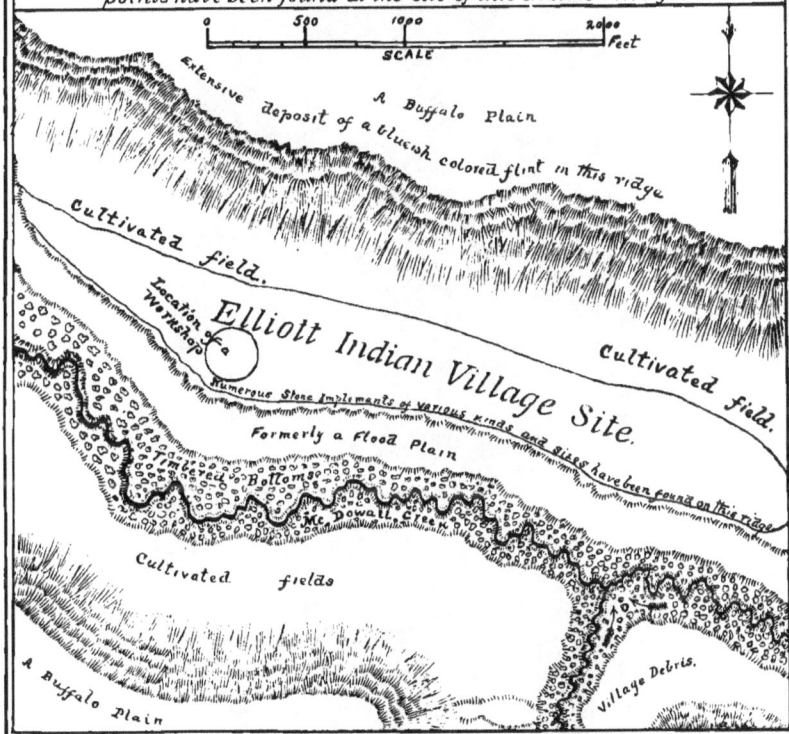

0   500   1000   2000
                                             Feet
              SCALE

Extensive deposit of a bluish colored flint in this ridge

A Buffalo Plain

Cultivated field.

Location of a Workshop

Elliott Indian Village Site.

Numerous Stone Implements of various kinds and sizes have been found on this ridge.

Cultivated field.

Formerly a Flood Plain

Timbered Bottoms

Mc Dowall Creek.

Cultivated fields

A Buffalo Plain

Village Debris.

IS THIS A VILLAGE SITE OF THE QUIVIRAN PROVINCE?

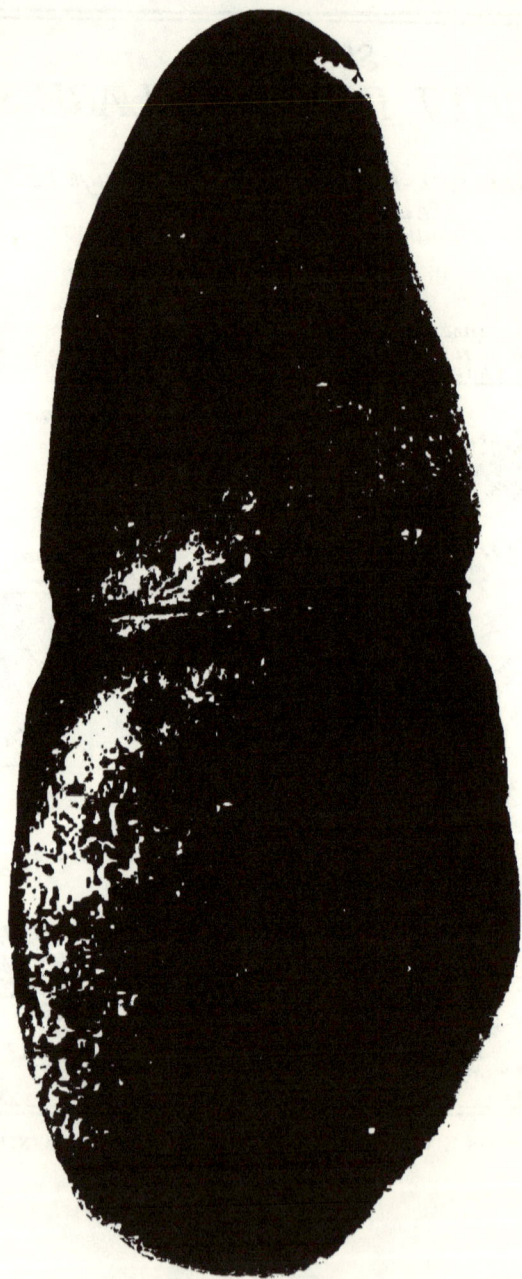

GROOVED LIMESTONE AXE.
From the Elliott Indian Village Site.
One-half natural size.

SINGLE FLINT TOMAHAWK.
From the Elliott Indian Village Site.
Natural size.

SINGLE FLINT TOMAHAWK.

From the Elliott Indian Village Site.

Natural size.

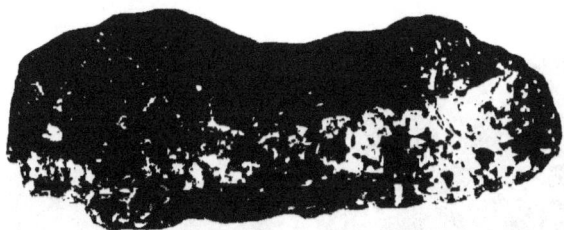

DOUBLE FLINT TOMAHAWKS.

From the Elliott Indian Village Site.

Natural sizes

4

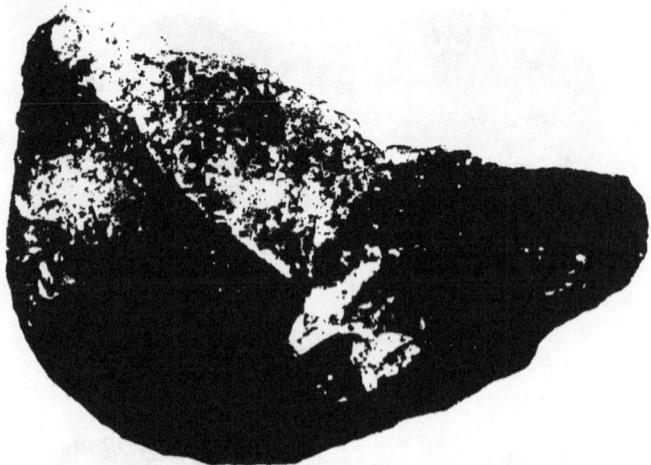

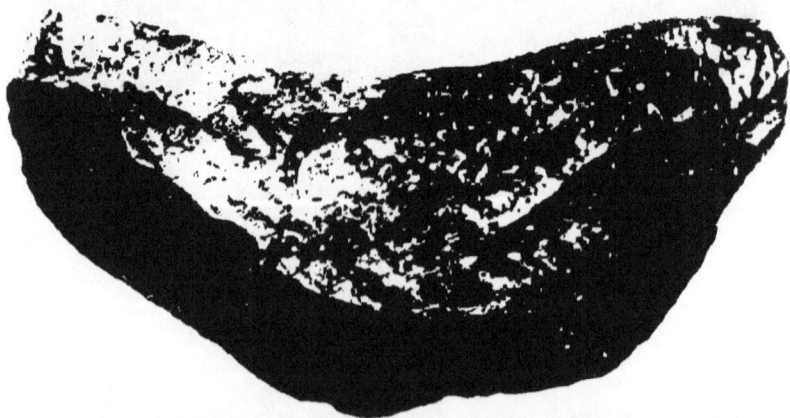

QUIVIRAN FLINT KNIVES.
From the Elliott Indian Village Site.
Natural sizes.

FLAT MOUTH.

Esh-ke-bug-e-coshe. Warren.
Esh-ke-bug-i-ko-zhi. Gilfillan.
Aish-ke-bug-e-koshe. Treaties, U. S. 1873.
Translation: Bill-like-a-new-leaf.
Comment: Mouth large and strong, like a new leaf.

———

Flat Mouth was the most noted chief of the Pillager band of Ojibway Indians, who were so infamously designated from a circumstance which happened to a very early trader. They pillaged his boats and confiscated his goods, and the name has since followed them without interruption.

Flat Mouth and other chiefs and head men sold to the United States the upper or head-water basin of the Mississippi, except portions reserved.

Fort Flat Mouth, a prehistoric inclosure in Northern Minnesota, was so named by the author of this work, in December, 1896, from a desire to perpetuate and preserve certain historic facts relating to a conference between Flat Mouth and Hon. W. W. Warren, one of his people, concerning prehistoric earthworks in the regions of the north about the headwater branches of the Mississippi, which, erroneously, they attributed to the Gi-aucth-in-in-e-wug, or "men-of-the-olden-time," the Gros Ventres.

BUTCHER KNIFE.
The oldest Missourias Indian living.

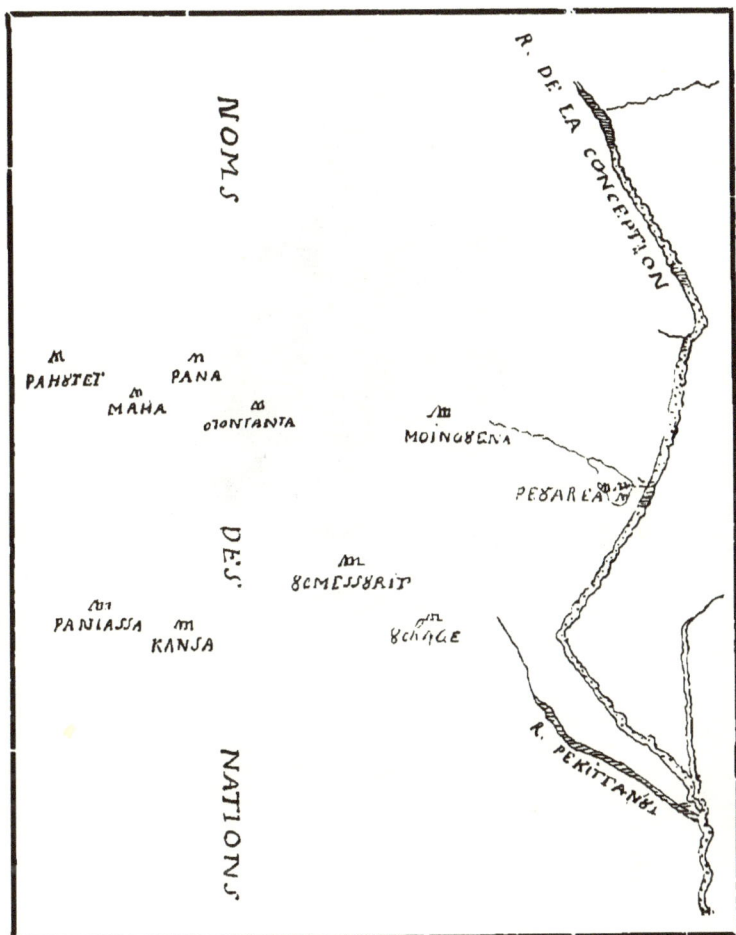

EXTRACT FROM MARQUETTE'S MAP OF R. PEKITTAN8I, 1673.

WHITE HORSE.

Chief of the Missouras Indians.

From a photograph by W. L. Sawyers.

(Identified by Mr. Sawyers, contrary to the Eleventh Census of the U. S. 1890.
Indians. p. 554.)

MISSOURIA INDIANS.

Represents present stage of tribal advancement.

From photographs taken in 1896, expressly for illustration.

REV. T. M. SHANAFELT, D. D.
In charge of over one hundred Baptist Churches in the Missouri Basin.

CONTENTS.

LIST OF ILLUSTRATIONS.

List of Illustrations.

List of Illustrations.

PERSONAL ACKNOWLEDGMENTS.

—

The following named gentlemen are entitled to sincere compliments for aid extended:

Prof. Warren Upham of St. Paul, Minn.

Prof. Henry W. Haynes of Boston, Mass.

Mr. Henry Gannett of Washington, D. C.

Prof. William H. Holmes of Chicago, Ill.

The Marquis de Nadaillac of Paris, France.

Dr. A. C. Peale of Philadelphia, Pa.

Mr. Geo. F. Gifford of St. Paul, Minn., Managing Editor of the Daily Globe.

Prof. George F. Becker of Washington, D. C.

M. Pierre Lefevre, Dautalie, of Paris, France.

Mr. David L. Kingsbury of St. Paul, Minn., Acting Librarian of the Minnesota State Historical Society.

Dr. Elliott Coues of Washington, D. C.

The Count de Bizemont of Paris, France.

Mr. Douglas Brymner of Ottawa, Canada.

Capt. Hiram M. Chittenden, United States Army.

Mr. Walter F. Cushing of Bismarck, N. D.

Mr. Nathaniel P. Langford of St. Paul, Minn.

Mr. William N. Culver of Magdalen, Mont.

Mr. D. F. Barry, Photographer of West Superior, Wis., who has permitted the use of valuable copyrighted photographs.

Mr. F. Jay Haynes, Photographer of St. Paul, Minn.

Hon. J. M. Page of Helena, Mont.

Mr. L. P. Sylvain of Ottawa, Canada.

Mr. Frederick I. Hanson of Magdalen, Mont.

Mr. L. R. Elliott of Manhattan, Kan.

Mr. James Blair of Magdalen, Mont.

Mr. J. P. Woolsey, Indian Service, Ponca, O. T.

Gen. Richard B. Hughes of Huron, S. D.

Mr. E. F. Higby of Bismarck, N. D.

Capt. J. A. Ockerson of St. Louis, Mo.

Mr. George H. Pegram, C. E., of Omaha, Neb.

Mr. O. C. Dallas of Helena, Mont.

Mr. Vic Smith of Anaconda, Mont.

Mr. James Hill of Newmarket, Ontario, Administrator of the estate of the late Alfred J. Hill.

Gen. John S. McNeill of Helena, Mont.

Mr. Harry Redfield of Twin Bridges, Mont.

Hon. W. W. Alderson of Bozeman, Mont.

Mr. William McCabe of Pocatello, Idaho.

Mr. R. R. Cummins of Glendive, Mont.
Mr. William Garland of Lima, Mont.
Mr. A. S. Garland of Lima, Mont.
Mr. Isaac Jaques of Lima, Mont.
Mr. William J. Seever of St. Louis, Mo.
Col. W. P. Clough of St. Paul, Minn.
Mr. Frederick Hein of St. Paul, Minn., who placed at my disposal the constant use of his private library.
Hon. Charles Aldrich, Curator and Secretary Historical Department of Iowa.
Capt. I. P. Baker, Bismarck, N. D.
Capt. William Braithwaite, Bismarck, N. D.
Rev. J. A. Gilfillan, White Earth, Minn.
Mr. M. W. Hutchinson, Bismarck, N. D.
Hon. J. T. McCleary, M. C., Washington, D. C.
Mr. J. B. Chaney, St. Paul, Minn.
Also to the following named ladies, I wish to render acknowledgments for their assistance:
Mrs. Lillian Hackett Culver of Magdalen, Mont.
Mrs. D. B. Fiske of Coldwater, Mich.
Mrs. S. B. Burnside of Monida, Mont.
Mrs. Mary J. Blake of Magdalen, Mont.
Mrs. S. M. Sterrett of Lake City, Minn.
N. B.—It can be readily understood, that the books, reports, maps, and authorities examined and digested, in the preparation of the following pages, are so numerous that a direct reference to each would deteriorate and unnecessarily burden the text, since it is needful to curtail the same to a limited paging and a minimum edition. It would, nevertheless, be unjust not to admit my gratitude for the privilege of carefully and constantly referring to the following books, most of which are on the shelves of the Minnesota State Historical Society's library, unlimited access to which has been cheerfully accorded by a resolution of the council of the society:
Croll's *Climate and Time*, 1875, i.--xvi. and 1--577.
Geikie's *Great Ice Age*, 1875, i.--xxv. and 1--545.
Wright's *Ice Age in North America*, 1891, i.--xviii. and 1--648.
Wright and Upham's *Greenland Icefields*, 1896, i--x. and 1--407.
The United States and the several state *Geological Reports*.
Geological and Natural History Survey of Canada.
Capt. Wheeler's *U. S. Geographical Surveys*, 1889, i. and 1--780.
Nadaillac's *Prehistoric America*, 1893, 1--566.
Coues' *Lewis and Clark*, 1893, iv. vols.
Irving's *Astoria* and *Captain Bonneville*.
Chittenden's *Yellowstone National Park*, 1895, 1--397.

Records of the Missouri River Commission.

Records of the Mississippi River Commission.

For comprehensive and scientific discussions on all questions *The Encyclopedia Britannica* (European Edition), *The Century Dictionary,* and the scientific works quoted, published by the D. Appleton Co., have been found to be unsurpassed in usefulness, and invariably of the most reliable character as indispensable works of reference.

It is also desirable to acknowledge my great obligations for the use of the following described volumes, among the very many examined:

CURTAILED BIBLIOGRAPHICAL REFERENCES.

[List limited to this page except as quoted in the text.]

Contributions to the Historical Society of Montana, vol. i., 1876, pp. 1-357, and vol. ii., 1896, pp. 1-409.

Annual Reports of the Bureau of Ethnology, vols. i.--xii.

Minnesota State Historical Collections, vols. i.--vi.

Langford's *Vigilante Days and Ways,* 1893, ii. vols., pp. 426 and 485.

Jean N. Nicollet's Report, intended to illustrate a map of the Hydrographical Basin of the Upper Mississippi, 1843. Senate Doc. 237.

Fremont's *Report of the Exploring Expedition,* etc., 1842, '43, '44.

Gen. Raynold's Report, *Exploration of the Yellowstone.* 1868.

Ross's *Fur Hunters,* ii. vols., 1855.

French's *Historical Memoirs of Louisiana.* Series.

Scharf's *History of St. Louis,* 1883, ii. vols.

The Historical Works of Francis Parkman. Series.

Winsor's *Narrative and Crit. History of America.* Series.

Smithsonian Contributions to Knowledge. Series.

Collections of the State Historical Society of Wisconsin. Series.

Catlin's *North American Indians.* 1842, ii. vols.

Winsor's *Mississippi Basin.* 1895.

Relation des Jesuites, etc., dans la Nouvelle France, 1632--1672.

The Historical Works of John Gilmary Shea. Series.

Transactions of the Nebraska, Missouri, and Kansas State Historical Societies. Three series.

Sully's Indian Expedition of 1864, unpublished MSS. by Lieut. David L. Kingsbury.

Charlevoix's *History of New France,* Shea. Series.

Various Spanish, French, English and American Charts and Maps, Official Reports, Treaties, and Records.

THE LATE MISS FRANCES ELIZA BABBITT.

Born Jan. 24, 1824; died July 6, 1891.

Miss Babbitt removed from her home in Otsego county, N. Y., to Michigan, and thence, in 1873, to Minnesota, returning to Michigan in 1886. From her twentieth year, she was a teacher in public schools. The only portrait of Miss Babbitt, known to exist, forms part of an ambrotype group, from which the accompanying miniature reproduction has been made, slightly enlarged from the original, through the courtesy of Mrs. Delia B. Fiske. The name "Franc," by which the deceased has been known in archaeologic history, was assumed as an abbreviation of her first name. Her discovery of palaeolithic quartz implements, at Little Falls, Minnesota, has been held, by competent scientists, to be genuine, and therefore important, as an affirmative conclusion that man existed in the basin of the Mississippi at the close of the last glacial epoch, about B. C. 5000. Mr. J. H. Rhodes of Little Falls, Minnesota, writes: "I much regret that I have no photograph of Miss Babbitt. I know she had an antipathy to having her photo taken." The above is reproduced from the only portrait known to exist.

THE MISSOURI RIVER.

§ I. PRELIMINARY REFERENCES.

Those who desire to study and adequately understand the physical conditions surrounding the ultimate source of the Mississippi and Missouri rivers, which, combined, constitute one of the most important and the longest river channel of modern times, are respectfully referred to vol. vii., Minnesota State Historical Collections, entitled "The Mississippi River and Its Source," a copy of which, now especially and specifically mentioned, is needed as a desirable preliminary to an adequate conception of the work presented herewith.

This subject is mentioned here for the reason, that, throughout the enlightened world, a deep-seated conviction exists, that the shorter channel,—i. e. the Mississippi,—has, by the force of circumstances surrounding Western discoveries, usurped and supplanted the longer channel in the contemporaneity of extant geographical history [1] by a premature acceptation of its nomenclature, as at present constituted, and it is unlikely that there may be an opportunity for any change while the English-speaking generations of this Western hemisphere survive; and that report compared with the contents of these papers, refer particularly to that question.

The true length of the Mississippi from its Greater Ultimate Reservoir above Itasca lake, to the Gulf of Mexico is 2,553 miles by the channel of the river, whilst, on the other hand, the distance from the Ultimate Reservoir of the Missouri at the summit of the Rocky Mountains, along the channel of the main Missourian stream-bed to the Gulf, is more than 4,200 miles.

Still another curious result of piecemeal exploration in the gradual Western migration of geographical discoverers is the peculiar fact, that this principal Missourian stream-bed, maintaining a perennial flowage from the summit of the Mountains to the Gulf, is known and is now designated by no less than five different names, while the most remote branch, far beyond

---

[1] "As a general rule, the river which heads farthest from the sea, or which has the longest course, retains its name, while the affluents entering it lose their identity when merged in the larger stream. There are various exceptions to this, one of the most remarkable of which is the Mississippi, which retains that name to its mouth although the affluent called the Missouri is much longer than the Mississippi and somewhat larger at the junction."—"The Century," vol. v., p. 5106.

Many similar references could be collected and inserted herewith, of the same general tenor, but the facts are so well known that it has seemed unnecessary to do so, only a few being reserved for a general reference in the text, or otherwise.

the mountains bordering the valley surrounding the Upper Red Rock lake in the Centennial Valley of Montana, was, up to 1895, unknown, unnamed, and undescribed in any historic or geographical writing, and no record can be found of any visit to it, previous to the explorations conducted by the writer of these pages during the month of August, last year, if any such exists.

Toward the results of those explorations and some subsequent studies, with accompanying papers, the attention of the reader is now directed, trusting that the same may be received in a kindly spirit of critical consideration, commensurate with the desire for a more extended information that prompts these preparations, which, no doubt, are not without error of various kinds.

§ II. ELEMENTS OF NATURE.

It is a very simple proposition to ask what constitutes a river, and a correct answer is as easily formulated; but the question, How was the first river formed? goes deeper into inosculated sciences than the present generation has been able to fathom. Barely four centuries have elapsed since it was believed that the ships of Columbus would sail over the edge of the Ocean to certain destruction, and yet, even in Minnesota, near where these lines are written, we have rock in place over which the waters have passed for more than 50,000,000 years —upwards of 500,000 centuries! and life has existed for a much greater period of time.

The transparent and tasteless fluid, which becomes a solid ice at 32 degrees Fahrenheit and a vapor at 212 degrees Fahrenheit, normally, a liquid between the two extremes mentioned, and which is, chemically, "a compound substance, consisting of hydrogen and oxygen," 770 times heavier than the air we breathe, is the water we drink [2]—a necessity to physical life.

Heat, which is a sensation thrown off from an energy created by the combination of specific elements, commonly proceeds from conflagration caused by carbon in connection with oxygen, and in its greatest intensity has an unknown limit of more than 6,300 degrees Fahrenheit.

---

[2] Prof. W. A. Noyes, in an address before the Indiana Academy of Sciences (December, 1894) upon Lavoisier, referring to the theory of phlogiston, suggested a "step in the constant endeavor of the highest minds to tear away from before our eyes the things which are fortuitous and misleading and to get a little closer to the realities which lie at the basis of all material existence." Lavoisier [born 1743; executed 1794] was a scientific manufacturer of gunpowder, and experimented in endeavors to convert water into earthy matter, to ascertain the character of combustion and oxidation. His execution was on a trivial complaint, under Robespierre, and while pleading for a short respite that his chemical experiments might be completed.

The element commonly called air "is a respirable fluid which surrounds the earth and forms its atmosphere. It is inodorous, invisible, insipid, colorless, elastic, possessed of gravity, * * * rarified, and condensed, essential to respiration and combustion, and is the medium of sound. It is composed by volume of twenty-one parts of oxygen and seventy-nine of nitrogen. * * * These gases are not chemically united, but are mixed mechanically."

The physical condition commonly described as "cold" is a normal temperature, and when uninfluenced by any modification, undoubtedly descends in intensity to —461 degrees Fahrenheit. Throughout all space (which is nothing, and therefore has no limit, and is inconceivably endless) a normal congealing influence exists, which is necessary, near our planet, in connection with obverse influences, to cause rainfall, by expansion, absorption, suspension, and condensation, and thence to precipitation, and the constant repetition of these natural phenomena sustains animate existence. When these forces shall have gradually exhausted the power to shower their sustaining influence upon the surface of the earth, all life will as gradually disappear, and a future age will descend upon this planet with an intense severity. The time will come when researches into the past may demonstrate some probability of the course of natural events sure to follow in the coming successive ages.[3]

Scientific descriptions of the causes which formed the sun, earth, and planets are all problematic. The most acute and philosophical minds have been, and must continue to be, utterly incompetent to correctly determine the time and manner, when and how a great natural law concentrated the elements into the visible and wonderful combination of solids and vapors and fluids, metals and matter, magma and material, which have been forcibly thrown together in the formation now constituting the earth as a planet. There are, however, some considerations which may be drawn upon to somewhat strengthen probabilities, in the study of sun-spots, the depth of the atmosphere, the law of gravity, the existence of an unknown electrical quantity, and the cyclonic tendency demonstrated in meteorological phenomena, as compared with information gained from the observation of other planets, and the nu-

---

[3] "It is necessary to have a great mastery over the past and present condition of things to have much keen insight into the future."—CH. V. de Bonstetten's "Man of the North and Man of the South" (Translator's Preface).
See, also, "The Search for the Absolute Zero."—"McClure's Magazine," vol. iii., pp. 557-562, November, 1894.
Absolute absence of all heat; that is, zero—which must be temperature of space—is computed as —461 degrees Fahrenheit.
A temperature of —346 degrees has been attained. This is solidified air!
Greatest heat yet measured, 6,300 degrees Fahrenheit.

merous solar conditions existing as made available by astronomic researches. Whether electricity can be generated equally within the space of a perfect vacuum, as in the presence of a surrounding atmospheric body, is yet to be determined, as also the minutest reality in the character of the condition of the central force of cyclonic demonstrations in nature. The distribution of extant natural matter undoubtedly always existed in space, and whether electricity could cyclonically create an energy sufficient to inaugurate the original power of gravitation is conjectural. In that manner or by some similar stupendous force all nature was upheaved in the heavens above and beneath, whence followed in an unknown, undeterminable manner the conflagration that threw off the vapors and gases and concentrated the solids and fluids. Thence the introduction of a systematic order out of chaos; and air, water and earth, heat and light, were precipitated from this union of forces, as the children of an Impersonal, Imperial Parent, forcibly uniting protoplasmic properties to an extent sufficient to cause the induction of life itself, with the power and qualities of sexual reproduction. The magnificently wonderful distribution of the gifts of nature in the formation of the solar system, of which the earth is an insignificant part, reduces the conception of humanity to a vile ignorance, powerless in its temporary existence to accomplish or fathom any of the great laws creating, governing, and regulating the necessary conditions precedent to the first production of physical life, and its subsequent development and expansion, and thence to an absolutely certain extinction in the future ages to come.

Some correspondence on this question is deemed of sufficient importance to justify reproduction:

HYDROGRAPHY OF THE MISSISSIPPI BASIN.

St. Paul, Minnesota, March 20th, 1896.
Professor Thomas A. Edison,

Dear Sir: Will you please advise me if electricity can be generated in a perfect vacuum, such as is believed to exist beyond the atmospheric properties surrounding the world?

The information is desired for legitimate purposes, in a consideration of the scientific question concerning the original condensation of vaporous elements into water.

Trusting you may reply,   Very respectfully,
                                                            J. V. Brower.

FROM THE LABORATORY OF THOMAS A. EDISON.

(Phonograph Dictation.)
Orange, New Jersey, March 27th, 1896.
J. V. Brower, Esq., St. Paul, Minn.,

Dear Sir: In reply to your favor of the 20th inst., I beg to state that Electric Waves undoubtedly travel through the ether throughout the Universe. Sun spots disturb the Magnetic lines of the Earth.

Yours truly,
                                         Thomas A. Edison.

Fortunately, in the furtherance of an enlightened desire for information, the scientific principles of astronomy and geology have been applied, which, in connection with chemical and other researches, have broadened and strengthened the human mind to such an extent that the narrow and beaten path of superstitious ignorance has recently been supplanted by a more accurate understanding of the laws of nature. The investigations which have brought about the strength to tear away the darkened canopy surrounding the original formation of material strength come almost entirely from the central intensity of the north temperate zone, in an isothermal delimitation encircling the earth scarcely five hundred miles in width; an important fact in a study of natural exigencies.

These allied sciences are not intended for a discussion in this paper: nevertheless in a consideration of the causes of ocean formation, constituting the present principal basis of evaporation, rainfall, and river channels, we would go back of all known conditions, if we could, to ascertain the original physical production of water.

It seems to be a problem impossible to solve, and yet, in a vaporous condition, in its separated properties, all water undoubtedly always existed in space previous to the formation of the earth and the birth of life in its different forms.

Extant substances may, in different ways, be overtaken by dissolution and dissemination, but absolute obliteration is impossible, and the weight of natural matter, in one or more forms, will always and eternally exist. Nothing whatsoever can add to or take from the bulk, existing in all space, notwithstanding the fact that physical transformations are of an uninterrupted natural sequence caused by the vicissitudes of climate, time, and conditions.

These brief considerations need to determine, that, in whatever manner the earth may have been precipitated as a molten mass of material solar detritus undoubtedly drawn from the particles everywhere present, in space, one is as competent as another to theorize, so far as actual facts are concerned, for philosophic minds still continue to remain simply an embodiment in human nature, incompetent to solve the deepest question in its own existence.

"I have said that a high degree of exhaustion of the air is necessary in the Crookes bulbs. We must not, however, obtain too high a degree of exhaustion; for in that case we should not be able to excite the rays in the bulbs. After we have once excited them, however, they will pass through a vacuum—at least a vacuum so perfect that no electrical discharge can be excited in it. This fact is of great interest to scientific men. The cathode rays can pass from the sun to the earth through the vacuum of space; yet they cannot be excited in that cold and lifeless region. The electrical energy enters the vacuum, traverses it, and reappears in ordinary air; it seems as if it must have traversed the vacuum by means of the ether. We have, therefore, in the manifestation of the cathode rays, a support of the hypothesis of an ether pervading all space."—Prof. John Trowbridge in "Scribner's Magazine," April, 1896, vol. xix., No. 4, p. 506.

GEOLOGIC TIME DIVISIONS AND FORMATIONS IN THEIR STRATIGRAPHIC ORDER.

(The older below, and the successively newer above, therefore to be read from below upward for the sequence of events in the order of time.)

BY WARREN UPHAM.

ERAS.	PERIODS.	EPOCHS.	FORMATIONS.
PRESENT OR PSYCHOZOIC. About 5,000 to 10,000 years.	HISTORIC AND PREHISTORIC.	PRESENT AND RECENT.	Alluvium, peat, etc. Erosion of the valley drift as terraces.
QUATERNARY. PLEISTO-CENE. Probably about 100,000 years.	Depression of the formerly uplifted lands.	CHAMPLAIN.	Modified drift, as eskers, kames, sand and gravel plains, loess and other valley drift.
	GLACIAL OR ICE AGE. High uplifts of areas that became ice-cov'd.	GLACIAL.	Till or boulder-clay, drumlins and moraines. The north half of North America covered by an ice-sheet.
		LAFAYETTE.	Loam, sand and gravel in the Southern Atlantic and Gulf states.
TERTIARY OR CENOZOIC. Durat'n probably 3 to 5 million years. Chief upheaval, folding and faulting of the Rocky mts. during the early part of this era.	NEOCENE. Volcanic beds of the Yellowstone park and Columbia r'g'n outpo'rd during Tertiary and Quater'y eras.	PLIOCENE.	Marine deposits adjoining the Gulf of Mexico, lacustrine beds on portions of the plains south of the Missouri river.
		MIOCENE.	Marine on the Atlantic coastal plain; fluvial and lacustrine on some areas south and north of the Missouri river.
	EOCENE.	Several; in total, much longer than the Neocene.	Marine on sea borders of North America; lacustrine in parts of Wyoming, Colorado, and Utah.
MESOZOIC (Secondary). Era of reptiles. Durat'n probably 10 to 15 million years.	UPPER CRETACEOUS.	LARAMIE.	Freshwater and brackish beds on large areas of the Missouri basin, including the chief productive seams of lignite coal.
		MONTANA (Fox Hills and Ft. Pierre).	Marine sandstones and mostly shales on the greater part of the northwestern plains drained by the Missouri.
		COLORADO (Niobrara and Ft. Benton).	Limestones and shales under the Montana strata; limited deposits of true chalk.
		DAKOTA.	Extensive sandstone deposits; land areas, with deciduous forests.
	LOWER CRETACEOUS.	Very long ages, scantily represented in Missouri dr'nage area.	Coal-bearing beds, of the Kootanie epoch, near Great Falls.
	JURASSIC.		Thin deposits outcropping on the flanks of the Black Hills and Rocky mountains.
	TRIASSIC.		
	PERMIAN.	All very long ages, producing thick marine deposits on the Appalachian area, but mostly thin on the western half of the United States.	Scanty North American deposits. Time of the chief upheaval and folding of the Appalachian mountain belt.
	CARBONIFEROUS.		Forests of ferns and allied cryptogamous plants. The greatest coal-forming period of the world's history. Coal measures of Pennsylvania, Ohio, and adjoining region.
PALEOZOIC (Primary). Exceedingly long, probably 75 to 150 million years.	DEVONIAN.		Long continued and gradual subsidence of the Appalachian region, keeping pace with the prolonged deposition of the alternating sandstones, shales, and limestones, to an aggregate depth of 30,000 feet or more. Well-developed marine faunas. The North American continent was outlined in these early periods, with land tracts along the present great Appalachian and Cordilleran belts.
	UP. SILURIAN.		
	LOW. SILURIAN.		
	UP. CAMBRIAN.	(Algonkian time was probably as long as all from that time to the present.)	
	MID. CAMBRIAN.		
	LOW. CAMBRIAN.		
	ALGONKIAN OR HURONIAN.		Earliest traces of life, beginning in the sea.
ARCHEAN OR AZOIC. Vast duration	LAURENTIAN.	Time of first encrustment of the cooling earth.	Granites, gneisses, and schists, everywhere overlain unconformably by the sedimentary (water-deposited) rocks.

An accepted theory, that the earth in its earlier condition was a molten mass, does not offer any certainty concerning the character of the phenomenal combination of the elements that precipitated it, as such; and the able sages of geological science, in an attempted solution of the origin of life, have partially determined the character of the transformation that followed during successive geological periods. Toward those periods an acute and determined examination has been extended in recent times, and it has gradually lightened the burden of the labor and thought necessary to solve many important and complicated questions.

Through the courtesy of Mr. Warren Upham, Secretary of the Minnesota State Historical Society, the opposite page, a tabular geological calendar of the probable duration of past eras, accepted as the latest estimated length of time in the world's evolutionary history, has been very ably and carefully prepared for presentation herewith.

Likewise, Mr. Upham has prepared the following interesting geologic history concerning the Basin of the Missouri:

GEOLOGIC HISTORY OF THE ROCKY MOUNTAINS AND GREAT PLAINS IN THE REGION DRAINED BY THE MISSOURI RIVER.

BY WARREN UPHAM.

[For Hon. J. V. Brower's Work on the Mississippi River and its Source.]

Many stages of mountain-building have left their impress on the great Cordilleran belt of the western part of the United States and the Dominion of Canada. As the Missouri river has its sources in the Rocky Mountains, which are the principal eastern range of this belt, we may best begin our description of the country tributary to the Missouri by a very brief review of these stages of growth and development of this greatest mountain belt of the world.

Extending our view to embrace the entire belt of which the Rocky Mountains are a part, we see that it forms the western side of both North and South America. Its length from Cape Horn to Alaska is about 10,000 miles of a great circle, from which the somewhat irregular course of the belt is nowhere widely distant. With this Andes-Cordilleran orographic belt is also associated the mountain system, consisting largely of volcanoes now active, which forms the Aleutian islands, Kamtchatka, the Kurile islands, Japan, Formosa, the Philippines, Borneo, and Celebes, lying nearly in the same great circle with the Andes and Rocky Mountains, and with them continuous in an arc of about two hundred and forty degrees. Along this circumferential line, having an extent of two-thirds of the girth of our planet, the great lateral stresses of the earth's crust, caused by the gradual cooling and contraction of the interior during long past geologic eras, and even up to the present time, have been relieved by plication, faults, and uplifts, in the processes of the formation of mountain ranges.

The Gold and Selkirk ranges of this Cordilleran belt in British Columbia, according to Dr. George M. Dawson, consist of Archæan, Cambrian, and Silurian formations, which were pushed up into moun-

tain folds before the close of these very ancient divisions of geologic
time. The auriferous slates of the Sierra Nevada, as Becker has shown,
were similarly built up in a folded mountain range at the close of the
Gault epoch in the Cretaceous period.

Mr. S. F. Emmons of the United States Geological Survey, from
his studies of the Rocky Mountains in Colorado, concludes that certain land areas existed along this belt before the Cambrian period;
that mountain ranges were thrust up at various times during the Paleozoic era, and in the Jurassic period near the middle of the ensuing
Mesozoic era; but that these mountains had been slowly worn away,
or reduced to very moderate heights, before the close of the Cretaceous
period, when the Mesozoic was succeeded by the Tertiary era.

During the later half of Cretaceous time a vast inland or mediter-
ranean sea, far surpassing the size of that which now divides Europe
from Africa, stretched from south to north across this continent, reaching from the Gulf of Mexico over the broad area called the Great
Plains to the Mackenzie river basin and the Arctic ocean. In the last
or Laramie division of the Cretaceous period the water of this sea became brackish and finally fresh, being shut off from its former connection with the ocean by the gradual rise of the land borders on the
south and north. A great depth of Cretaceous sediments, marine below and lacustrine above, had been laid down on all the area of the
plains, and upon much of the country which is now traversed by the
Rocky Mountain chain, but which had sunk in this period beneath the
sea level.

At the end of the Laramie epoch came great movements of uplift,
folding, and overthrusting of the Cretaceous and older strata along all
the belt of the Rocky Mountains, which, with reference to the date
of these disturbances of mountain-formation, has been called the Laramide range. The great orogenic movements of this time are similarly
named the Laramide revolution. For the western half of North America, this time of vast mountain-building was comparable with the
much earlier Appalachian revolution in the eastern United States, at
the end of Palæozoic time, by which the Appalachian mountain belt
was formed.

Emmons writes of this grand stage in the development of the
Cordilleran mountain belt as follows: "The post-Cretaceous movement,
as has been almost universally recognized, was that which produced
the main plication and faulting, and played the most important part
in determining the present orographic features of the Rocky Mountain
region. But, as it is evident that these features had been in a great extent already outlined in the movements that went before, it is also more
than probable that the post-Cretaceous folds and faults have been further
emphasized along the principal lines of disturbance in the less violent
movements that have affected the region since, even into very recent
times. It is therefore manifestly impossible to determine with absolute accuracy how much of the present displacement of Cretaceous beds
in folds and faults was produced in the first post-Cretaceous movement
and how much in those that have supervened in Tertiary and Recent
times. * * * I have laid stress upon the importance of the movement at the close of the coal-bearing Laramie in the Rocky Mountain
region. * * * It is unquestionably one of the most important events
in the orographical history of the entire Cordilleran system. With the
exception of the great unconformity between the Archæan and all over-
lying sediments, * * * no movement has left such definite evidence
as that which followed the deposition of the coal-bearing rocks, to
which the name Laramie has by universal consent been applied."

Dr. George M. Dawson, now the director of the Canadian Geological
Survey, writes: "In the mountains, the Cretaceous rocks have been
involved in all the flexure, faulting, and overthrust suffered by the

Palæozoic; and both in the mountains and foothills these rocks are found at all angles up to vertical and even overturned. It is thus difficult to know to what elevations these rocks may have been thrust up in some places, but a minimum estimate may be arrived at by tracing the continuations of the beds over the less disturbed anticlinals or by adding their volume to the elevation of the flat-lying ranges of the older rocks. About latitude 50° it may thus be shown that the base of the Cretaceous must in several places have considerably exceeded 10,000 feet in altitude, while in Mr. McConnell's section along Bow Pass (51° 15′) * * * the same horizon must have been about 15,000 feet above sea-level, the beds at this place being nearly flat. To ascertain the uplift of the beds which were at sea-level at the close of the Cretaceous, the volume of the Cretaceous strata must, of course, be added to such figures as the above. This was, in the eastern part of the mountains, at least 17,000 feet, and may well have been 20,000 feet * * * giving as a minimum estimate of greatest uplift for the region say 32,000 to 35,000 feet. * * * It is probably impossible to ascertain exactly how long the main uplifting process continued or to what extent its effect was counteracted by concurrent denudation." This author states it as his belief, however, that the mountain uplifting and folding may have continued through the very long Eocene and Miocene periods, which may be estimated to have comprised together about nine-tenths of the Tertiary era. During the early part of the Miocene period Dr. Dawson thinks that the Rocky Mountains adjoining the west side of the Canadian portion of the Great Plains were "a range comparable to the Himalayas in height."

The geologic strata of this northern portion of the plains are the Dakota, Colorado, Montana, and Laramie formations, of late Cretaceous age, whose deposition took place during the closing part of the Secondary or Mesozoic era. Southward, in the United States, the plains comprise extensive deposits of Tertiary lacustrine beds, representing the continuation of the brackish water and finally lacustrine conditions which prevailed over large areas of the plains during the Laramie period; but in the northern region, crossed by the Missouri river and extending to the Peace and Mackenzie rivers, no Tertiary beds are found. Since the beginning of the Tertiary era this region has been a land surface undergoing denudation. When its marine and lacustrine deposits were first raised to be dry land they had a monotonously flat surface. A very long cycle of base-leveling ensued, beginning as soon as this northern part of the plains was uplifted at the end of Cretaceous time and continuing nearly or quite to the end of the Tertiary era. During this time the surface was gradually lowered by the action of rains, rills, rivulets, creeks, and rivers, until it was mostly reduced to a base-level of subaërial erosion.

Across an area 700 or 800 miles wide from east to west on the international boundary, and of much greater extent from south to north, the processes of base-leveling were at work through the vast duration of Tertiary time, cutting down the plains far below their original surface. But here and there isolated areas of hills and even mountains remain, consisting of remnants of the horizontal Cretaceous strata which elsewhere have suffered erosion.

The most noteworthy eastern highland area of this kind is the Turtle Mountain, lying in the north edge of North Dakota and the south edge of Manitoba, its extent on the international boundary being about forty miles, with two-thirds its great width. This high tract, diversified by many subordinate hills and short ridges, 50 to 300 feet above adjoining depressions, rises with a massive general form suggesting, as seen from some distant points of view, the rounded back of a turtle; but as seen from the south or north, its many hills and buttes present a serrated outline. Its altitude above the surrounding country is 300 to 800 feet, the summits of its highest hills being about 2,500 feet above the sea. Beneath a veneering of glacial drift, which is in large part morainic and generally strewn with many boulders, averaging perhaps fifty to seventy-five feet in thickness, Turtle Mountain consists of nearly horizontally bedded Laramie strata, chiefly shales, with very thin seams of lignite. At or below the base of this highland, the freshwater Laramie formation rests on the marine Cretaceous series. A thickness of not less than 500 to 1,000 feet of the Laramie and marine beds has been carried away from the surrounding eastern part of the plains.

Westward the depth of the Tertiary base-leveling was greater. About the west end of the Cypress hills in Assiniboia, Dr. Dawson finds that the general surface of the plains is now some 2,200 feet lower than in early Miocene time, when rivers from the mountains deposited the gravels which now cap these hills. Around the Highwood and Crazy Mountains, in central Montana, according to Prof. W. M. Davis and Dr. J. E. Wolff, the erosion of the plains has a vertical extent of 3,000 to 5,000 feet. Perhaps the most striking evidence of this great erosion is afforded by the range of the Crazy Mountains, which lies immediately north of the Yellowstone river, near Livingston, and is conspicuously seen from the Northern Pacific railroad. These mountains trend slightly west of north, and extend about forty miles with a width of fifteen miles, attaining an elevation of 11,178 feet above the sea, and 5,000 to 6,000 feet above the prairies at their base. Their structure has been thoroughly studied by Wolff, who finds that they consist of late Cretaceous strata, soft sandstones, nearly horizontal in stratification, intersected by a network of eruptive dikes. The more enduring igneous rocks have preserved this range, while an average denudation of not less than one mile in vertical amount reduced all the adjoining region to a base-level of erosion. The Highwood Mountains, about twenty-five miles east of Great Falls, having a height of 7,600 feet above the sea or about 3,500 feet above their base, are described by Davis as displaying the same structure, and therefore similarly testifying of great denudation.

The epeirogenic or continental uplift at the beginning of the Tertiary era appears to have raised this portion of the Great Plains to a height above the sea equaling or exceeding the vertical extent of their Tertiary erosion; that is, to a height of at least 1,000 to 5,000 feet, increasing from east to west. This uplift, however, beginning at the end of Cretaceous time, may most probably have progressed through the first half or a longer part of the Tertiary era. Toward the end of this era, the base-leveling had reduced the country mostly to a plain which was probably only a few hundred feet above the sea, lying much below its present altitude.

Between the general Tertiary cycle of base-leveling and the Glacial period there intervened a second great epeirogenic uplift, as shown by the present elevation and westward ascent of the Great Plains, and by a return of the conditions of vigorous stream erosion and a new cycle of partial base-leveling, by which wide, flat valleys were cut in the eastern part of these Cretaceous plains. This latest uplift of the Rocky Mountains and of the country eastward I believe to have extended to the Atlantic coast, and there to have caused the erosion of the now deeply submerged continuation of the channel of the Hudson river, which reaches a hundred miles beyond Sandy Hook to a maximum sounding of 2,844 feet near the submarine margin of the continental plateau, though a nearly uniform depth of only about 600 feet of water is found on each side. The late Tertiary and early Quaternary uplift of nearly all our continent to a height from 2,000 feet to, probably in part, 5,000 feet higher than now appears to me the most probable explanation of the Ice age, bringing a cold and snowy climate throughout the year, with consequent deep accumulation of snow and ice. But under the great weight of the ice-sheet the continent sank to its present height, or, for most of the northern region which had been ice-enveloped, from 100 to 500 or 600 feet lower.

Many changes in the courses of rivers were produced by the upward and downward and again upward epeirogenic movements associated with the Ice age, and by the deposition of the glacial and modified drift. In the case of the Missouri river, Gen. G. K. Warren remarked, nearly thirty years ago, that it flows through all its course on the marginal part of the northern drift-bearing region; and he therefore attributed the location of this great river to the obstruction of the ice-sheet, which he supposed to have turned it from a more northerly and easterly preglacial course. It seems very probable that the present Missouri is made up by the union of the courses of several independent preglacial rivers, and that some of these old avenues of drainage underwent great changes of location, as Prof. J. E. Todd has shown from his explorations and studies of the glacial geology of South and North Dakota. Much further exploration, however, including the present watershed which divides the most northeastern part of the Missouri river from the Souris and Assiniboine rivers and the lakes of Manitoba, will be needed to ascertain whether the upper Missouri was permanently turned far away from its preglacial lower course by the vicissitudes of the Ice age.   W. U.

§ III. MAGMA.

A few references seem now to be in order, concerning the condition of the interior of the earth's crust and the foundation upon which it rests.

The interesting theory, now accepted as being based upon a foundation of probable fact, that a molten and moving mass of magma constitutes at least a portion of the inner formation of the earth upon which an outer, cooled crust has its downward bearing, is very important in the light of the conclusions of the authorities hereinbefore cited.

Magma is described as a "molten or plastic material lying beneath the surface,[4] which it is desirable to speak of without any specific indication of its mineral character, in discussing the phenomena of volcanism, metamorphism, or the ground-mass or basis of a rock."

The moving magma has caused the uplifting of the continents to such an extent, that the rarification of the atmosphere produced the glacial epochs, when a variously estimated thickness of the ice-sheet, similar to the present condition of Greenland, by the force of its enormous weight, depressed the surface covered, gradually, until the climatic conditions again moderated, and the glacial covering disappeared to the northward. The thickness of the crust of the outer portion of the earth has been variously estimated[5] at from twenty to eighty

[4]"The Century," iv., p. 3573.
[5]Capt. George M. Wheeler, in a note, vol. i., p. iii., United States Geographical Surveys, west of the one hundredth meridian, makes the following very concise statement:

"One of the most interesting of the many phenomena presented by the workings of the Comstock mines is the great heat encountered at the lower levels, and it was to the investigation of the sources of this heat supply that Mr.

miles, [6] while the depth of the atmosphere encircling the earth is unknown, but believed to be at least one hundred miles.

Church devoted much of his time. As is readily seen, the question of future increase or decrease of the temperature is a most important one in its bearing upon the prosperous workings of the mines. As the result of his investigation, Mr. Church reached the conclusion, that the usual explanation of the heat that exists in the eruptive rocks of many localities—namely, that it is the last manifestation of the heat which fused the rocks—does not apply here, because of the persistence with which the supply is maintained under conditions that make extraordinary draughts upon it. He considers the true source to be the chemical alteration of the feldspathic minerals in the rocks, or the process technically known as kaolinization—the changing of feldspar to clay. As to the question of increase of heat, he is of the opinion that it is subject to a steady and moderate increase as greater depths are reached."

6A recent letter, by Prof. Alexander Agassiz, published in the December "American Journal of Science," concerning rock temperatures at great depths on Keweenaw Point, Michigan, which demonstrates very different results from "accepted figures for the downward increase of temperature," was republished as follows in the January (1896) "American Geologist:"

"For several years past I have, with the assistance of our engineer, Mr. Preston C. F. West, been making rock temperature observations as we increased the depth at which the mining operations of the Calumet and Hecla Mining Co. were carried on. We have now attained at our deepest point a vertical depth of 4,712 feet, and have taken temperatures of the rock at 105 feet, at the depth of the level of Lake Superior, 655 feet, at that of the level of the sea, 1,257 feet, at that of the deepest part of Lake Superior, 1,663 feet, and at four additional stations, each respectively 550, 550, 561, and 1,256 below the preceding one, the deepest point at which temperatures have been taken being 4,580 feet. We propose when we have reached our final depth, 4,900 feet, to take an additional rock temperature and to then publish in full the details of our observations. In the mean time it may be interesting to give the results as they stand. The highest rock temperature obtained at the depth of 4,580 feet was only seventy-nine degrees Fahrenheit; the rock temperature at the depth of 105 feet was fifty-nine degrees Fahrenheit. Taking that as the depth as unaffected by local temperature variations, we have a column of 4,775 feet of rock with a difference of temperature of twenty degrees Fahrenheit, or an average increase of one degree for each 223.7 feet. This is very different from any recorded observations; Lord Kelvin, if I am not mistaken, giving as the increase for one degree Fahrenheit, fifty-one (51) feet, while the observations based on the temperature observations of the St. Gothard Tunnel gave for an increase of one degree Fahrenheit, sixty (60) feet. The calculations based upon the latter observations gave an approximate thickness of the crust of the earth, in one case of about twenty miles, the other of twenty-six. Taking our observations, the crust would be over eighty miles, and the thickness of the crust at the critical temperature of water would be over thirty-one miles, instead of about seven and eight and one-half miles, as by the other and older ratios. With the ratio observed here, the temperature at a depth of nineteen miles would only be about 470 degrees, a very different temperature from that obtained by the older ratios of over 2,000 degrees Fahrenheit. The holes in which we placed slow registering Negretti and Zambar thermometers were drilled, slightly inclined upward, to a depth of two feet from the face of the rock, and plugged with wood and clay. In these holes the thermometers were left for from one to three months. The average annual temperature of the air is forty-eight degrees Fahrenheit; the temperature of the air at the bottom of the shaft was seventy-two degrees Fahrenheit."—vol. xvii., p. 60-61.

Also, there appears in the same publication for February, vol. xvii., p. 100, the following comment by Prof. Alfred C. Lane: * * * "The two chief factors of cost (in mining) are the increased length of time in hoist and the increasing temperature. The escape of compressed air helps to overcome the latter difficulty. Figures were given from the Tamarack and the Calumet and Hecla mines, showing that nearly down to 5,000 feet the increase has been a little less than one degree Fahrenheit for each hundred feet, so that a depth of 10,000 feet can probably be reached there with no great difficulty. One Calumet shaft is now down 4,800 feet vertically, and one Tamarack shaft is started which will not reach the lode until it is down 5,000 feet."

"In discussion, Professor Shaler suggested that the very low temperature gradient thus found in the Lake Superior copper mining district may be largely the effect of compressed air. The temperature gradient for the Calumet and Hecla mine recently published by Alexander Agassiz appears to give only one degree Fahrenheit of increase for each 223.7 feet down to 4,580 feet. To supply this gradient a mean rock temperature at 105 feet of fifty-nine degrees Fahrenheit is used, whereas the mean annual temperature of that district is about forty degrees, and approximately this temperature of forty degrees has been

Between these two limited extremes, within the delimitation of a few thousand feet, all that is known to exist of fauna and flora life is visible, while above or below that line all living forms in nature perish, and it is not an unknown fact that the surface channeled by river flowage, and thence to the ocean depths, is the natural home of every living species, according to the requirements of a varied nature of existence.

It is, then, toward the inner movement of the magma[7] formation, in its gradual uplifting of the outer crust of the earth, that the attention is directed, as the primal cause of surface elevations, as variously influenced by mountain-uplifts, volcanic eruptions, and glacial periods,[8] and those natural forces have changed the geoid surface of the mean sea level, until about one-fourth of the original bed of a single ocean (?) has been uplifted into continents[9] and islands, dividing the

determined at slight depths in other neighboring mines. A mean annual temperature of fifty-nine degrees Fahrenheit is not met north of Kentucky, and this fact makes corroboration desirable before important inferences are based on these exceptionally low gradients. Professor Lane suggested, that, as the Wheeling record indicates, the low gradient may be due partly to a rise in the surface temperature since the glacial period, or may also in part be due to the cooling effect of downward percolating waters. He urged the advantage of an exploratory boring from the bottom of one of the copper mining shafts, which might penetrate to a total depth of nearly 15,000 feet below the surface."—Reported by Prof. Warren Upham from proceedings of the Philadelphia meeting of the Geological Society of America, 1895.

7"As in all the North American districts noted, these upward movements seem attributable to the rise of the earth's crust, upborne by inflow of a molten magma beneath."—Upham in Wright's "Ice Age," 1891, p. 582.

8"Combined with oscillations of the earth's crust, which are here regarded as the primary cause of the growth and decline of ice sheets, many other concomitant conditions, notably changes in aërial and oceanic currents, and the earth's cycles of twenty-one thousand years through precession and nutation, enter into the complex causation of recurrent glacial and inter-glacial epochs."—Wright's "Ice Age," 1891, p. 587.

9"The history of the mountain chains is almost co-extensive with that of the continent itself. In the sea the beds were deposited horizontally, or nearly so; and at certain intervals the deposition was arrested in consequence of the beds being uplifted above the sea. Each successive submergence and emergence occupied a very long period of time, during which the rocks were at one time faulted, folded and metamorphosed, and at other times denuded both by the sea and by meteoric agents."—"Ency. Britannica," vol. i., 670. America.

"In comparison, however, with the physical conditions and laws familiar to us upon the earth's surface, the subsidence and elevation of extensive areas, as of nearly all glaciated regions, seem to demonstrate a mobility of the earth's interior, as if it were fused rock. The same conclusion is indicated by volcanoes, which are probably the openings of molten passages that communicate downward through the crust to the heavier melted interior, thence deriving their supply of heat, while their outpours of lavas consist largely or wholly of fused portions of the crust, the phenomena of eruption being caused by the access of water to the upper part of the molten rock near the volcanic vent."—Upham in Wright's "Ice Age," 1891, p. 575.

"By far the most important of all these [physical] agencies, and the one which mainly brought about the glacial epoch, is the deflection of ocean currents."—Croll's "Climate and Time," 14.

On p. 222 of the same volume (Plate iii.) appears a very interesting and instructive chart as to temperatures in the mid-Atlantic, from the equator, north and south. An actual sounding by the admiralty shows that the temperature at the bottom of the ocean at the equator is thirty-four degrees seven minutes; not far removed from the freezing point.

"According to this explanation, the accumulation of the ice sheets was due to uplifts of the land as extensive high plateaus, receiving snowfall throughout the year. It may therefore be very properly named the epeirogenic theory."—Upham in Wright's "Greenland Icefields," 1896, p. 344.

"Not until we go back to the Permian and Carboniferous periods, are numerous and widely distributed proofs of very ancient glaciation encountered. The

waters, and constituting river channeling, a natural consequence that followed, by the precipitation of rainfall upon the
face of the uplifted earth, and which, seeking its level toward
the geoid line at the sea-shore, channeled every river bed that
has ever existed, paving the way for the birth of mammalia and
man. In that manner the great Mississippian-Missourian river
system was inaugurated upwards of 500,000 centuries since,
and every passing day has witnessed a change in its physical
features, by the eroding qualities of precipitated water, or
other natural causes.

§ IV. THE EARLY APPEARANCE OF MAN IN THE BASIN OF THE MISSISSIPPI.

Only a brief reference can now be made to the early existence of humanity in the Western World.

It has come to be an accepted fact, that palæolithic man
existed in Europe and America at the date of the disappearance of the last glacial epoch. The evidences are accumula-
tive, and certainly extend in the direction of a final confirm-
ation of that theory, for very able scientists, who have carefully studied all these accumulated indications, principally
very old stone implements,[10] have gone on record in the most
positive terms in favor of the theory stated. On the other
hand, another school of theoretical scientists are on record in
just as positive terms in the opposite direction, holding fast
to an original standpoint, that all the old and new stone implements found east of the Rocky Mountains and north of the
Gulf of Mexico are of historic Indian origin.

No fixed and certain chronological time has been agreed
upon or accepted for the final disappearance of the last ice-sheet
in the United States, and on that account, principally, no actual
date can be designated to show the real age of the palæolithic

---

atmosphere had been purified by the formation of Palaeozoic limestones of great
thickness, and by the storing up of the principal coal deposits of the world;"
* * * —Wright's "Ice Age," 1891, pp. 591-92.

"The great terminal moraine stretching across the United States from Cape
Cod to Dakota and thence northward to the foot of the Rocky Mountains, marks
the limit of the ice invasion in the second glacial epoch."—Mr. H. W. Haynes,
in "Nar. and Crit. History of America," i., 332.

10Among these ancient and apparently authenticated evidences may be men-
tioned the following limited number of references:
The Boucher de Perthes discoveries on the river Somme.
The Thomas Wilson collection of Palaeolithic types in North America.
The flints, described by Frere, found in Suffolk, England.
The important Trenton discovery by Dr. C. C. Abbott.
The Madisonville discovery in Ohio by Dr. C. L. Metz.
Mr. H. T. Cresson's Indiana deposit of similar types at Medora.
Miss Franc E. Babbitt's Little Falls, Minn., Palaeolithic discovery.
The Claymont discovery by Mr. Cresson on the Delaware river.
The Table Mountain collection by the late Dr. Snell.
The noted Calaveras crania.
Man and extinct mammalia in contemporaneous existence.

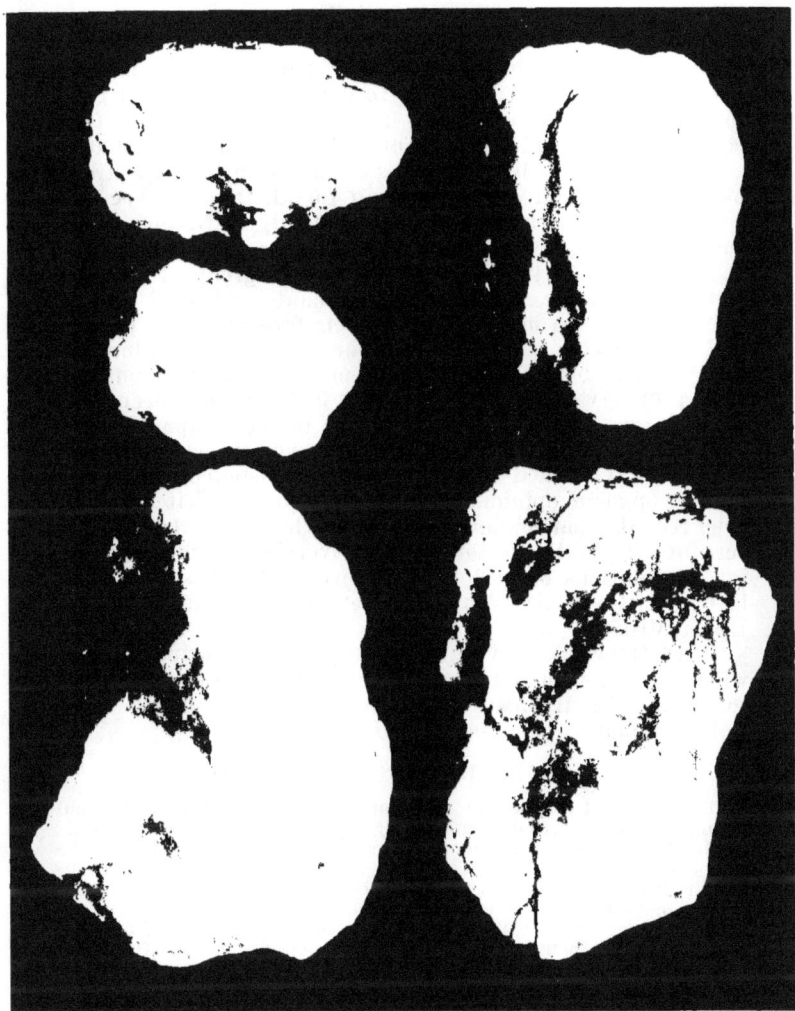

SPECIMENS OF THE BABBITT PALAEOLITHIC QUARTZ IMPLEMENTS.

Observed at Little Falls, Minnesota; said to have been deposited by Glacial Man B. C. Exactly one-half natural size. Photographed by Baldwin Coolidge of Boston, Mass., through the courtesy of Mr. Henry W. Haynes, expressly for Illustration.

evidences collected in this country;[11] hence, no scientist is as
yet amply competent and able to determine the actual truth
in a matter of such historic interest. When the full facts
come to be known after careful and mature disinterested investigation, the written record of those who have so strenuously insisted that a historic limit for all that has been un-
earthed in America[12] exists, may probably find their records
successfully impeached and utterly valueless, for there can be
scarcely a doubt that all the interesting group of very old
stone implements, crania, and remnants collected in the
United States do not bear upon their face any such positive
and indisputable evidence of recent and historic Indian origin,[13] as has been claimed for them; and the final outcome
must probably follow, that America in its earliest occupancy
by man was certainly prehistoric, for the contemporaneity of
man and mammalia in this western hemisphere has been quite
definitely established and as persistently disputed.

Two opposite opinions, however, have been solicited for this
brief record, from eminent gentlemen, who are thoroughly con-
versant with both sides of the controversial arguments touching the relations borne by the discoveries by Miss F. E. Babbitt at Little Falls, Minn., in the immediate valley of the
Upper Mississippi.

Prof. Henry W. Haynes of Boston, Mass., enjoying a world-
wide reputation in the scientific field of palæolithic research,
to whom Miss Babbitt submitted a collection of the Little
Falls old quartz relics, says:

PALAEOLITHIC MAN IN MINNESOTA.

The abundant evidence of the existence of man upon this continent
during the glacial period, furnished by the discovery at Trenton, N. J.,
by Dr. C. C. Abbott and others, of large numbers of palæolithic implements, fashioned out of argillite, has been strikingly corroborated by
similar discoveries made in the State of Minnesota.

In the year 1879 the late Miss Franc E. Babbitt, in the vicinity
of the town of Little Falls, came upon a bed or stratum of fragments
of white quartz lying buried in the glacial deposits of the Mississippi
river, in an ancient terrace elevated some twenty-five feet above the
present bed of the river and about forty rods to the east of it. This
stratum was at a depth of some twelve or fifteen feet below the summit of the terrace, and was made up of pieces still perfectly sharp,
although occurring in a water-worn deposit. Among these fragments

---

[11]"M. de Quatrefages awarded to Lund, the learned Dane, the honor of
having discovered fossil man on the American continent."—Nadaillac's "Prehistoric America," p. 26.

[12]"But when the bones of man and the results of his very primitive industry
are associated with the remains of animals which have been extinct for a period
of time of which it is difficult to estimate the length, it is impossible not to
date the existence of that man from the most remote antiquity."—Nadaillac's
"Prehistoric America," 1884, p. 37. See, also, Bancroft, vol. iv., p. 607.

[13]"Those whom we are disposed to call aborigines are perhaps but the conquerors of other races that preceded them; conquerors and conquered are forgotten in a common oblivion, and the names of both have passed from the
memory of man."—Nadaillac's "Prehistoric America," p. 14.

were several implements of the palæolithic type, some of which bore
traces of use. A number of these were submitted to my inspection
by Miss Babbitt, and they are still in my possession. I stated, that,
in my judgment, they are genuine palæolithic implements, and this
opinion was quoted by her in an account of her discoveries in "The
American Naturalist," 1884, p. 705. The greater portion, however, of
the objects discovered by her are now deposited in the Peabody Museum, Cambridge, Mass.; and they are regarded by Prof. Frederic W.
Putnam as unquestionably authentic palæolithic implements.

The question of the geological age of these objects has been fully
discussed by Mr. Warren Upham, of the United States Geological Survey, in a paper to be found in the "Proceedings of the Boston Society
of Natural History," vol. xxiii., p. 436, etc. His conclusion is, that
"the rude implements and fragments of quartz discovered at Little
Falls were overspread by the glacial flood-plain of the Mississippi
river, while most of the northern half of Minnesota was still covered
by the ice."

This view has been generally accepted by all those men of science
who are satisfied with the proofs of the existence of palæolithic man
on this continent. It had been questioned, however, by Mr. Wm. H.
Holmes in "The American Geologist," April, 1893, who claims that
these quartz fragments are merely relics of our historical aborigines.
His arguments, however, seem to me to be singularly disingenuous and
inconclusive. He insists that there never was any "stratum" or layer
of quartz fragments found, notwithstanding Miss Babbitt's most positive and unequivocal statements to the contrary. He drove a trench
into the terrace for a distance of over thirty feet, near the supposed
site of those discoveries (although the locality has been obscured by the
subsequent erection of a dam and the flowing of the banks), and found
fragments of quartz scattered throughout it from the surface down
to a limit of five feet in depth. By this discovery he claims that he
has disproved the existence of a bed of fragments lying at the depth
of twelve or fifteen feet from the surface-level of the terrace. He then
proceeded to carry a line of pits more than one hundred feet from
the margin of the terrace, and in every one of them he states that
he discovered "shaped quartzes" uniformly distributed through the
loam to the depth of three and a half feet. By this very misleading
expression he must be understood to mean not implements, but fragments, and he accounts for their presence there by supposing that they
had been introduced from the surface by the uprooting of trees caused
by a tornado, which had buried them to this depth "in the unstratified
superficial loam." He insists, also, that the objects discovered were
not implements at all, and that "they were rude because mere shop
refuse." He has made the same assertion also with regard to the universally accepted palæolithic implements of Europe.

Mr. Holmes takes occasion to state that Prof. N. H. Winchell now
fully acquiesces in his views although in the "Sixth Annual Report
of the Geology and Natural History of Minnesota," 1877, p. 54., he has
formally put himself on record as believing, that, not far from the site
of Miss Babbitt's discoveries, he has found a spot where there once
dwelt "a chipping race * * * which preceded the spreading the
material of the plain, and must have been preglacial." Mr. Upham,
however, in "The American Geologist," May, 1894, p. 363, states that
he sees no reason to change his opinion in regard to the importance of
Miss Babbitt's discoveries at Little Falls, notwithstanding Mr. Holmes'
skepticism; and he particularly calls attention to the inaccurate manner
in which that gentleman cites and comments upon the geological section by which Mr. Upham's views were illustrated.

HENRY W. HAYNES.

Boston, Dec. 28, 1895.

Prof. W. H. Holmes of the Field Columbian Museum, on the other hand, offers the following in an opposite opinion to that expressed by Professor Haynes:

OF HISTORIC INDIAN ORIGIN.

Dear Sir: I have quite dropped out of the controversy in regard to glacial man, but still take enough interest in the subject to sincerely desire that the truth may prevail. As to the Little Falls site, I have no hesitation in saying that Miss Babbitt was wrong in every feature of her observations, and she, Professor Winchell, and myself are the only persons that have made observations on the spot, and it may be added that I am the only one that has ever attempted to explore beneath the surface of the ground. I feel very strongly that you will do a wrong to science and to the history of the Northwest if you adopt in your publications the views of anyone who has not personally examined the site.

If you feel sufficient interest in the question I will join you at Little Falls when the period of low water arrives, and we will dig another trench, if the site is still free to us. I am sure that if Mr. Haynes or Mr. Upham would visit Little Falls they would find that Miss Babbitt was wholly wrong and that Professor Winchell was right, and that my own interpretations must finally be accepted by the world.[14]

The section given on page 228 of my paper is a clear presentation of the conditions under which the quartzes are found. Miss Babbitt found specimens outcropping at the base of the terrace, but did not dig into the ground to find out whether the undisturbed glacial gravels came to the surface or not. All the quartzes are in slide material descended from above and never were involved in the glacial deposits.

W. H. HOLMES.

Field Columbian Museum, Chicago, Feb. 29. 1896.

The early part of the twentieth century will undoubtedly witness a final and affirmative solution of this important question, for the remote antiquity of man on the American continent cannot be successfully changed to a later and historic date by an obliteration of facts which opinions and interpretations cannot change.

---

[14]Holmes' "Vestiges of Early Man in Minnesota," "American Geologist," 1893, xi., 228. Mr. Holmes further states, p. 240: "There is no available evidence of either a paleolithic or glacial man in any part of the upper Mississippi Valley. So far as my own observations and interpretations go, the vestiges of early man in Minnesota are confined exclusively to ordinary traces of Indian occupation."

The quoted statement includes, of course, the remarkable tumuli of the Mound-Builders. In historic times North American Indians have not been known as original constructors of effigy mounds.

"But when the bones of man and the results of his very primitive industry are associated with the remains of animals which have been extinct for a period of time of which it is difficult to estimate the length, it is impossible not to date the existence of that man from the most remote antiquity."—Nadaillac's "Prehistoric America." 1884. p. 37. See, also, Bancroft, vol. iv., p. 697.

The quotations are not those of Professor Holmes, but were made by the editor of these papers.—J. V. B.

THE MOUND-BUILDERS.

Now comes the necessity of briefly referring to the prehistoric Mound-Builders, for their remnants, remains, tumuli, pottery, stone and copper implements, arrow points, spears, village sites and effigies are everywhere found in the upper portion of the basin of the Mississippi, and far up toward the mountain sources of the Missouri and its branches.

They were a courageous people, industrious, possessed of ability, were geographers of no limited ideas, penetrating to the utmost limits of the central and western portions of the United States and across the continental divide into Canadian territory, maintained mines in the copper regions of Superior, and discovered portages leading to and from all the principal water courses in the territory occupied.

No individual member of the present generation of the Anglo-Saxon race can truthfully state who the Mound-Builders were, where they came from, or whence they departed. There seems to be an unfathomable mystery surrounding their former existence, and it is not probable that it will ever be solved satisfactorily. Opinions differ, and the controversy, which has continued for nearly a century in contemporaneous archæological history, has been so unfortunate and vindictive that misleading and deceptive assertions, based only upon set opinions that may be entirely erroneous, have been forced upon unwilling readers who are cheerfully searching for accurate information, until the point has been reached where the record made is almost draped in the folds of acrimony and distortion.

MRS. M. J. BLAKE.

Standing aside from these acrimonious controversies, which deteriorate the value and reliability of conclusions drawn and opinions formulated, the unbiased course is left open for all those who seek for the most reliable information concerning an extinct race of men, of whom we know so little. Builders of mounds have existed from time to time for many centuries,[15] in various parts of the world, but none more systematic and uniquely interesting than prehistoric man in the upper basin of the Mississippi.

---

[15] "The famous mound of Marathon, raised over the bodies of those Athenians who fell in repelling the invading Persians. * * * Very frequently a mound covering and inclosing a more or less elaborate structure of masonry. The raising of mounds over the tombs of the dead, particularly of distinguished persons, or those slain in battle, was a usual practice among very many people from the most remote antiquity."—"The Century," vi., 6528.

In 1894, in company with Dr. Shanafelt and Rev. S. Hall
Young, the editor of these notes had the pleasure of exploring
the remarkable Tascodiac effigies, situated in Northern Minnesota, at the most northerly course of the Mississippi, approximately, lat. 47° 30′, lon. 94° 45′, west of Greenwich.[16]

On the west bank of Apple creek, at the Sibley rifle-pits,
near Bismarck, N. D., in July, 1895, a genuine prehistoric
mound was discovered by the writer, upon section 27, township
138, range 80, west of the fifth principal meridian. The attention of Mr. Walter F. Cushing, secretary of the State Historical Society at Bismarck, was called toward this discovery. On
the 12th of September last Mr. Cushing caused this mound to
be excavated and explored,[17] and the evidences were sufficient
to determine that the mound was not of Mandan origin but prehistoric in all its surroundings, 1,436 miles above the mouth
of the Missouri. This class of mounds are found in many
parts of the two Dakota states, but systematic exploration has
not yet been extended sufficiently toward the upper branches
of the Missouri to certainly ascertain how far up those streams
the Mound-Builders extended their occupancy previous to the
advent of the North American Indian.

It is now known as a certainty that they penetrated northward to Itasca lake and every branch of the Mississippi in its
upper or headwater basin.

As the Yellowstone National Park is situated immediately
east of the most remote branch of the Missouri, numerous
explorations near the Obsidian quarries of that wonderful
locality[18] are pertinent, and Capt. Hiram M. Chittenden,
United States Army, has considerately furnished for these
pages the following condensed account of the researches of
Colonel Norris,[19] formerly superintendent of the park, and who
divided the honor of the discovery of the Obsidian cliff with
Mr. W. H. Holmes:

[16]Vol. xi., Nos. 1-3. January to March, 1895, p. 54, of "The Manchester
[England] Geographical Journal."

[17]In a letter, dated at Bismarck, September 13th, Mr. Cushing says: "Yester-
day afternoon a party of us went over to investigate your mound at the Sibley
field. It is a prehistoric affair all right enough, but our search did not develop
any human remains. We dug two cross-section trenches down to the level of
the terrace upon which it was constructed and excavated between these trenches.
In several places we found streaks of gray substance pointing toward the center,
but no skulls or other evidences of bones. In the center of the mound we found
a large pile of burned stones, mixed with ashes. We also found a number of
small pieces of pottery and many flint chippings but only one arrow point.
Digging in one of the Sibley trenches I found a broken table plate and the top
half of an old cavalry boot, in a good state of preservation, thirty-two years
after its deposit in the trench."

[18]"The Century" (p. 4065) says: "[* * * Obsius, erroneously Obsidius, the
name of a man who, according to Pliny, found it in 'Ethiopia.'] A volcanic
rock, in a vitreous condition, and closely resembling ordinary bottle-glass in
appearance and texture. * * *."

[19]"Near these lakes, the basaltic terraces back of Bottler's and in Trail
Creek Pass, are long, often parallel, lines of small rude stone-heaps, and near
the latter many mining shafts and drifts of some prehistoric race for a rare,
wavy, ornamental rock, the first evidence of ancient mining discovered in these
regions. From their adjacent burial cairns, discovered by me in 1870, specimens
of this rock, arrowheads, and other implements and tools of obsidian or volcanic
glass were found."—Norris' report upon the Yellowstone National Park, 1877,
p. 6.

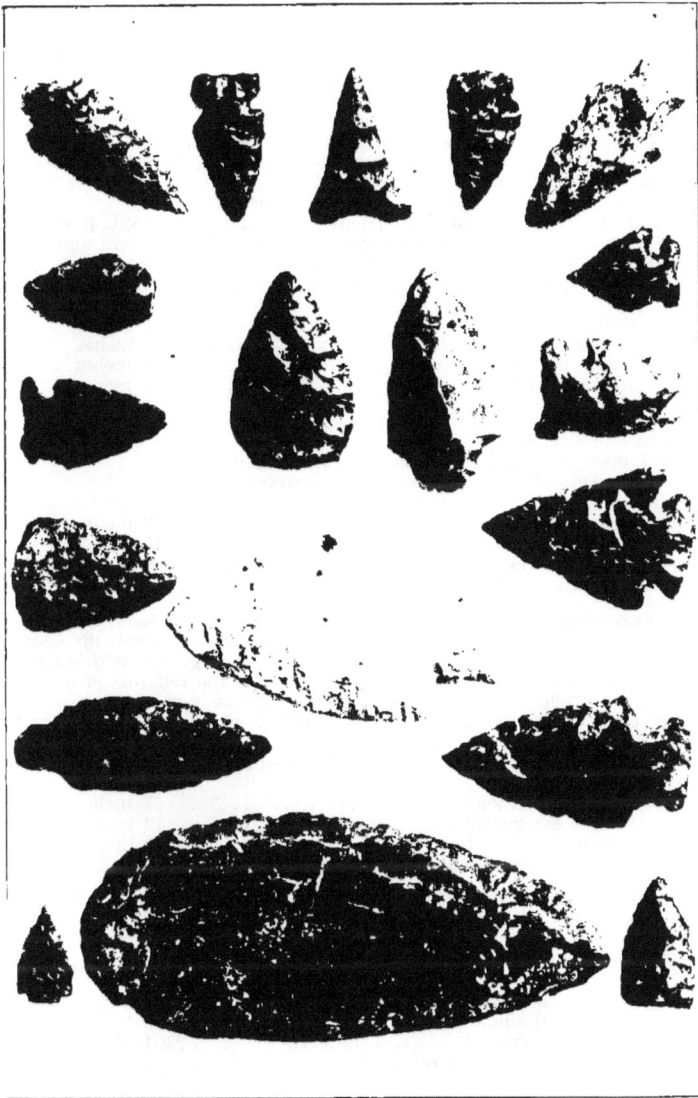

OBSIDIAN AND OTHER STONE RELICS FROM MONTANA.

(One-Half Natural Size).

Identification of locality, at the Centennial Valley, perfected as to most of them. Photographed by Swem, St. Paul, Minn.

RESEARCHES OF COL. P. W. NORRIS, SECOND SUPERINTENDENT OF THE YELLOWSTONE PARK.

"I will only here add that there is proof positive of the early and long occupancy of these mountain parks and valleys [in the Yellowstone National Park] by a people whose tools, weapons, burial cairns, and habits were very unlike those of the Red Indians and who were the makers of the steatite vessels, etc., we discovered."

(Annual Report of Superintendent of the Park for 1881, p 34.)

The steatite vessels are then described by Colonel Norris and four restorations are represented by cuts in the text. These are:

"Fragment of steatite vessel, size restored about as follows:

Greatest diameter	11 inches
Height externally	10 inches
Depth of vessel inside	8 inches
Breadth of rim	1 inch

"Much thicker in the bottom, pecked into oval shape outside. No evidence of fire, but some pestle marks in the bottom of the cavity. Found upon the surface in the Upper Madison Canon.

"Fragment of steatite vessel, size restored:

Greatest diameter	8 inches
Height externally	10 inches
Depth of vessel inside	9 inches
Breadth of rim	1-2 inch

"Very uniform throughout and finely finished, but not polished or ornamented; showing very evident fire marks. Found outside up, nearly covered with washings from the volcanic cliffs, together with various rude stone lance heads, knives, and scrapers, in the remains of ancient camp fires disclosed by the recent burning of the forest border of the upper end of Pleasant Valley, on the right of where our road enters it from the cliffs.

"Fragment of a steatite vessel, size restored:

Greatest diameter	7 inches
Height externally	12 inches
Depth of vessel inside	10 inches
Breadth of rim	5-8 inch

"Very uniform, well finished outside, but showing much evidence of fine tool marks inside. Found upon the surface of the mines at the head of Soda Butte.

"Soapstone or very soft steatite vessel, fragment:

Greatest diameter	5 inches
Smallest diameter	3 1-2 inches
Height externally	2 3-4 inches
Depth of vessel inside	2 inches
Breadth of rim	1-2 inch

"Well finished inside and out, with flat bottom. No evidence of fire; found with fragments of pottery and rude lance heads at an ancient camp on the eroding bank of the Blacktail creek.

"It may be mentioned that these steatite vessels are the first found between the Atlantic and Pacific coasts, and are entirely different in form from those found in either direction."

In attempting to draw conclusions from evidence like the foregoing, it is necessary to take into consideration the personal characteristics of its author. Colonel Norris had a large admixture of Quixotism in his nature, and the park was just the place to draw it all out. He saw everything there through a magnifying glass; and, like Don Quixote, beheld in what he saw the embodiment of all his overwrought fancy had led him to expect. It was an impossibility for him to talk or write of that region without exaggeration—not intentional, but the natural overflow of his exuberant imagination. All his distances, descriptions of scenery, personal achievements, are grossly overstated. It is indeed refreshing to follow the old mountaineer in his exhilarating literary rambles through a region which is wonderful enough on the plain basis of fact; but like Don Quixote's faithful squire, we must sooner or later strip off the outside vesture of fancy and measure our hero's visions by the humbler scale of actual reality.

The steatite vessels which Norris found were none of them intact. He has "restored" them all in the text, and the restorations are generally the larger part of the whole. After applying Norris' personal equation of overstatement, the basis of these restorations becomes insignificant. It is like restoring a cask from a mere fragment of a single stave. The result might vary according to the fancy of the restorer, from a nail keg to a railroad water tank.

It is wholly impossible to accept Norris' discoveries as affording the least support to the conclusions which he draws from them. Even admitting that he did find remnants of hand-wrought vessels, it is to be observed that they were found in the valleys of the Madison or the Yellowstone and its principal eastern tributary—in both cases along routes of travel. They were evidently dropped by migrating parties and were brought from points outside the park. Considering the nature of the Park climate, which can hardly be supposed to have been less rigid than now since the advent of man upon the earth, it is clearly impossible that this region could ever have been occupied by races pursuing the arts of civilized life.

But while there is nothing on which to base a conclusion that a more civilized race once dwelt in the Park, there is conclusive evidence that the ancestors of the present Indian races resorted to that region for the manufacture of implements of war and of the chase. Since the time when Obsidius discovered the volcanic glass which now bears his name, that material has been wrought into innumerable devices for ornament and use. Obsidian is an opaque, black, glassy substance, breaking with a conchoidal fracture and yielding sharp-edged fragments which have long been used in the manufacture of primitive weapons of destruction. Perhaps no better or more abundant quarry for this material is to be found in the world than in the now celebrated Obsidian cliff in the Yellowstone National Park. It is a massive outcrop two or three hundred feet high and half a mile long, apparently composed of no other material than an excellent quality of this obsidian glass.

To those who first saw it, the probability of its early use as an implement quarry promptly suggested itself, and led to a search for evidence of such use. Prof. W. H. Holmes, author of the geological report in the twelfth annual report of Dr. Hayden, published in 1883, explored this cliff in 1878. He says, p. 31, Hayden's report:

"It occurred to me, while making examinations at this point, that the various Indian tribes of the neighboring valleys had probably visited this locality for the purpose of procuring material for arrow-points and other implements. A finer mine could hardly be imagined; for inexhaustible supplies of the choicest obsidian, in flakes and fragments of most convenient shapes, cover the surface of the country for miles around.

"Having climbed the promontory, I observed that an old but quite distinct trail passed along the brink of the ledge and descended the broken cliffs to the valley above and below. In the vicinity of the trail the glistening flakes proved to be more plentiful than elsewhere, and were also apparently gathered into heaps. After a short search a leaf-shaped implement of very fine workmanship was found; it is made of the black opaque obsidian, and is four inches in length, three inches in width and one-half inch in thickness. * * * Having continued the search as long as the time at my command would permit, I was amply rewarded in the possession of ten more or less perfect implements. Three are leaf-shaped and nearly the same in size as the first specimen found, but imperfect from having been broken. * * * If we are to suppose that the great quantities of minute flakes are the fragments left from the manufacture of implements, we must conclude that extensive supplies have been obtained here, but by what tribes or at what period it will be quite impossible to determine."

Colonel Norris, who also discovered this quarry during the same season, and probably before Holmes saw it, describes it in his usual effusive style. (Report of Secretary of the Interior for 1878, part i, p. 982.)

"An impure obsidian, black, with white flecks and cavities, is common in the park, notably at the Great Falls; but chips, flakes, arrow-heads, and other Indian tools and weapons have been found by all recent tourists and explorers, in burial cairns, and also scattered broadcast in all those mountain valleys, of a different and much superior kind of obsidian, and from a source unknown until my discovery of it this season. I had seen the canon [near Obsidian cliff] from Sepulcher Mountain, some twenty miles distant, and specimens of obsidian increasing in number, size, and beauty as I neared it, only in wonder and admiration there to find the eastern palisade—for two miles in distance and many hundred feet in height, literally towering vertical pillars of glistening black, yellow, and mottled or banded obsidian,—basaltic columns in form, but volcanic glass in fact,—ever for the aborigines a vast weapon and implement quarry of obsidian, of a quality unequaled and a quantity elsewhere unknown."

The facts set forth in these extracts have since been abundantly verified. Arrow and spear heads and similar instruments, generally composed of obsidian, have been found throughout the Park in considerable numbers. Their discovery does not in any way establish an early occupancy of this region by Indians. Being generally found on the lines of trails, they may have been, and probably were for the most part, dropped by wandering bands who were crossing the Park or visiting this quarry. The Sheepeaters, sole aboriginal occupants of the Park country, are also to some extent responsible for their presence.

Columbus, Feb. 21, 1896.

HIRAM M. CHITTENDEN,
Captain of Engineers, U. S. Army.

Prof. E. L. Berthond, in proceedings of the Davenport Academy of Natural Sciences, also gives an interesting description of Obsidian leaf-shaped implements, found at Tahgee Pass, 7,470 feet above the sea level, and on the Madison Fork, where he noted peculiar old works and small piles of stones set at regular intervals. He also describes small stone mounds as having been found upon his route of travel through Idaho.[20]

[20] Vol. III., part ii., p. 83.

In many places in Southern Montana and along the course of the upper branches of the Missouri numerous obsidian and other stone relics, bearing the unmistakable markings of human manufacture by discoidal flaking, have been discovered in unlimited quantities.

Near the headwaters of Snake river, Mr. Nathaniel Pitt Langford and Mr. James Stevenson,[21] the first two white men to ascend to the summit of the Grand Teton in 1872 (13,833 feet above the sea), made a remarkable discovery. Mr. Langford says:

"We found on one of the buttresses, a little lower than the extreme top of the mountain, evidence, that, at some former period, it had been visited by human beings. There was a circular inclosure about seven feet in diameter formed by vertical slabs of rough granite, and about three feet in height, the interior of which was half filled with the detritus that long exposure to the elements had worn from these walls."[22]

At that time Mr. Langford thought this old stone structure might have been erected half a century before. He is now inclined toward the opinion that its construction and occupancy by man occurred before the eroding influences of the elements in nature had eroded and cut the chasms, canons and gulches into the uplifted surface, and when the country thereabouts was more nearly a level plain; not an impossibility, for human remains have been found in that part of the world deeply imbedded below the surface.

Mr. L. R. Elliott of Manhattan, Kan., has forwarded thirty-one specimens of stone implements collected on a branch of the Missouri, twelve miles south of that city. Most of these old relics show great age, and some of them a unique shaping into the form of a hand-ax or hoe, with oval, chipped extremities. They show some of the unmistakable forms made and used by the Mound-Builders, and constitute a valuable addition to the present collection.

As it is not intended to take up a discussion of all these evidences at this time, they are left over to appear in another essay upon the life work of the late Mr. Alfred J. Hill, my lamented associate in examinations at the source of the Mississippi.

In drawing this section to a termination, already more extended than was at first arranged, some reference must be made to archæological indications near the utmost source of the Missouri.

21"His part [Stevenson's] in the Yellowstone explorations of 1871 and 1872 is second to none in importance. It will not be forgotten that he was the first to build and launch a boat upon the Yellowstone lake, nor that he and Mr. Langford, who was with him, were the first white men to reach the summit of the Grand Teton."—Chittenden's "Yellowstone," 1895, p. 309.
22Sixth Annual Report, United States Geological Survey, 1872, p. 89.

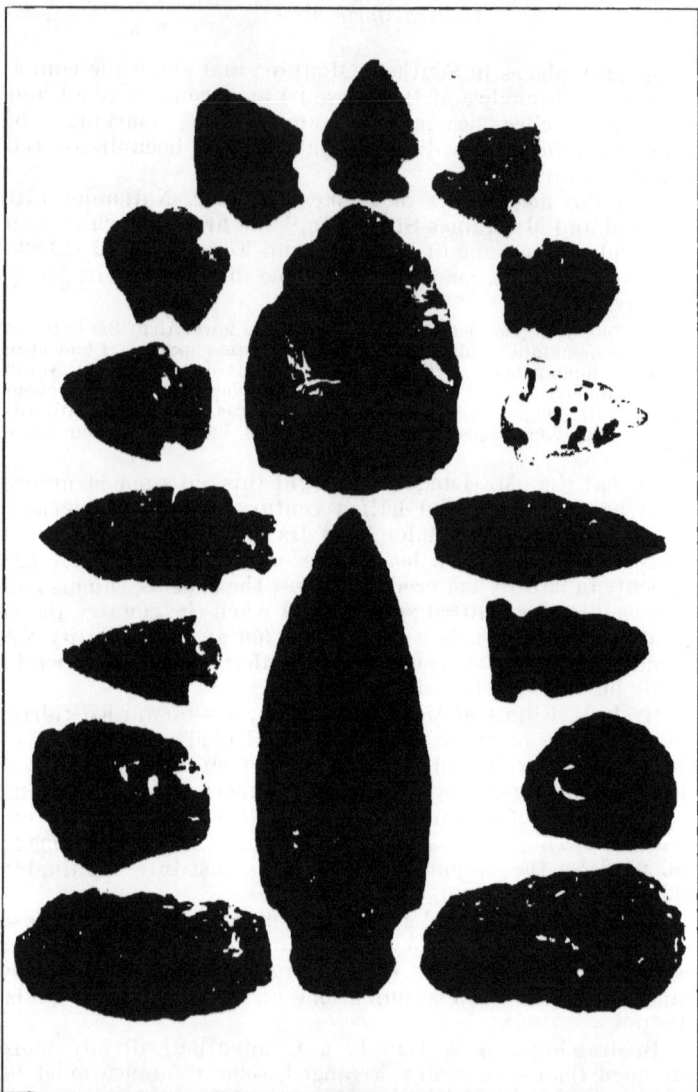

OBSIDIAN AND OTHER CHIPPED STONE IMPLEMENTS FROM NEAR
THE UTMOST SOURCE OF THE MISSOURI RIVER.

(One-Half Natural Size.)

Excavated by Mr. James Blair and others, near Red Rock Lake, Montana.
Identification of locality perfected. Photographed by Swem, St. Paul, Minn.

Mrs. Mary J. Blake, only seventeen years of age, and for nearly the whole of her brief life an equestrienne at her father's home at the base of the Rocky Mountains, near Lower Red Rock lake, has from time to time gathered, in the Centennial valley, where she lives, a collection of Obsidian spears and arrow points as they have been plowed up in the fields or washed out by rain storms, and she has also collected, from time to time, broken pipes and spalls at the pipe-stone quarry near by, on the north side of the valley. Several of these stone relics appear in the accompanying illustrations. At her father's home on Shambow creek a stone hammer was excavated, but not preserved.

STONE HAMMER.

From Upper Red Rock Lake, Montana.

Presented by Mr. A. A. Hayden, through the courtesy of Mr. James Blair.

Mr. James Blair, at his home near Upper Red Rock lake, has made a considerable collection of a more varied nature, but of the same character, and he furnishes the stone hammer illustrated, as having been found near his residence by Mr. Hayden.

Mr. and Mrs. W. X. Culver, at their mountain home in the same locality, on Picnic creek, which flows directly out of the base of a mountain, have gathered from time to time the obsidian and slate spearheads and arrow points common in the region.

Mrs. S. B. Burnside, likewise, has made a collection of the same class of relics in the neighborhood of Henry's lake and Tar-ghé pass,[23] named after the chief of the Lemhi Bannocks, the band of Indians who occupied the Centennial valley when it first became known to civilized man.

At the mouth of Long creek, below the Lower Red Rock lake, is an embankment that has every appearance of being artificial in its nature; probably a work for defense during some unknown warfare of the remote past. In that same neighborhood is a very old irrigated field with symmetrical rows and ditches, but of such an age that the practiced eye only would detect its outlines. No one in the locality had any knowledge of its existence.

Obsidian spalls and debris are scattered far and wide throughout the Red Rock lake locality, indicating an occupancy by man in the remote past, the earliest date of which remains undetermined.

The indications are, that, probably, they were North American Indians, but unfortunately no scientist has been able to penetrate the mystery surrounding the advent of this remarkable race of savages, and their earliest history remains enveloped in the most impenetrable obscurity, legitimately prehistoric in its nature, and if the unduly strenuous efforts to force an acceptance of the proposition, that the Mound-Builders were the immediate ancestry of certain tribes of North American Indians, shall finally prevail, that result will utterly fail to determine the identity of their origin, which is the most important question involved, almost lost sight of in the acrimonious discussion, touching a supposed tribal relationship by ancestral descent, not known to exist between the ancient Mound-Builder and the modern Indian. The Indians of the present time, in the Upper Mississippi Basin, have no legendary information concerning the people who built the mounds, and all will admit that the Indians mentioned and their ancestors have resided in Wisconsin, Minnesota, Dakota, and Iowa localities since the very earliest time of which we have any historic knowledge, and not within that time have they themselves been builders of mounds.

23This old chief, who has been a frequent visitor at the home of Mr. Culver, gave his name as Tar-ghé, and that is the proper pronunciation of the name and of Tar-ghe pass. The name as signed to the official treaty of cession is: "Tag-gee, chief of the Bannock tribe of Indians." See Revision of Indian Treaties, 1873, p. 931.

SIOUX TREE BURIAL AT STANDING ROCK, NORTH DAKOTA.
From a photograph by D. F. Barry.

CHIEF JOSEPH (The Shahaptian Warrior).
From a photograph by F. Jay Haynes.
(30)

§ V. INDIAN OCCUPANCY OF THE MISSOURI BASIN AND THE NOMENCLATURE OF ITS PRINCIPAL RIVER.

"The sun is my father and the earth is my mother, and I will rest on her bosom."

These were the words said to have been spoken by Tecumseh, Aug. 15, 1810, to Gen. William Henry Harrison, at Vincennes, Indiana, in council, when no chair was provided for that noted Indian's accommodation, and he seated himself upon the bosom of the earth; a silent and intrepid chieftain, the embodiment of autochthonic characterization in aboriginal mythology.

His oratory and his courage were insufficient to save his people the land of their birth, and they turned their faces toward the setting sun, disappearing into that realm of elements, mysterious and unfathomable, which gave them their temporary existence upon the face of the earth.

Mute pages of history indicate the sequel, from New England to the Pacific slope; the grandest land in all the world. The sun of the white man rose in the East, and the night of the Indian enveloped the West.

Under the very able direction of Maj. J. W. Powell, the ethnologic history of the American Indian has assumed a scope commensurate with the highest purpose involved in the official investigations for which the Bureau of Ethnology was established; and time will demonstrate that perhaps an hundred volumes of carefully prepared public reports will be necessary to unfold and display all that can be learned of the origin, existence, character, habits, and fate of the numerous cognate nations, tribes, and bands, articulating probably four hundred languages and two thousand dialects,[24] who legitimately possessed the larger part of the northern portion of the Western hemisphere when discovered under Spanish auspices; and much of that unfolding must necessarily rest upon the basis of individual opinions, as variously influenced by impressions, interpretations, and purposes, gained in the fields of ethnologic research.

No hope exists of throwing any new light upon any of the intricated questions enveloping Indian history, at this time; yet they have been the most important and eventful epochs affecting civilization in the Basin of the Missouri.

The Iberian, Gaulish, and Anglo-Saxon conquests, approaching successively the coasts of the Gulf, the river St. Lawrence, and the Atlantic seaboard, registered the com-

---

24 Ellis' "Indian Wars of the United States," 1893, p. 3.

mencement of the downfall of tribal life in North America.
This beautiful and bounteous land, probably uplifted from the
depths of the ocean, had been the scene of active and warlike
life for so many centuries that its population had lost all
knowledge of its origin, except the traditionary recitals,
handed down from tribe to tribe and from father to son, incidentally conformable to mythic or religious beliefs, inherited
from an ancestry unknown in the history of enlightened civilization. According to the "Map of Linguistic Stocks," the Basin of the Missouri[25] had been principally occupied by the Siouan, Algonquian, Caddoan, Kiowan, and Shoshonean linguistic divisions of the Indian tribes, when the fortunes of war
and the vicissitudes of wealth precipitated an intromission of
foreign occupancy as persistent as has been the disappearance
of these children of nature, until occasional reservations with
a diminishing people are all that remain to indicate where the
light of the fire of the Indian went out. His lodge-poles are
missing, his game is all gone and his squaws are half-white,
licentiously tainted with the blood of a more formidable race.[26]
The history of the past four hundred years practically covers
the period of about all that can be said of the Indians of America; their discovery, the exciting scenes of a warlike dispos-
session, and their downfall, absorption, and final disappearance.

Incidentally there is another question of historic moment:
tribal names and designations.

Every word spoken in the original tongue of the Indian
has its direct meaning. Modern ethnologic writers seem determined to systematically modify and change about all the
names found in tribal nomenclature to such an extent that
the not distant future will witness an established interruption
in pronunciation and orthography that seems to foreshadow
the obliteration and abandonment of all the old original
names of the different stocks and tribes.

The great Dakota nation and related tribes occupied nearly
the entire Missouri Basin. Each band was named according
to the character of the place or location where they resided, as

25Annual Report, Bureau of Ethnology, 1886, vol. vii., and Eleventh Census
of the United States (1890), Indians, p. 36.

26This is a more important question than has ever been admitted, for only
in scattered lines has the real truth received attention. From New Scotland to
Mexico and from the Carolinas to the Pacific coast, without interruption or cessa-
tion, prohibition or punishment, this miscegenation has been eventful and morbid.
Only one quotation is given from a list of many hundreds noted in various
publications: "Nevertheless, adultery is not reckoned any great crime among
them, and there are women who make no secret of having had to do with
Frenchmen. Yet are they not sufficiently addicted to that vice to offer themselves, and they never fail unless they are sued to, when they are none of the
most difficult in the world to be prevailed on."—French's "Jontel's Historical
Journal," 1846, p. 188, in Historical Collections of Louisiana.

BANNOCK INDIANS, NEAR THE UTMOST SOURCE OF THE MISSOURI.
Shoshonean Linguistic Stock.

SIOUX GHOST DANCERS AT THE STANDING ROCK, NORTH DAKOTA.
From a photograph by D. F. Barry.

described by Riggs in his "Dakota Language," 1851 ("Smithsonian Contributions to Knowledge"), from Mille Lacs in Minnesota to the Black Hills and the Upper Missouri.

Mr. Riggs and his associates were missionaries, and they lived among the Dakotas almost an entire lifetime, and the information preserved by them is of the most reliable nature, coming as it does direct from the Indians themselves.

Mr. Riggs says:

"Dakota; feeling affection for; friendly.
"Dakota: The name of the Sioux Indians. They are divided into seven principal divisions — Mdewakantonwans, Wahpetonwans, Wahpekutes, Sisitonwans, Ihanktonwans, Ihanktonwannas, and Titonwans [Damakota, Danikota, Daunkotapi, Dawicakota].
"Their name, the Dakotas say, means 'leagued' or 'allied.'
"Also: Oceti-sakowin—Seven council fires."

Most of these names are practically obliterated from use, and a century hence will be referred to as ethnological curiosities.

On the other hand, the designations now in use, to a very great extent, were unknown and unheard of among the Indians, until the modifications were adopted by the whites and extended to them in written descriptions.

These modifications are very numerous. A few are noted:

Naudowessioux [Sioux], Nation of the Bœff [Buffalo].

Ozaukiuk, Ozaukies, Sauks, Sac [Sprouting].

Oumissourites, Missourites, Missouria, Missouri.[27]

Anishinaubag,[28] Ojibway, Chippewa, Chippeway [Spontaneous].

The word "Indian," so universally adopted, was never heard of or spoken until after the landing of Columbus, when it was supposed he had reached India, and the natives were thence known as Indians; now, in vulgar parlance, called "Injun," even by many of the natives themselves. This question is too broad and far-reaching to permit of an attempt to fathom its causes and scope at this time.

Other considerations, such as origin, ancestral relations, cannibalism, slavery, flesh-eaters, root-diggers, fish-netters, lodge and troglodytic life, religious traditions and instincts, mortuary rites and practices, marriage customs, polygamy, migrations, origin and secrets of clans, climatic influences, and those various and numerous conditions of Indian existence, life, warfare, habits, customs, and languages, might be referred to, were it not for want of space and opportunity at this time.

27The true meaning is explained in following pages.
28Hoffman gives this name as Ani Shinâ bég, in Seventh Annual Report, Bureau of Ethnology, 1885, p. 179. Gilfillan, the ripest and most accomplished Ojibway student, states it differently, from White Earth, where he has resided among them for a quarter of a century.

A BANNOCK INDIAN.

RUNNING DEER.
A Crow Indian.
(37)

The Missourias Indians, said to be of the same linguistic stock,—Siouan,—and after whom the name Missouri has come down to us, are now practically an extinct tribe or band, having been consolidated with the Otoes, now at Ponca, Oklahoma. The name of these Indians will be referred to for information concerning the true meaning and origination of the tribal designation conferred upon them.

It is evident, and more than probable, that they are the descendants of that ancestry who located somewhere upon the Missouri river prior to the advent of the French, and, increasing in numbers, developed into the numerous bands known to exist,[29] some of which passed up the river and some down toward its mouth. In that way the habitat of the Missourias became fixed near the junction of the Missouri with the Mississippi; hence they were known as people "Living on the Mouth of the Waters."

Their reduced numbers, from a powerful and savage tribe, came from warfare, and the destructive influences of smallpox,[30] which depleted their ranks until they were no longer able to withstand the onslaughts of their enemies, and claiming the protection of the Otoes, consolidation and extinction as a separate tribe followed.

Like all other North American Indians, they knew nothing concerning their origin, save only those traditionary lines of uncertainty, which their successors in the Western country have been unable to fathom.[31]

As bloodthirsty savages, they figure in contemporaneous history,[32] treacherous and cunning in modes of action to an extent equaling the later tribes of the same stock, who have plundered, murdered, and mutilated the frontier settlers, and

[29]Col. Garrick Mallery has determined that there were at least 126 bands.
[30]Catlin's "North American Indians," vol. ii., p. 24.
[31]"If the character of the Indian is enveloped in mystery, how much more so is his origin. From his earliest history to the present time learned men have striven to unravel this mystery, and to trace the genealogy of the red man to its original source. But in spite of all study and the deepest research capable of being brought to bear on this subject, it is to-day surrounded by a darkness almost as deep and impenetrable as that which enfolded it centuries ago. Various writers of ability have attempted to prove that the Indians came from Eastern Asia; others trace them to Africa; others to Phoenicia, while another class believes them to be Atochthones. In favor of each of these beliefs strong circumstantial evidence can be produced."—General Custer's "My Life on the Plains," p. 13.
[32]"As it was known that the company in France readily favored any proposition made for the advancement of the colony of Louisiana, an officer represented that it would be advantageous to form a post on the river of the Missouris, in the vicinity of an Indian tribe of that name. This project was approved, he was named commandant of the new post, repaired to New Orleans, showed his orders, received three boat-loads of provisions and necessaries for the execution of his plan, and some soldiers, to act first as boatmen, then as garrison of the fort he was to build. They sailed up [the Mississippi and Missouri] in 1720, and on arriving were well received by the Missouris, who gave them a suitable site for the new establishment. A palisade fort was at once thrown up, with a cabin within for the commandant and officers and another for the soldiers' barracks. All went on peaceably at the new post, where they lived in perfect harmony with the Indians, when the commandant, who had formerly rambled much in those parts, and spoke their language very well, endeavored to persuade some of them to go with him to France, where he told them he would show them everything fine. At the same time he told a thousand

ravished their wives and daughters, until retaliation followed with the same vengeance; and rifle-pits and trenches for defense are scattered on the plains nearly the entire length of the Missouri and many of its branches, now relics of past decades; for the Indian, becoming subdued, likewise became submissive, and the graves of the dead mark the progress of the change.

Captain Wheeler has aptly said:

"The Indian has been denominated and treated as a ward, and at the same time as ostensibly a sovereign, treaty-making power. He has been met by the government, through its War Department, sword in hand, to suppress outbreak, and as sustaining the Interior Department, whose emblem has been the olive branch, while the citizen has too often stood ready to rob him of his morals and his land. It is not at all strange that this child of wonder and fear, viewing nature and man more through the external senses, should resist the approach of civilization that apparently despoils him of most that life holds dear."[33]

The name Missouri has come down to the present generation in a modified form, and with a misinterpretation of its real and true original meaning, as named after a tribe of the Siouan stock residing upon its banks when first seen by Europeans. The preparation of a detailed list of the different forms of this name was arranged for, but owing to an unforeseen disappointment only a partial and curtailed showing can now be made; sufficient, however, to indicate the origin, meaning, and use of the word as applied to the Indians, the river, and a state of the Federal Union.

The original meaning of the word Missouri was "Living on the Mouth of the Waters." So stated by the Indians themselves.

The following references are deemed of sufficient interest to warrant preservation in this form:

---

wonderful stories of that country, so that by dint of presents and promises he succeeded in getting eleven to follow him, with the great chief's daughter, who was, it was said, his mistress. The voyage being thus decided on, the commandant embarked in some piraguas with these twelve Indians, and a sergeant named Dubois, leaving his lieutenant in command of his fort and garrison; then descending the River St. Louis, they landed at New Orleans, whence after some days rest they embarked for France. * * * The girl became a Christian and was baptized at Notre Dame, after which Sergeant Dubois married her and in consequence of this alliance was made an officer, and commandant of the Missouris. * * * The voyage of M. and Mme. Dubois and their suite to America was a very prosperous one; all arrived in good health at New Orleans, and while they remained there to rest, were supported at the expense of the company, which also furnished them a boat, with soldiers and boatmen, to carry them to their village. On their way they passed to the Natchez, then to the Arcancas, and at last arrived at the Missouris. What joy for those Indians to see once more their countrymen, whom they had given up for lost, and see them return rich and loaded with presents! * * * Mme. Dubois remained at the fort and went, from time to time to visit her family. But, either because she did not love her husband, or that her own people's way of living suited her better than the French, the boats which brought them had scarcely left, when the Indians massacred the Sieur Dubois and butchered the whole garrison, not one escaping; after which Madam Dubois renounced Christianity, and returned to her former mode of life, so that the past no longer exists."—Historical Memoirs of Louisiana, series v., 1853, pp. 37-39.

[33] Geographical Report, 1889, vol. I., p. 219.

THE NAME—MISSOURI, DEFINED.

"R PEKITTANSI."   From fac simile of the autograph map of the Mis-
[Pekitanoui.]   sissippi or Conception river, drawn by Father Mar-
[Peketanoui.]   quette at the time of his voyage. From the original
preserved at St. Mary's College, Montreal.—Histor-
ical Collections of Louisiana, 1852, part iv., p. 268.

"I have seen nothing more frightful; a mass of large trees, entire, with branches,—real floating islands,—came rushing from the mouth of the river Pekitanoui, so impetuously that we could not, without great danger, expose ourselves to pass across. The agitation was so great that the water was all muddy and could not get clear."—Marquette.

"SeMESSSRIT."   To the northwestward, up the Missouri river, on
[Oumessourit.]   the same map, at a point indicated as an Indian
village, the foregoing word was placed by Mar-
quette, demonstrating that he then heard of the
Indians, now known as Missourias.

DEPARTMENT OF THE INTERIOR,
UNITED STATES INDIAN SERVICE.
PONCA, ETC., AGENCY, PONCA, OKL., Feb. 11, 1896.

Dear Sir: In reply to your communication of Dec. 24, 1895, I submit the following information relative to the Missouria Indians:

The name of these Indians appears on the records of this agency now, and for quite a number of years back, as "Missouria." Whether this is the correct spelling of this word or not I am unable to say. This word means "Living on the Mouth of the Waters."

Pekitanoui belongs to the Missouria Indians who consolidated with the Sac and Fox Indians, and the Missourias of this agency do not know the meaning of this word. You could perhaps get the meaning of this word by making application to the agent for the Sax and Fox Indians, Sac and Fox Agency, Oklahoma. Only a very few of the Missouria Indians are now living, and they have progressed but very little in the arts of civilization. They oppose the allotment of land in severalty, preferring to still cling to the old tribal customs. Financially these Indians, together with the Otoes, are well fixed; in fact, too well for their own good. The head chief of the confederated tribe of Otoe and Missouria Indians claims to be a full-blood Missouria. His name is White Horse, and he wields great influence over the tribe, and is a typical Indian. The Missourias as a distinct people will soon pass away, as they have inter-married with the Otoes. I hope you will pardon the delay in giving this information, for it has taken a longer time than I at first anticipated it would.

Very respectfully,
J. P. WOOLSEY,
United States Indian Agent.

Missourias.   }
Oumissourias.   }
Oumissourites.   } Living on the Mouth of the Waters.
Oumissourits.   }

HYDROGRAPHY OF THE MISSISSIPPI BASIN.
ST. PAUL, MINN., Feb. 14th, 1896.

Indian Agent, Sac and Fox Agency.

Dear Sir: Mr. J. P. Woolsey, the agent at Ponca, suggests that I write to you to ascertain the meaning of the name "Pekitanoui," one of the names applied to the Missouri river. White Horse, the chief of the Missourias, at Ponca, says it is a Sac and Fox name. Also, do you know the meaning of the word Sac or Sauk? Your early reply will be thankfully received.

Very sincerely,
J. V. BROWER.

UNIDENTIFIED CHARACTERISTIC PORTRAIT.
From the Bannock Region in the Rocky Mountains.
Reduced from a photograph forwarded from Pocatello, Idaho.

SAC AND FOX AGENCY, Feb. 21, 1896.
Dear Sir: The meaning of the word "Peketanoui" is "Missourian." The word "Sauk" means "Growing Up"—"Sprouting." White Horse is called "Wah-pe-ske-na-ko-to-kow-show."
The above is given by

WILLIAM HURR,
Interpreter.

"When in 1673, Marquette descended the Wisconsin and the Mississippi, and was going along with the current in clear water at a speed of twelve miles an hour, he noticed a great change in the body of the stream, which was produced by the much more rapid influx from the west of a great volume of eddying sediment. He learned from the Indians that this polluting stream was called the Pekitanoui. At a later day, when the tribe of the Missouris was found to be a leading race among the fourteen nations of savages which inhabited the banks of this great river, it was easy for it to become better known as the Missouri, thus distinguishing it as an affluent of the Mississippi, when the volume of its current entitled it, rather than the Mississippi, to be called the principal stream. At this time Marquette indulged the hope that one day he might be permitted to ascend its turbid course and solve the great problem of the West. It was reserved, however, for the eighteenth century to begin the solution of that geographical riddle which was made clear in the nineteenth. It was then found that the springs of the Platte, which fed the Missouri, were adjacent to those of the Colorado, which debouched into the Gulf of California. Other explorers discovered that the sources of the Yellowstone and portages to those of the Snake while an upper affluent of the Missouri was contiguous to the headwaters of Clark's Fork. The Snake and this fork were ultimately found to pass their united waters into the Columbia * * *."—Winsor's "Mississippi Basin," p. 32.

Riviere des Osages.
[Emissourites.]
[Oumessourits.]

"The Missouri is called Pekitanoui by Marquette. It also bears on early French maps the names of Riviere des Osages and Riviere des Emissourites, or Oumessourits. On Marquette's map a tribe of this name is placed near its banks, just above the Osages. Judging by the course of the Mississippi that it discharged into the Gulf of Mexico, he conceived the hope of one day reaching the South Sea by way of the Missouri."—Parkman's "La Salle," page 60, note.

"We now come to the map of Marquette; which is a rude sketch of a portion of Lakes Superior and Michigan and of the route pursued by him and Joliet up the Fox river of Green Bay, down the Wisconsin, and thence down the Mississippi as far as the Arkansas. The river Illinois is also laid down, as it was by this course that he returned to Lake Michigan after his memorable voyage. * * * The Mississippi is called 'Riviere de la Conception;' the Missouri, the 'Pekitanoui.' * * * On or near the Missouri he places the Ouchage (Osages), the Oumessourit (Missouris), the Kansa (Kanzas), the Paniassa (Pawnees), the Maha (Omahas), and the Pahoutet (Pah Utahs?)."—Parkman's "La Salle," appendix, 457.

Forked River.

"Wee mett with severall sorts of people. Wee conversed with them, being long time in alliance with them By the persuasion of some of them we went into ye great river that divides itself in two where the hurrons with some Ottanake and the wild men that had warrs with them had retired. * * * The river is called the forked, because it has two branches: the one towards the West, the other towards the South, which we believe runs towards Mexico by the tokens they gave."—"Radison's Voyage" by the Prince Society, 1885, pp. 7-8.

Thus wrote Peter Esprit Radisson about the year 1660, a short time before or afterward; actual date unknown. Two conclusions are drawn from the Radisson papers: (1) Radisson and Groseilliers reached and crossed the Upper Mississippi in Northern Minnesota at that time, and thereby discovered it. (2) They heard of the Missouri river, which was described as "Forked River."

"le Missouri ou R de Pekitanoui." On "Carte de la Louisiane et du Cours du Mississippi," found in Historical Collections of Louisiana, 1850, by B. F. French, the above designation is found at the point on the river where Mandan is now situated. The map is De l'Isle's. This seems to definitely connect the two words of Marquette, as given on his original map.

Ozage. On the thirteenth day of February, 1682, the Sieur de la La Salle reached the mouth of the Missouri. In the narrative of his voyage down the Mississippi, Father Zenobius described this occurrence as follows:

"The floating ice on the river Colbert [Mississippi] at this place, kept us till the 13th of the same month, when we set out, and six leagues lower down found the Ozage (Missouri) river, coming from the west. It is full as large as the river Colbert [Mississippi] into which it empties, troubling it so, that. from the mouth of the Ozage, the water is hardly drinkable. The Indians assure us that this river is formed by many others, and that they ascend it for ten or twelve days to a mountain [Rocky Mountains] where it rises; that beyond this mountain is the sea where they see great ships; that on the river are a great number of large villages of many different nations and there are arable and prairie lands, and abundance of cattle and beaver. Although this river is very large the Colbert [Mississippi] does not seem augmented by it; but it pours in so much mud * * * that the water is more like clear mud than river water."—Narrative of Father Zenobius, p. 165, Historical Collections of Louisiana. Part iv., 1852. French.

Minanghenachequeke. "Extract from the Memoire of Bougainville on the State of New France, 1757."

The late Mr. Alfred J. Hill, my associate, writing, probably in 1894, noted this name for the Missouri river, in his historical researches.

Mr. Hill's written extract says:

"The fort Dauphin, eighty leagues [220.8 miles] from the preceding [the fort la Reine], is situated upon the river Minanghenachequeké, or Muddy Water [De l' Eautrouble]."

QUERY.—May not this have been during the time of the journey of the Chevalier de la Verendrye, or his successor, Jacques Repentigny de Saint Pierre, about one hundred and fifty years ago, the origination of the name Muddy Water river [Big Muddy], as applied to the Missouri?

Missisourie.
Missesourie.
Mississoury.
Missisoury.
Missourites.
Missourias.
Missourie.
Dr. Elliott Coues has called attention to the foregoing different forms of the name Missouri, taken in part from the writings of David Thompson, the astronomer, 1798, at the Mandan country, near Heart river. The source of the Missouri was calculated by Thompson on Indian information as follows: Lat. 45 deg. 30 min. 37 sec., long. 110 deg. 49 min. .08 sec. In his communication Dr. Coues says:

"SMITHSONIAN INSTITUTE, WASHINGTON, March 20, 1896.

"Dear Sir: I may note here the prevalence of an additional syllable in the name, very common in the N. W. country writings late in the last and early in the present century, during which time such forms as above stated were very frequent if not the rule. Sir Alexander McKenzie, David Thompson, and others used such forms. My present author, Alexander Henry, Jr., 1799-1814, usually has Missourie, which is again a different style of variation; also, Missoury.

Sincerely yours,

ELLIOTT COUES.

River St. Philip. The letters patent from the French King to Sieur Anthony Crozat, 1712, granting the commerce of Louisiana, after extraordinary and sweeping authority extended, says, among other things, in describing the territory covered by the grant:

"* * * And do appoint the said Sieur Crozat solely to carry on a trade in all the lands possessed by us, and bounded by New Mexico and by the lands of the English of Carolina, all the establishments, ports, havens, rivers, principally the port and haven of the isle Dauphine, heretofore called Monacre, the river St. Louis heretofore called Mississippi from the edge of the sea as far as the Illinois together with the river St. Philip heretofore called Missouri, and St. Jerome heretofore called Onabache, with all the countries, territories, lakes within land, and rivers which fall directly or indirectly into that part of the river St. Louis," * * * with all necessary powers to discover, open and operate mines of the precious metals within the territory granted by the favor of the crown. Thus every gold, silver and copper mine within the basin of the river St. Philip (Missouri) was granted to one individual; not, however, in perpetuity, but for a term of years, and even this term was curtailed by failure in 1717.

Missourias.
Missouries.
Missouri.
Mud River.
Muddy River.

MISSOURI HISTORICAL SOCIETY.
1600 LUCAS PLACE.
ST. LOUIS, Jan. 13, 1896.

Dear Sir: Replying to yours of the 8th inst. I have been unable to satisfy myself of the true meaning of Missouri, whether a name in the true sense of the word or merely descriptive I cannot learn. The first mention I find is by Marquette mentioning a tribe of Indians, the Missouries, living at what is now known as the mouth of the Missouri river. The Missouri country, as designated by the French, was that portion of this state bordering on the river of the same name, and on which the Missourias were located. Lewis and Clarke, Pike, and others, interpret the word Missouri as "Mud" or "Muddy," i. e., "Missouri river," "Mud River," "Muddy River," and this is the generally accepted meaning. I believe that the Sioux Indians called the river Pekitanoui. If you have access to a Sioux dictionary the Sioux meaning may help you out. Missouri Territory and Missouri State was retained from the French, and which referred to the tribe of the same name. I should be pleased if you will advise me of anything more definite if you find it.

Very truly,

WILLIAM J. SEEVER,
Secretary.

Missury. Peter Pond, upon his map of April, 1785, found upon p. 52, Report on Canadian Archives, by Douglas Brymner, 1890, says:

"Here, upon the branches of the Missury, live the Maundiens, who bring to our factory at Fort Epinett, on the Assinipoil river, Indian corn for sale. Our people go to them with loaded horses in twelve days."

At a representation of mountains on the same map, farther to the westward, the following appears in colors:

"Hereabouts the Missury takes its source out of the mountains."

Other notes characterize different tribes of Indians by name such as "Nottowases or Sious," "Bigg Bellys," "Near these mountains live the Sweet Mouth Indians."

Ni-u-t'a-tei.
New-dar-cha.
Ne-o-ta-chu.   } "Said to mean 'Those who settle at the mouth of a
Ne-o-ge-he.   river,' i. e., the Missouri."

"The Missouri or Missouria Indians (Ni-u-t'a-tei) were one of the principal tribes of the great Siouan linguistic stock or family. In Powell's classification they are enumerated as the tenth of eighteen Sioux tribes. Lewis' "Statistical View" (1806) spells this native name New-dar-cha. Some of the many forms of this name are Neotacha and Neogehe. The word is said to mean 'those who settle at the mouth of a river,' i. e., the Missouri. They later moved up where they were found by the French in about 1700. They lived in one village with the Otoes, mustering a total of 300 persons, with eighty warriors. They traded with the merchants of St. Louis, and their commerce was substantially the same as that of the Otoes. They were at peace with the Pawnees proper, Sacs, and Foxes, but warred with the Omahas, Poncas, Sioux, Osages, Kansas, and Pawnee Loups. At that date they were already the mere remnant of a numerous nation inhabiting the Missouri when first known to the French. Their ancient and principal village was on an extensive and fertile prairie on the north bank of the river, just below the mouth of Grand river. * * * In 1752 D'Auville called the Missouri the Pekitanoui, or Reviere des Missouris." Coues' "Lewis and Clark," 1893, p. 22, note 49.

Niut'atei.
Teiwere.
(Che wa-ra).   "A tribe of the Teiwere division of the Siouan stock
Ni cud je.   of the North American Indians. Their name for themselves is Niut'atei, 'Those who reached the mouth' (of the river). Called Ni cudje by the Kansa, which appellation may have been corrupted into Missouri. For many years they have been consolidated with the Oto. The population of the two tribes is given as 358." * * *

"Teiwere [an Oto term meaning Autochthon]—A division of the Siouan stock of North American Indians, composed of three tribes: The Iowa, Oto, and Missouri."—Col. Garrick Mallery, in "Century Cyclopedia of Names, 1894."

Ne-u-chaeta.   "The Missourians, 'Encamped at the mouth of the
Ne-u-tach.   stream;' Ne-u-chaeta, 'At the mouth of the stream;' hence, Ne-u-tach, the name they go by. But this seems to contradict the saying that they were escaped prisoners within the recollection of the older ones, unless it refers to previous history. The Otoes derive their name from a transaction or love scrape between an Oto chief's son and an Iowa chief's daughter, Watota.[34] * * * The Omahas have a similar tradition about the Missourians, except, that, instead of encamping at the mouth of the stream, there were two persons drowned in the stream, and hence the name ne, 'water,' and u-chae, 'to die in,' i. e., 'to drown,' ta, 'at a place,' as Ne-u-chae-ta, 'to be drowned at.'"—Father William Hamilton in Transactions Nebraska State Historical Society, vol. i., p. 75.

---

[34] "Otoe," or "Lovers of the sexual pleasure."

Mi ni-So sa.
Me Ne-Suchae. } Missouri River

"The Missouri, I think, derives its name from the Sioux language in which 'water' is Me-Ne; smoky or roily is Suchae in Iowa, Zheda in Omaha, and something like it in Sioux, as all speak of it under a term signifying smoky or roily or foggy, as the word often signifies."—Father William Hamilton in Transactions Nebraska State Historical Society, 1885, vol. i., p. 74.

"Mi ni, 'water;' So sa, 'roiled.' "—Rigg's "Dakota Language," 1852, "Smithsonian Contributions to Knowledge," vol. iv.

NAMES OF STATES ON THE MISSOURI.

Missouri. From a tribe of Indians, who were known as a people. "Living on the mouth of the Waters." The river having been named after this tribe, the stream was known by the Indians on the lower portion of the river as "Living on the Mouth of the Waters River," from which the word Missouri has been corrupted from the original pronunciation. North American Indians usually name localities, lakes, and rivers in like manner and after some circumstance or feature.

Kansas. From a tribe of Indians variously known as Kaws, Kanza, Kansa, Kanzas, Konza, Kanse, said to be "a reference to the wind."

Neshnebottany.
Nesh-un-pachae-o-wae-ne.
Nodaway, Iowa. "Neshnebottany signifies a stream on which a canoe or boat may pass: Nesh-na, 'stream;' pachae, 'a boat,' o-wae-ne, to make a way or passage.' Nodaway is Ne-a-ta-wae, Iowa, 'a stream that can be jumped over,' or it might mean 'jumping water."—Father William Hamilton, in Transactions Nebraska State Historical Society, vol. i., p. 74.

Nebraska.
Nebrathka. "The Platte is, as you are aware, a French word signifying 'broad,' and is a translation of the Indian name signifying the same thing, Ne-brath-kae, or Ne-prath-kae, in Iowa, and Ne-brath-kae, in Omaha, or, as some speak it, Nebraska."—Father William Hamilton, in Transactions Nebraska State Historical Society, vol. i., p. 73.

North Dakota.
South Dakota. } Formerly Dakota Territory.

Named after the Sioux Indians—"Leagued" or "Allied;" "Seven Council Fires."

Montana. "The name was given by the Committee on Territories in the House of Representatives. Hon. James M. Ashley, in answer to a question as to the meaning of the word replied: 'It is a Spanish word, meaning mountainous.' "—Congressional Globe, March 19, 1864, p. 1169; Report of the Internal Commerce of the United States, 1889, p. 481.

(See Appendix.)

YELLOW DOG.
A Crow Indian.
From a photograph by F. Jay Haynes.

CURLEY, A CROW SCOUT.
Only Survivor of the Custer Massacre.
From a photograph by F. Jay Haynes, St. Paul.

CURLEY (The same Indian).

As a Crow Savage.

From a photograph by D. F. Barry.

SITTING BULL.
The noted Medicine Man of the Sioux.
Shot by Indian Police
Dec. 15, 1890.
From a copyrighted photograph by D. F. Barry.

SITTING BULL (The same Indian).
In modern Tribal Costume.
From a copyrighted photograph by D. F. Barry.

(51)

OLD CROW.
A Crow Chief.
From a photograph by D. F. Barry.

§ VI. THE SPANISH AND FRENCH DISCOVERIES.

Some references seem now desirable concerning the approach of civilization toward the Missouri.[35]

Years before Soto, the "Hernand of the Grove," had crossed the Mississippi, at some unknown point below the site of the city of Memphis, Nunez Cabeza de Vaca, the treasurer of the unfortunate Narvaez expedition, landing probably on the shores of Texas, had wandered with his three companions northward to the plains and mountains of the West. After about nine years of hardships and privations, alternating between captivity and freedom, they hailed with sentiments of delight, in April, 1536, the Spanish settlements in Mexico. This is referred to here not that they had gone as far as the Missouri, but that they had found the tribes, the buffalo, the mountains, and the plains to the northward under such remarkable circumstances as to lead to the presumption that they were probably the first Europeans to learn of the existence, from tribal sources and by actual discoveries, of the grand river system, supplying the freshets that had formerly driven their boats into the sea at the delta of the Mississippi, when their shirts were the sails and the lanyards the manes and tails of their horses, of which system the Missouri is an important part. Wherever Soto may have marched with his army from the 18th of June, 1541, until the 17th of the following April, no one has yet successfully fathomed the identity of the actual localities traversed, except that the direction was northerly and the position west of the Mississippi, which they had called the Rio Grande. It is unlikely that an army would march to the north, under such circumstances and in search of gold, without learning from the natives the character of the country beyond, and yet no certainty exists concerning the actual localities penetrated. Had they marched farther to the westward they would have learned, from their own kindred, of Coronado's northward march to the Seven Cities of Cibola, and unques-

---

[35] In the library of the Historical Society of Montana and of the Manchester Geographical Society of England will be found vol. vii. of the Minnesota State Historical Collections, "The Mississippi River and Its Source," which describes in detail the Spanish and French accounts of the discovery of the Mississippi, which will not be repeated here.

tionably, to the valley of the Missouri,[36] in 1540-42. Coronado marched with his mixed army from Culiacan in April, 1540, reached the famed cities of Cibola in the following July, overcoming with force and arms every opposition of the natives, and, searching for gold, penetrated far to the northward, across mountains and plains under the guidance of "The Turk," an Indian of that region, who represented, faultlessly in description, but recklessly in fact, for which he was strangled, the wealth of the country and the cities beyond.

The identity of the localities, owing to the Spaniard's greed for gold and contempt for geography, cannot be certainly fathomed; but the description they have left of the rivers and nations, the mountains and plains, leave no doubt whatever that they were the real discoverers of the Basin of the Missouri, if not of the river itself.

This question of discovery by Coronado's marching horde, living upon the flesh and milk of the buffalo, upon one of the most remarkably bold and daring marches recorded in the annals of American history, has been slow to penetrate to the importance it deserves, antedating as it does any known exploration toward the interior as far as the hydrographic system of the Missouri Basin.[37] The cause for this may be found in the conflicts of authority, the diversity of languages and the zones of temperature. The Spanish were Catholic, exclusive, cruel to a fault, and avaricious. Their state papers seldom saw the light of day. In discoveries the natives were made, not companions but slaves; and while an ambitious priest might strive to plant the cross of Christ in the Western World, the marches were by armies and the subjection was by force; not yet ended, while Cuban independence is suspended in the balance.

For these reasons, we have been loth to either know or acknowledge the greater importance of the Spanish discoveries north of New Mexico and west of the Mississippi until

36"* * * An army of 300 Spaniards and 800 Mexican Indians, under Francisco de Coronado, started for Cibola. They visited the Zuni and Moqui pueblos, discovered the grand cañon of the Colorado, and marched northward as far as a village called Quivira, concerning the site of which there is some diversity of opinion. The farthest point reached by Coronado may have been somewhere near the boundary between the states of Kansas and Nebraska, or perhaps farther west at some point on the south fork of the Platte. * * * Many subordinate explorations were undertaken by detached parties, and a vast extent of country was visited."—Fisk's "Discovery of America," 1894, ii., p. 508.
See, also, article by Henry W. Haynes, "Narrative and Critical History of America," vol. ii., chap. vii.
37Mr. Henry W. Haynes, in a note, vol. ii., p. 494, Winsor's "Nar. and Crit. History of America," says: "General Simpson, however, * * * argues against this view and maintains that 'Coronado reached the fortieth degree of latitude, or what is now the boundary line between the states of Kansas and Nebraska, well on toward the Missouri river.' Judge Savage believes that he crossed the plains of Kansas and came out at a point farther west, upon the Platte river. * * * Prince thinks that Coronado traversed parts of the Indian Territory and Kansas, and finally stopped on the borders of the Missouri, somewhere between Kansas City and Council Bluffs." See, also, "Critical Essay on the Sources of Information," by the same author, same volume, pp. 498-503.

very recent times. The papal grant was followed by the
royal grants, and the maps of this republic, to the fortieth
degree, continue to indicate the result. The rest is history,
from the conquest of Mexico to Santa Fé and the Federal
Union, and from the Aztecs to Cortés, Juan de Oñate, and
the butchered Spaniards of 1720.[38]

Nothing better could be expected from the cruelties, the
greed for gain, the overbearing insolence of the Spanish explorers, whose only procedure seemed to be for gold and
glory, through the channel of the downfall of a less powerful
race of men; and that, too, when millions of the precious
metal remained at their very feet, unmined, in the mountains
they traversed, and which, since, has become the wealth of
a more powerful nation.

Spaniards lived in a different atmosphere, and the man of
the North succeeded the man of the South in the sequence of
time and events. One tortured and robbed the natives, the
other rounded him up on reservations.

We can now notice concisely the advance of the French
west of the Mississippi.

The voyage of M. Nicollet, in 1639, to within a short distance of the Mississippi, paved the way for the march of discovery by Radisson and Groseilliers, about twenty years later,
to and across the Great River, in Northern Minnesota, where
they heard of the Missouri from the lips of the Sioux Indians,
which Radisson called the "Forked River." Joliet and Marquette, with their voyageurs and canoes, the 17th of June,
1673, floated out from the mouth of the Wisconsin to the
"broad bosom of the Great River of the West." They found
another name, that of Buade· for the Mississippi, and upon
reaching the mouth of the Missouri, July 1, 1673, they heard
of that river as the PekittanSi, and upon Marquette's map is
indicated, above its mouth, a tribe of Indians which he called
8emessSrit, as before stated. From these two words, which
have been fully explained, the first an Ozaukiuk (Sac) name
and the last an Oumessourit name, has been derived—Missouri: "Living on the Mouth of the Waters River."

38"In Illinois, through the arrival of a band of Missouris, who had come to
chant the calumet, bedecked in chasubles and stoles, and tricked out in the
paraphernalia of the altar, Boisbriant learned that a Spanish expedition from
Sante Fé, in 1720, had been completely annihilated by these savages."—Winsor's
"Nar. and Crit. Hist.," vol. v., p. 39.
It has been related that the Spaniards, mistaking the Missouris, whom they
had come to chastise and annihilate, were entertained as guests, when, their
purpose becoming known, the chuckling savages easily became the annihilators.
Englishmen had previously reached the Mississippi by way of Kentucky
(1654), as Scharf has related, and that Gravier had found swords and guns of
English make among the Arkansean Quapaws in 1700, years after Colonel Wood,
and later, Captain Batt, had traversed Kentucky to the Mississippi. It is also
related by Stone, in the life of Thay en dan e ga (Brant), that a Spanish pros-
pecting expedition, in 1669, proceeded up the rivers Mississippi, Ohio, and
Allegheny in search of silver, and found salt.

The results of the explorations of Joliet and Marquette, with their five voyageurs, who turned back after descending the Mississippi to the mouth of the Arkansas, or near there, need not here be further referred to. They were prompted not to proceed on account of the Spanish occupancy and other obstacles beyond; for, should they not return, all the fruits of their labor would be lost to the world. Not so the intrepid Sieur de la Salle, who, a few years later, passed down the Mississippi and took possession of the country in the name of the King of France. To him is accorded the honor of establishing Fort St. Louis on the Illinois, and on his arrival at the mouth of the Mississippi, in 1682, named the country Louisiana, that vast territory reaching from the mouth of the Mississippi to the Lake of the Woods and the Pacific Coast. The vicissitudes of European warfare changed its possession from France to Spain and from Spain to France, and, in 1803, to the United States, for Bonaparte was afraid to retain it in the event of certain war with England. St. Louis and New Orleans had been founded and the Spanish and French had alternated in possession according to the vicissitudes of maritime expeditions and international treaties.

In the meantime penetration westward from the Mississippi had actively commenced, and the fur trade of the French had taken the place of the greed for gold on the part of the Spanish. Western migration became the order of the day for traffic with the tribes of the plains. The voyage of Hennepin and Accault to St. Anthony, and La Hontan's River Longue bear but little or no significance as regards the Missouri, although La Hontan's fanciful fiction might seem to refer to that stream, unless comprehensively understood. But another character appeared in 1701 with such a fabulous story that the wild ideas of western wealth caused his hoax to be entertained. As this is closely a part of the history of the Missouri region, a quotation from the works of the lamented Parkman concerning Sagean's story, of sixty pages, is admitted here as a historical curiosity.

From Parkman's *Lasalle*, appendix ii., p. 458, the following is quoted, with full credit and acknowledgment to the memory of that author:

THE ELDORADO OF MATHEW SAGEAN.

"Mathew Sagean is a personage less known than Hennepin or La Hontan; for, though he surpassed them both in fertility of invention, he was illiterate and never made a book. In 1701, being then a soldier in a company of marines at Brest, he revealed a secret which he declared that he had locked within his breast for twenty years, having been unwilling to impart it to the Dutch and English in whose service he had been during the whole period. His story is written down from his dictation, and sent to the Minister Ponchartrain.

"It is preserved in the Bibliothèque Nationale, and, in 1863, it was printed by Mr. Shea.

"He was born, he declares, at La Chine, in Canada, and engaged in the service of La Salle about twenty years before the revelation of his secret; that is, in 1681. Hence, he would have been at the utmost only fourteen years old, as La Chine did not exist before 1667. He was with La Salle at the building of Fort St. Louis of the Illinois, and was left here as one of a hundred men under command of Tonty. Tonty, it is to be observed, had but a small fraction of this number; and Sagean describes the fort in a manner which shows that he never saw it. Being desirous of making some new discovery, he obtained leave from Tonty, and set out with eleven other Frenchmen and two Mohegan Indians. They ascended the Mississippi a hundred and fifty leagues, carried their canoes by a cataract, went forty leagues farther, and stopped a month to hunt. While thus employed, they found another river, fourteen leagues distant, flowing south-southwest. They carried their canoes thither, meeting on the way many lions, leopards, and tigers, which did them no harm; then they embarked, paddled a hundred and fifty leagues farther, and found themselves in the midst of the great nation of the Acanibas, dwelling in many fortified towns, and governed by King Hagaren, who claimed descent from Montezuma. The king, like his subjects, was clothed with the skins of men. Nevertheless, he and they were civilized and polished in their manners. They worshiped certain frightful idols of gold in the royal palace. One of them represented the ancestor of their monarch, armed with a lance, bow, and quiver, and in the act of mounting his horse; while in his mouth he held a jewel as large as a goose's egg, which shone like fire, and which, in the opinion of Sagean, was a carbuncle. [A beautiful gem found chiefly in the East Indies.] Another of those images was that of a woman mounted on a golden unicorn, with a horn more than a fathom long. After passing, pursues the story, between these idols, which stand on platforms of gold, each thirty feet square, one enters a magnificent vestibule, conducting to the apartment of the king. At the four corners of this vestibule are stationed bands of music, which, to the taste of Sagean, was of very poor quality. The palace is of vast extent, and the private apartment of the king is twenty-eight or thirty feet square; the walls, to the height of eighteen feet, being of bricks of solid gold, and the pavement of the same. Here the king dwells alone, served only by his wives, of whom he takes a new one every day. The Frenchmen alone had the privilege of entering, and were graciously received.

"These people carry on a great trade in gold with a nation believed by Sagean to be the Japanese, as the journey to them lasts six months. He saw the departure of one of the caravans, which consisted of more than three thousand oxen, laden with gold, and an equal number of horsemen, armed with lances, bows, and daggers. They receive iron and steel in exchange for their gold. The king has an army of a hundred thousand men, of whom three-fourths are cavalry. They have golden trumpets, with which they make very indifferent music; and also golden drums, which, as well as the drummer, are carried on the backs of oxen. The troops are practiced once a week in shooting at a target with arrows; and the king rewards the victor with one of his wives, or with some honorable employment. These people are of a dark complexion and hideous to look upon, because their faces are made long and narrow by pressing their heads between two boards in infancy. The women, however, are as fair as in Europe; though, in common with the men, their ears are enormously large. All persons of distinction among the Acanibas wear their finger-nails very long. They are polygamists, and each man takes as many wives as he wants. They are of a joyous disposition, moderate drinkers, but great smokers. They entertained Sagean and his followers during five months with the fat of the land; and any woman who refused a Frenchman was ordered to be killed. Six girls were put to death with daggers for this breach of hospitality. The king, being anxious to retain his visitors in his service, offered Sagean one of his daughters, aged fourteen years, in marriage; and, when he saw him resolved to depart, promised to keep her for him till he should return. The climate is delightful and summer reigns throughout the year. The plains are full of birds and animals of all kinds, among which are many parrots and monkeys, besides the wild cattle, with humps like camels, which these people use as beasts of burden. King Hagaren would not let the Frenchmen go till they had sworn by the sky, which is the customary oath of the Acanibas, that they would return in thirty-six moons, and bring him a supply of beads and other trinkets from Canada. As gold was to be had for the asking, each of the eleven Frenchmen took away with him sixty small bars, weighing about four pounds each. The king ordered two hundred horsemen to escort them, and carry the gold to their canoes; which they did, and there bade them farewell with terrific howlings, meant, doubtless, to do them honor. After many adventures, wherein nearly all his companions came to a bloody end, Sagean, and the few others who survived, had the ill luck to be captured by English pirates at the mouth of the St. Lawrence. He spent many years among them in the East and West Indies, but would not reveal the secrets of his Eldorado to these heretical foreigners. Such was the story, which so far imposed on the credulity of the Minister Ponchartrain as to persuade him that the matter was worth serious examination. Accordingly Sagean was sent to Louisiana, then in its earliest infancy as a French colony. Here he met various persons who had known him in Canada, who denied that he had ever been on the Mississippi, and contradicted his account of his parentage. Nevertheless, he held fast to his story, and declared that the gold mines of the Acanabas could be reached without difficulty by the river Missouri. But Sauvolle and Beinville, chiefs of the colony, were obstinate in their unbelief; and Sagean and his King Hagaran lapsed alike into oblivion."

OTHER EXPLORATIONS.

There are other records concerning early explorations up the Missouri.[39] Sieur de Bourgmont was charged with erecting a fort, on an island in the Missouri, as an advance for the fur trade with the Indians, and settlements were established, the earliest grant being that to Sieur Renard. Bourgmont claimed to have ascended the river 800 leagues, and to its source, but such a claim is impossible of proof and is absurd in the extreme.

The story of the Yazoo Indian, Moncachtabe ("Moncacht-Ape"), claiming to have passed up the Missouri as early as 1700, and across the Continental Divide to the Columbia, gained some credence at the time, and in contemporaneous

---

[39]"In October, 1717,the Sieur Hubert made a report to the minister of the marine upon an alleged route by the Missouri through a rich mining country, and he supposed it to lead to a mountain barrier, where the springs of eastern and western flowing rivers could not be far apart. The notion was not a novel one, but it had always been veiled in conjecture. * * * Bourgmont [Bourmont, Boismont, Bournion], a trader, who had been for fifteen years trafficking on the Missouri, was responsible for a story that the Panis (Pawnees) and their kindred in the remote West were trading with other peoples living about a

writings during the eighteenth century received consideration. The occupancy of the Hudson Bay country by the English, Louisiana by the French, and Mexican provinces by the Spanish in lines of trade and traffic greatly influenced and disturbed the advance of civilization to and beyond the Missouri, and the complicated history of all the intrigues, expeditions, forts, and outposts figure largely in the final adjustment of international boundaries.

EARLY EXPLORERS.

Since the preparation of this work emanates from a desire to more fully learn of the earliest discoveries of the utmost waters of the Missouri, and of its geographic distinctions in the Mountain region, the length of the river, its ultimate source and geographical importance, more attention has been extended toward that region than to the well-known and understood historical record of its lower course.

Toward the Verendrye discoveries from Lake Superior to the Rocky Mountains, and the following voyages, interesting accounts have been secured for this work, as given in following pages.

great lake. This far-away race was represented as small of stature and dressed like Europeans. * * * In a memorial, which was prepared at Paris in 1718, outlining a plan for giving Louisiana a dominating position in North America, it was made a part of the means to that end that the mines on the Missouri should be worked. * * * In the summer and autumn of 1719, there were two adventurers, incited by such stories as these, endeavoring to discover the meaning of them. One, La Harpe, had gone up the Mississippi in August with a small escort, and was soon among the Osages on the Missouri, finding unicorns and other creatures. * * * The other explorer, Du Tisné, had followed another branch, and reached the Panis at a point supposed to be where Fort Riley now stands. Here he planted the French standard forty leagues beyond the Osages."—Winsor's "Mississippi Basin," 1895, 111-114. This last explorer reached the Padoucas Sept. 27, 1719.

Le Page du Pratz, addressing M. Dumont concerning Moncachtabe's travels, said:

"He ascended the St. Louis [Mississippi] to the Illinois; thence, crossing the river either on a raft or by swimming, he began to travel by land north of the Missouri, a river which the Sieur de Bourgmont, who ascended it to its source, gives a course of eight hundred leagues, from its rise till it empties in the Mississippi."

WILLIAM N. CULVER'S CABIN
At Base of the Rocky Mountains,
Madison County, Montana.

CHIEF LITTLE JOHN.

A Mandan.

From a photograph by D. F. Barry.

§VII. DISCOVERY OF THE ROCKY MOUNTAINS.

We now come to a consideration of the early approach of the French toward the Pacific slope, to and across the continental divide separating the Basin of the Missouri from that of the hydrographic system of the Saskatchewan, and of Hudson Bay, to a discovery of the Rocky Mountains. Dr. Edward D. Neill, the accomplished divine and historian, gave this question, during his lifetime, careful attention, and his writings have come down to us with little that can be complained of and very much that is historically valuable. The late Mr. Alfred J. Hill, during his career, also made a study of the La Verendrye voyages, but his writings remain unpublished. Now that opportunity offers an occasion to revere the memory of his scholarly accomplishments, the consent to publish the following has been obtained from Mr. James Hill of Newmarket, Ontario. These abstracts and references by Mr. Hill, now first published, read in connection with the article in Volume I. [1876, pp. 301-316] of the Contributions to the Historical Society of Montana, throw considerable light upon the route of travel and the estimated distances accomplished by the earliest exploration of the French from the Lake of the Woods to the Rocky [Shining] Mountains. The following is my authority for publishing Mr. Hill's Abstracts:

NEWMARKET, Canada, Feb. 17, 1896.
Dear Sir: You have my permission to publish the MSS. referred to in your letter of the 13th inst. thereby crediting the same to the memory of the writer, the late Alfred J. Hill.

Very respectfully,
JAMES HILL,
Administrator.

The Abstracts referred to, translated from the French, are as follows:

ABSTRACT OF THE JOURNAL OF THE CHEVALIER DE LA VERENDRYE, KEPT WHILST SEARCHING FOR THE WESTERN SEA.

ADDRESSED TO THE MARQUIS BEAUHARNOIS.

[Sent by him to the Minister, Oct. 27, 1744.]

BY ALFRED J. HILL.

On the 29th of April, 1742, the Chevalier with one of his brothers and two Frenchman left the fort de la Reine, and arrived at the Mantanes May 19. They remained there till July 23, waiting for the promised guides from the Gens des Chevaux ("tribe of the Horses") who did not come. They then engaged two Mantanes to conduct them to the lands of said tribe, hoping to find some village [of these people] near the Mountain or upon their route. They travelled twenty days W. S. W., seeing no one, only wild beasts. They saw in many places earths of different colors, such as blue, vermilion, meadow green, shining black, chalk black, and other ochreous colors. They arrived on August 11 at the Mountain of the Gens des Chevaux. They were afraid to go any further so they built a little house to wait for any savages that might come along. Every day they made fire signals on neighboring heights and observed in all directions. On Sept. 14 the scouts saw a smoke to the S. S. W. One of the Frenchmen and the Mantane who had remained with them were sent out to it. They found a village of the Beaux Hommes ("Handsome Men") and were well received. On the 18th the whole party went to the Indian village, where they paid off the remaining Mantanes who wanted to go home. They remained with the Beaux Hommes twenty-one days. On November 9th [October evidently] they left, with guides, to hunt up the nearest village of the Gens des Chevaux. Their course was to the S. S. W. The second day they met a village of the nation of the Petits Renards ("Little Foxes") who were glad to see them. He told them that they were searching for the Gens des Chevaux to show the party the way to the sea, when the whole village took up the line of march with them, which made him feel that he would find a known sea. On the second day of march they met a populous village of the same nation and were well received there too. They were conducted to a village of the Pioya, arriving there the 15th [October] where they were also well received. [It would appear as if this village, too, then went along.] The route was continued to the S. W., and on the 17th [October] another big village of the same nation was met with. All marched together in a southern direction till the 19th [October], when they finally arrived at a village of the Gens des Chevaux, but found the people in great distress, all their villages having been destroyed by the Gens du Serpent ("Snake tribe" [or nation]) a very populous nation; and one having no other for a friend. The travellers were told that in 1741 these people had entirely defeated seventeen villages, killing all the men and old women, and making slaves of the rest, whom they sold at the sea for horses and merchandise. He was told by the Gens des Chevaux that none of their nation had visited the people who lived on the sea, the Gens du Serpent barring the way, but that later they could see, on making a great circuit, people who traded with the whites of the sea. He got the village to march with him to the Gens de l' Arc, the only nation not afraid of the Gens du Serpent. Always marching S. W. they came on Nov. 18 to a very large village of the Gens de la Belle Riviere. From them they learned of the Gens de l'Arc [before mentioned here—"People of the Bow"] who were near there. All together they marched to the S. W., and on the 21st, discerned the sought-for village, which seemed very large. All the natives of these countries have great quantities of horses, asses and mules for hunting, travelling, and carrying purposes. The chief received them very kindly, putting all their effects in his lodge which was very large, and taking great care of their horses. He said that he only knew the people of the sea through what was said of them by prisoners taken from the Gens du Serpent—that he must not be surprised to see so many villages assembled for they were just going to march along the side of the great mountains which are near the sea to hunt there for the Gens du Serpent. The chief seemed to think that the whites of the coast were French, but the few words of their language that he had heard and remembered showed them to be Spaniards. He also told the Chevalier of the massacre of the Spaniards who were looking for the Missouri, of which Verendrye had already heard; all of which a little cooled the latter's desire to find a known sea. The march was now continued, sometimes S.S.W., sometimes N.W., the crowd continually increasing by the junction of many villages of different nations. On the 1st of January, 1743, they came in sight of the mountains. The number of warriors was 2,000. The French, though not consenting to take part in the war, had now to accompany the army, for it seemed the only course to pursue. Continued the march till January 8. On the 9th they quitted the village, he leaving his brother to guard the baggage which was in the lodge of the Arc chief. The greater part were on horseback, marching in good order; at last, on the 12th day they arrived at the mountains, which are mostly wooded with all kinds of trees and are very high. Being near the greater part of the village of the Gens du Serpent, the scouts reported that they had all fled with precipitation, abandoning their cabins and most of their property. The Indians now fearing an attack in the rear (on their families and camp presumably) could not be induced by the chief to go farther, and so he and the French had to make up their minds, unwillingly, to return. Thus Verendrye was not able to even ascend the mountains for such western views as he could have thence. The return was not made in as good order as the outward march. The French got separated from their companions and had a slight skirmish with a few hostile Indians. They arrived first at the village of the Gens de l' Arc, on the 9th of February, which was the second day of their retreat (deroute). The prairies were bare and dry (rare et sèche), so that their horses' hoofs left no trace, and the chief who thought them lost hunted unavailingly for them, but found them at the village when he returned. The day after their arrival two feet of snow fell, and there was a frightful storm. They continued to march with the Gens de l' Arc to the first day of March, going always E. S. E. The Chevalier sent one of the French with a savage to the Gens de la l'etite Cerise, having learned that they were not far off. They were ten days on their journey and brought back an invitation for the French to visit the tribe. Verendrye promised the Arc chief he would come back to see him if he would establish himself near a little river he pointed out to him, build a fort there and raise grain, which he promised to do, on the expectation that the Chevalier would return to him next spring after having seen his father at Fort la Reine.

Seeing no chance of getting guided to the Spaniards, and fearing his father was becoming anxious about the party, he took his leave of the Gens de l'Arc. Arrived March 15, at the Gens de la Petite Corise (before mentioned—"People of the Little Cherry") who were returning from their winter quarters, and were two days' march from their fort, which is on the bank of the Missouri. They arrived on the 19th at the fort and were well received. They found there one who had been brought up among the Spaniards, who stated that it was very far to those people, and many dangers to run by reason of the Nation du Serpent, and that it would require at least twenty days to go there by horse. He said that three days' journey from them was a Frenchman, who had been established there many years. Verendrye would have gone to see this man had their horses been in good condition; as it was he wrote to him that they would wait for him to the end of March, and that if he could not come by that time he should at least send them word. "I laid down upon an eminence, near the fort, a plate of lead with the arms and inscription of the king, with stones in a pyramidal form for the Governor General. I told the savages, who did not know anything about the plate of lead that I had put in the ground, that I was placing these stones as a memento of our having come in their country." (Original is: "Je posai sur une eminence, pres du fort, une plaque de plomb aux armes et inscription du Roy, et des pierres en pyramide pour Monsieur le Général—Je dis aux sauvages, qui n'avaient pas connaissance de la plague de plomb que j' avois mis dans la terre, que je mettois ces pierres en mémoire de ce que nous étions venus sur leurs terres.") Unfortunately he could not take the latitude of this place as the circle of his astrolabe was broken.

No news had arrived from the Frenchman by April, and the guides having become impatient and the horses being in good condition, they left these people on the 2d, with a message to the Frenchman if he should come to follow them to the Mantanes, for Verendrye would have liked to take him out of that country. It appears that this tribe and the Mantanes were enemies, but the Chevalier guaranteed the safety of the young men who were to go along as guides.

On the 9th they met at noon a village of 25 cabins of the Gens de la Fleche Colleé ("People of the Stuck Arrow") otherwise called Sioux of the Prairies. Next day they pursued their route, sometimes N. N. E., and N. W., to the Mantanes, without meeting anything further, and arrived there May 18. It had been the intention to stay with this tribe about fifteen or twenty days to rest themselves and their horses, but learning, on the 26th, that there were Assiniboels at the fort de la Butte ("Hill Fort") who were going to set out for fort la Reine, they got ready promptly to take advantage of travelling in company with them. In the morning of the 27th they went to the fort la Butte, but the Assiniboels had gone; they hurried up a little and joined them at their camp, where there were more than one hundred of them. On the way the Sioux attempted to ambuscade them, on the 31st, but on having to meet French also, after a skirmish they fled. On June 2 came to the village near the mountain (pres de la montagne). "As our horses were tired we delayed our march and remained with the village to the 20th" (nous restâmes à marcher avec le village, &c). They arrived at fort la Reine July 2 (1743).

[End of the summary of the Chevalier's journal.]

*Time Basis:

        Outward—Fort la Reine to Mandan villages, April 29 to May 19, 1742—22 days;

        Outward—Petite Couse village to Mandan, April 2 to May 18—47 days.

        Return—Mandan villages to Fort la Reine, May 27 to July 2 (less 18 days)—19 days.

        N. B.--Call Ft. la Reine to Mandan, 20 days time at . . . . miles per day.

EXTRACTS FROM THE MEMOIRE OF BOUGAINVILLE ON THE STATE OF NEW FRANCE—1757.

In his catalogue of forts, he goes on to describe—

"La Mer d'Ouest [the Western Sea] post which includes forts Saint Pierre, Saint Charles, Bourbon, de la Reine, Dauphin, Poskoia, and des Prairies, all stockaded forts, formidable [respectable] only as regards the savages.

"The fort Saint Pierre is situated upon the left bank of the lake of Tekamamiouen or Rainy Lake, five hundred leagues [1,380 miles] from Michilimakinak and three hundred [828 miles] from Kamanistiguoia or the Three Rivers to the north-west of Lake Superior.

"The fort Saint Charles is sixty leagues [165.60 miles] from that of Saint Pierre, situated upon a peninsula, quite prominent [presqu' isle fort Avancée] in the L. of the Woods.

"The fort Bourbon is one hundred and fifty leagues [414 miles] from the preceding situated at the entry of Lake Oimpeg.

---

*There seems to be an error in the time basis.

"The fort la Reine is upon the right bank of the river of the Assiniboels, seventy leagues [193.20 miles] from fort Bourbon. These regions offer everywhere vast prairies; there is the route to go to the upper part of the Missouri.

"The fort Dauphin, eighty leagues [220.80 miles] from the preceding, is situated upon the river Minanghenachequeké or Muddy Water [de l'Eau Troublé].

"The fort Poskoia is upon the river of this name one hundred and eighty leagues [496.80 miles] from the preceding; from this fort you can go in ten days to the Nelson river.

"The fort des Prairies ["Prairie fort"] is eighty leagues [220.80 miles] from fort Poskoia in the upper part of the river of that name. This post has been farmed for eighty thousand francs; the commandant is the farmer and he has a fourth in the post. The savages who come to trade there are the Cristinaux and the Assiniboels; these two nations form each twelve villages of two hundred and fifty men taking one with the other; in an ordinary year there is made in this post from three to four hundred packets of beavers, pekans, martins, otters, lynxes, carcajoux, fouines, foxes; there must also be counted fifty to sixty slaves red or panis de Jatihilinine, nation situated upon the Missouri which plays in America the role of the negroes in Europe. Only at this post is the trade in them carried on.

"Le poste de la mer d' Ouest ["the post of the Western Sea"] deserves particular attention for two reasons, the first of which is that it is the nearest of all to the English establishments on Hudson's Bay, whence their movements should be watched; the second is that it is from this post that the Sea of the West may be discovered; but to make this discovery it will be necessary for the voyageurs to abandon their interested views.

"Voyage de la Véranderie.—The one who most forwarded this discovery is the Sieur de la Véranderie; from the fort de la Reine he reached the Missouri, he met first of all upon this river the Mandannes or Blancs Barbus ["Bearded Whites"] to the number of seven villages fortified by terraced stockades with a ditch, next the Kinongewiniris or the Brochets ["Pikes," i. e., fish] to the number of three villages; in the upper part of the river, he found the Mahantas making also three villages, and along the Missouri, in descending it to the mouth of the river Wabiek or Shell [Coquille], twenty-three villages of Panis.

"To the south-west of this river and upon the two banks [of the?] Ouonaradeba or à la Graisse ["Fat River"] are the Hactannes or Gens du Serpent ["Snake People"]. They extend as far as the foot of a chain of very high mountains, which run north, east, and south, and to the south of which is the river Karoskiou or Cerise Pelée ["Peeled Cherry"], which is supposed to run towards California.

"He continued his route, and found in those immense countries which are watered by the Missouri, opposite to and about forty leagues [110.40 miles] from the Mahantas, the Ouriliniock or handsome men [Beaux Hommes], four villages; opposite the Brochets, the Macateoualasites or Pied Noirs ["Black Feet"], three villages of about one hundred cabins each; opposite the Mandannes are the Ospekakaerenousques or People of the Flat Bluff? [Gens de la côte platte] four villages; opposite the Panis are the Gens de l'Arc ["people of the bow"] Atchapcivinioques in Cristinaux and Utasibaoutchactas in Assiniboels, three villages; next are found the Makesch or Petite-Renards ["Little Foxes"], two villages, the Piwassa or Great Talkers, three villages, the Kakakoschena or Gens de la Pie ["Magpie" people?] five villages, the Kiskipisounouinini or People of the Garter [Gens de la Jarretiére] seven villages.

"He could go no farther by reason of the war which was then raging between the Garter people and the next nation. However I have somewhat improperly used the name village for all the nations who inhabit the prairies: they form, like the Tartars, but wandering hordes; they follow the animals whose hunting is their subsistence, their homes are cabins of skins."

[End of all that pertains to the Verendryes and the territory they travelled in.]

EXTRACT FROM MR. NEILL'S WRITINGS.

"Father Coquard, who had been associated with Verendrye, says that they first met the Mantanes and next the Brochets. After these were the Gros Ventres, the Crows, the Flatheads, the Blackfeet, and Dogfeet, who were established on the Missouri, even up to the Falls, and that about thirty leagues [82.80 miles] beyond the rapids they found a narrow pass in the mountains."[16]

"ABRIDGED MEMOIR OF THE MAP WHICH REPRESENTS THE ESTABLISHMENTS AND DISCOVERIES MADE BY THE SIEUR DE LA VERENDRYE AND HIS SONS.

The map begins at the shore of Lake Superior and shows the portage thence to the river of the Natohouagannes which is three leagues [8.28 miles] long. From the shore of the lake to the height of land it is 25 leagues [69 miles] in distance.

From the height of land to the first establishment, called Fort Saint Pierre at the outlet of Rainy Lake, it is 95 leagues [262.20 miles]. The savages there are called Gens de la Graisse d' Ours [Bear's fat tribe] and Monsonis.

The second establishment is fort Saint Charles to the south west of Lac des Bois, 80 leagues [220.80 miles] distant from fort Saint Pierre. The savages of this region are the Monsonis and Cristinaux, long-time allies.

The third establishment is Fort Maurepas, at the lower part of the river of the same name, near the entry of Lake Ounipigon, on the north side, 100 leagues [276 miles] from the north side. The nation is Cristinaux du Bois fort (of the "Big Woods").

The fourth establishment is the fort de la Reine, 100 leagues [276 miles] from fort Maurepas, on the north side of the river of the Assiniboels.

There was formerly a fort on the Red river built by the Sieur de la Verendrye ainé five leagues [13.80 miles] from the lake. It is now abandoned like that at the fork of the river of the Assiniboels, on account of the nearness of the fort de la Reine to that of Maurepas.

The savage nations of the fort de la Reine are Assiniboels. Only the banks of the river are wooded. All the rest is prairie, but there are wooded "islands" there, of oak and plum trees.

From fort de la Reine there is a portage of three leagues [8.28 miles] to the N. E. to reach the lake of the Prairie. You follow along the south of the lake to the mouth of a river, which comes from the great prairie, at the lower part of which is the fort Dauphin, the fifth establishment, required by the Cristinaux of the Prairies and the Canoe Assiniboels.

16"The entire sentence as quoted by Margry in a letter dated July 5, 1875, reads: 'Trouvent les gorges des Missouri entre des Montagnes, et le Missouri est la decharge des Lac dont on ne connait pas l'entendue.' " [I. e., found the narrows of the Missouri amongst some mountains, and the Missouri is the outlet of the lake whose extent is unknown.]

There is a route thence to the fort Bourbon, which is the sixth establishment, but the way is not good. The custom is, leaving fort Maurepas, to pass by the north of Ouinipegon up to its first narrows where you pass to the south from island to island, then you coast the lands as far as the river aux Biches, where is fort Bourbon, near to the lake of the same name. The nations are the Cristinaux of the Lakes and Little Rivers.

From fort Bourbon to the Poskoyak river is thirty leagues [82.80 miles]. There is a fort at the lower part of this river, abandoned in the winter on account of the scarcity of provisions.

This is now the most convenient route by which to follow up the discovery of the Sea of the West. The Cristinaux extend to the heights of land which can only be got at by the way of the prairies.

The Chevalier de la Verendrye was the first to discover the Poskoyak and ascended it to the fork, where is the rendezvous every spring of the Cristinaux of the Mountains, Prairies, and Rivers, to deliberate whether they shall trade with the English or French. There it was that he was told that the river came from very far, from a height of land where there were very high mountains, and that they knew of a great lake on the other side of them of which the water was not drinkable.

The Poskoyak river comes from the W. N. W. It is proposed to establish a fort on this divide, or in its neighborhood.

[End of the memoir on the map.]

MEMORANDUM OF THE VIEWS OF FRANCIS PARKMAN CONCERNING THE JOURNEY OF THE VERENDRYE BROTHERS, AS GIVEN IN HIS ARTICLE IN THE ATLANTIC MONTHLY, JUNE, 1888, ENTITLED "THE DISCOVERY OF THE ROCKY MOUNTAINS."

Pierre Gaultier de Varennes de la Verendrye was his full name. In 1728 he was in command of a small post on Lake Nipegon. Here he was told by an Indian of a great lake which discharged itself by a river flowing westward till it reached a tidal water.

Speaking of the journey of the brothers to the Mountains he says "The Black Hills lay at a distance to their left, and the upper Missouri on their right."

He thinks that where they saw the "earths of different colors—blue, green, red, or black, white as chalk or yellow like ochre," was probably in the "bad lands" of the Little Missouri.

Thinks the hill, or group of hills, they reached on the 11th August, apparently not far west of the Little Missouri. Thinks that the Beaux Hommes were probably Crows. Thinks that the Bow Indians were one of the bands of the western Sioux. Quoting from the report, "We continued our march sometimes S. S. W. and now and then N. W.," he says: "The variations of the course were probably due to the difficulties of the country."

Thinks the mountains they saw on January 1, 1743, were probably the Big Horn Range 120 miles east of the Yellowstone Park.

Thinks that the southern Snakes at that time haunted the valleys of Wind and Green rivers, in which case the war party could not only have reached the Bighorn Mountains but have pushed further on till within full sight of the great Wind River Range.

Thinks that the Choke Cherry Indians [Gens de la Petite Berris] were probably a branch of the Sioux.

Here ends the Hill abstracts.

Mr. Douglas Brymner, in *Report on Canadian Archives,* 1886, published the "Memoir or Summary Journal of the Expedition of Jacques Repentigny Legardeur de Saint Pierre, Knight of the Royal and Military Order of St. Louis, Captain of a Company of the Troops detached from the Marine in Canada, charged with the discovery of the Western Sea."

"In consequence of the orders of the Marquis de Lajonquière, Commodore, Governor and Lieutenant General in New France, I left Montreal the ———, 1750, to proceed to my destination for the discovery of the Western Sea," says Captain St. Pierre in his journal.

Captain St. Pierre was the successor of Laverendrye, who preceded him to the Western country, and curiously enough Mr. Brymner publishes this journal, with an opposite page translation, in 1886, while the Laverendrye journal follows in the report of 1889.

A condensed abstract of the St. Pierre journal is of sufficient importance to present at this time:

Captain St. Pierre proceeded to Michillimakinac from Montreal in the earlier part of 1750, thence through Lake Superior to Rainy Lake, passing thirty-eight portages. He found the Indians at Rainy Lake impertinent and dissatisfied with whatever presents were given. He extolled the goodness of the king, testifying the pain felt on the subject of the war unceasingly waged against the Sioux, whom to conciliate their father had sent M. Marin, to bring them also to peace. A great scarcity of food existed at the Lake of the Woods and at the lower part of the Winnipeg river, which greatly injured the health of the party. That fact and the war which still continued, "engaged in against Hyactchèjline, the Brochets and the Gros Ventres," practically prevented a consummation of official orders. The Chevalier de Niverville was dispatched to the river Paskoya to make an establishment three hundred leagues higher than that. There was some fear that the party would land at Hudson's Bay, but the intention was to turn to the west in order to find the sources of the Missouri river, in the hope that they would lead to a discovery of other streams leading to the Western Sea. The order to establish a post three hundred leagues above that of Paskoya was executed by Niverville May 29, 1751. He sent off ten men in two canoes, who ascended the river Paskoya as far as the Rocky Mountains, where they made a good fort which was called Lajonquiera. Niverville's continued illness prevented him from proceeding from Paskoya to Lajonquiera, where, at the latter fort, the Assinipoils gathering for the purpose of trade, found the Yhatchelini there to the number of forty-five lodges, feasted five days with them, and noticing their superiority of strength in numerical numbers, slaughtered them, and no mention is made of a single person saved, except a few women and children carried off as prisoners. This occurrence disarranged all the plans of St. Pierre, and he commenced an inquiry among the Indians for tidings from the Great Sea beyond. An old man of the nation of the Kenougèonilini assured him, that, a short time before, an establishment had been made at a great distance from them, where they go to trade; that the merchandise brought there was almost similar to that of Canada; that they were not absolute English; that the road to them is directly where the sun sets in the month of June. The Indians had horses and saddles obtained there. Several Indians having been engaged to penetrate the dangerous country to this post, the English were feared, on the ground that they incited hostilities against all who traded with the French. It is stated that there were upwards of fifty thousand Indians, bearing arms who preferred to trade at the French posts, and the English, annoyed at not receiving a large amount of furs at Hudson's Bay sent collars to the Indians, forbidding them to carry furs elsewhere under penalty of death. Several hundred dying from illness they were all seized with fright at the manifest destiny wreaked by the devil in answer to the prayer of the English. M. de Niverville returning from his new settlement near the Rocky Mountains, gave an account of a party of Indians, who, when they were going to war, met with a nation loaded with beaver, who were going by a river which issues from the Rocky Mountains to trade with the French, who had their first establishment on an island at a small distance from the land where there is a large storehouse. These Indians positively asserted that the traders were not English.

For the disappointments encountered by St. Pierre, in his utter failure to penetrate the continent to the Western Sea, the reader of his journal can supply the missing lines that were never written. None of his people went farther than the eastern slope of the Rocky Mountains, and St. Pierre himself was not of the number who penetrated even that far toward the aim of their ambition,—the Western Sea.

ROCKY MOUNTAIN COYOTE.
From a Photograph by James Blair, at Upper Red Rock Lake, Montana.

§ VIII. NATIONAL TERRITORIAL CHANGES.

A brief consideration seems now appropriate concerning the general advance of civilized life from the East toward the West across the Mississippi. The treaty of Utrecht had enlarged, in 1713, the British possessions in America.

At Fontainebleau, Nov. 3, 1762, the sixth article of the Preliminary Treaty of Peace entered into by England, Spain, and France, irrevocably fixed the middle of the channel of the Mississippi as an international boundary between the possessions of England and France, in America; Spain abandoning to England all claims east of that river, which meant her Floridan possessions, which were afterwards again relinquished. On the same day, by a secret donation and a later acceptance, Louisiana, west of the Mississippi, passed from France to the Spanish crown, and practically the whole of the basin of the Missouri, with an undetermined and indefinitely described limit, became Spanish territory.

The Revolutionary War, which brought into existence the Federal Republic as the United States of North America, came next.

It was a prophetic destiny, foreshadowed by the effect following the cause, for the peace of the East had been almost constantly disturbed by avaricious influences emerging from opportunities more or less directly connected with colonial possessions in America, and England had few sympathizers in the loss of the brightest gem in the crown of her realm, and a Washington and the 4th of July decorate the pages of an irrevocable history. As secretly as Louisiana had been ceded to Spain in 1762, the treaty of San Ildefonso, in 1800, retroceded the same to France, and Napoleon Bonaparte ordered its sale and cession to the United States, which was consummated April 30, 1803, and then followed an end to the distinct territorial possessions as divided by the channel of Mississippi, and the broad plains and valleys, mountains and streams of the Missouri Basin became a territorial possession of the United States, only slightly infringed by a British dominion in the remote northwest.

The following brief monetary statement of that transaction (all honor to Jefferson and his advisers!) may be summarized here:

Louisiana, area, in 1803, acres...................... 766,733,440
(Reduced from Wheeler's square-mile estimate.)
Stipulated price $15,000,000
    Price per acre, a fraction less than two cents.
Price per section, of 640 acres each...................... $12.52
Value at the government price, $1.25 per acre........... $958,416,800
    Present value, vast and incomparable.
In capabilities of natural sustenance, a population of 200,000,000, from the Mississippi to the Pacific Coast, can be maintained.

When this remarkable domain, augmented afterward in the southwest, came into the possession of the Federal Union, that grand array of fur companies, too numerous to mention and too complicated to describe in this unpretentious address, sustained in traffic a horde of traders, trappers, hunters, and voyageurs, limited only by the extent of the frontier. Their customers were the Indians and their trade was in pelts, while their approaches were the rivers and their highways the plains. Stockaded posts dotted the line from Saskatchewan to the Gulf, from St. Louis to the mountains, and from Superior to the Missouri, and the Mississippi assumed the importance foreshadowed by the impetuous boldness of its original discoverers, not now as of the Spaniards nor the French, but by that American nation of men, whom to the English were a star in the West and to the Red Indian a shadow in the East.

There are reasons for this. The inherent ambition for an advance by man, from whatever motives and in numerous ways,—national, international, religious, economic, political, personal,—and from those various causations particularly influencing the separate characteristics of diversified life.

The Indian and his bison, the beaver and bear gave way, and the aptitude of events inspired the memorable words:

"Westward the march of empire takes its way."

FEDERAL AUTHORITY IN THE MISSOURI BASIN.

There are three conspicuous and historic names connected with the assumption of federal authority in the Missouri Basin —Merriweather Lewis, William Clark, and Zebulon Montgomery Pike.

Appropriately have they been sumptuously remembered, after nearly a century, by an accomplished writer, Elliott Coues.[40]

Thomas Jefferson, the president, as soon as the purchase of Louisiana was an accomplished fact, proceeded deliberately in taking peaceable possession of the acquired domain from the channel of the Mississippi to the Pacific Coast.

The City of St. Louis had been founded by the French in 1764, on the west bank of the Mississippi, seventeen miles below the mouth of the Missouri, and on the 10th of March, 1804, as the principal rendezvous of the Missouri Valley, it was formally transferred to the United States.

Captains Lewis and Clark had been commissioned to ascend the Missouri, cross the mountains, and descend the Columbia

---

[40]Coues' "Lewis and Clark," 1893, iv. vols., pp. 1-1364, and Coues' "Zebulon Montgomery Pike," 1895, iii. vols., pp. 1-955, which see for remarkable results in Western explorations, and as the most exhaustive and comprehensive works on the subjects discussed.

to tide water on the Pacific Coast, as officers of the United States government. Their able and successful exploratory labors, the most remarkable in the annals of the Great West, and the vast store of information gathered, constituted them historic personages, and the most important if not the first explorers on the upper waters of the Missouri river.

The detachment of forty-five officers and men in one batteaux and two periogues commenced the ascent of the Missouri, May 14, 1804, and, wintering near the Mandan villages, fifteen hundred miles from the mouth of the river, proceeded with remarkable success to the Three Forks, which they reached July 25, 1805,[41] twenty-five hundred and fifty-one miles from the united waters at the mouth of the Missouri.

Selecting the larger river as the main stream, they ascended the same, changing the name from Missouri river to Jefferson Fork, in honor of the president who had honored them.

It was now that, inadvertently and unadvisedly, a great geographic error was committed in changing the name of the parent river.

This question has been importantly considered by geographers, historians, and map-makers for nearly a hundred years, during which time only estimates of the true length of the river have been made, in the absence of any authoritative information upon which to rely; and even on that basis, nearly all who have considered the question neglect and refuse to admit that the source of the Missouri is at the mouth of the Jefferson, where the waters of the Madison are united with it.

The proposition that the Missouri takes its rise in the middle of its own principal channel because another river comes in at the side, is a geographic absurdity.

The best evidence of the circumstances surrounding the change of the name has been discovered by Dr. Coues, and is as follows:

[20]"Though the Three Forks and some of their branches have been named in the narrative before it reaches this date [Aug. 9, 1805], it seems from Gass' journal that the names were not determined, or at least announced, till now. His entry of August 9th, p. 118, reads: 'This morning our commanding officers thought proper that the Missouri should lose its name at the confluence of the three branches we had left on the 30th ultimo. The north branch, which we went up, they called Jefferson; the west or middle branch, Madison; the south branch (about two miles up which a beautiful spring comes in), Gallatin! and a small river above the forks they called "Philosophy." Of the three branches we had just left, they called the north "Wisdom," the south

---

[41]"The next morning, Thursday, July 25th [1805], at the distance of a few miles he [Wm. Clark] arrived at the Three Forks of the Missouri. * * * After breakfast he examined the rivers, and finding that the north branch, though not larger (?) contained more water than the middle branch, and bore more to the westward he determined to ascend it."—Coues' "Lewis and Clarke," 1893, ii., pp. 437-38.

"Philanthropy," and the west, or middle fork, which we continued our voyage along, retained the name Jefferson.'"—Coues' "Lewis and Clark," 1893, vol. ii., note 20, p. 470.

The Montana Historical Society has presented evidence of definite measurements, indicating the relative importance of each stream, as follows here:

"After securing a camping place * * * immediately at the junction of the Jefferson and Madison rivers, we proceeded to calk and pitch our boat. While here we gauged the volume of the rivers, not only to discover which of the three was the largest or parent stream (a point that had never before been definitely determined), but also to ascertain how much water there was to deal with at that season of the year for purposes of navigation. * * * We found that the Jefferson discharged 226,728 cubic feet per minute, the Madison 160,277 and the Gallatin 125,480. There can, therefore, be but little doubt that the Jefferson is the father of the Missouri, which fact makes it, by fair inference, the grandfather of the Mississippi, a distant but noble relative."—Thomas P. Roberts, in "Contributions to the Historical Society of Montana," 1876, vol. i., pp. 236, 237.

This change of the name of the main Missourian stream-bed need not be further considered here, except to refer to two other changes in the name of the same principal channel, which have almost universally come into use—Beaver Head river and Red Rock creek (the last more properly a river).

The following are quotations and the best record of the manner in which one principal river has been divided up to suit a fanciful taste in descriptive nomenclature:

"On our right is the point of a high plain which our Indian woman recognizes as the place called Beaver's Head."—Coues' "Lewis and Clark," 1893, ii., p. 468.

Appended is the following note:

" * * * giving name to the county, and with some geographers to the river itself, above the forks."—[Mouth of Big Hole river.]—Coues' "Lewis and Clark," 1893, ii., p. 469, note 19.

After passing the mouth of Big Hole river (the second forks reached), Lewis and Clark proceeded on their way up the main stream-bed until they reached still another fork and the following is the record concerning this third discovery:

"* * * At the distance of fifteen miles from Rattlesnake cliffs they reached a handsome, open, and level valley, where the river divided into two nearly equal branches."[23]

[23]"A western branch on Captain Lewis' right, and a southeastern on his left. It is important to fix this point in mind; for here is the end of the navigation of the Jefferson by the expedition. Here the canoes are to be left, to be picked up on Captain Clark's return next year. Here is the westernmost point in the course of the Jefferson, for here the river begins to turn southwestwardly and then sweeps eastwardly along the Atlantic base of the Great Divide to its heads

about Red Rock lake, near the Yellowstone National Park. This branch is, of course, the main Jefferson or Missouri, though it was not so regarded by Lewis and Clark, who will follow up the western branch (Prairie creek) into Shohone cove, and so to one of its sources on the main divide, of which the text will speak as the "fountain-head" of the Missouri. The point where Captain Lewis stands at this moment may be called the Two Forks of the Jefferson."—Coues' "Lewis and Clark," 1893, ii., text and note, p. 472.

It is now to be shown that Captain Lewis himself placed no great reliance on the error committed in abandoning the name of the river, for he claims to have discovered "the most distant fountain of the waters of the mighty Missouri."

The accurate record of that interesting event of Aug. 12, 1805, is too valuable to be left out, and is as follows:

"From the foot of one of the lowest of these mountains, which rises with a gentle ascent of about a half a mile, issues the remotest water[9] of the Missouri. They have now reached the hidden sources of that river, which had never yet been seen by civilized man. As they quenched their thirst at the chaste and icy fountain—as they sat down by the brim of that little rivulet, which yielded its distant and modest tribute to the parent ocean—they felt themselves rewarded for all their labors and all their difficulties."[42]

[9]"Which gives rise to that western fork of the Jefferson which Lewis thus traced up Shoshone cove; but he would have had to be many miles eastward of this spring, at the highest fountain which feeds Red Rock lake [Upper Red Rock lake], near the Yellowstone National Park, in order to verify the text literally. However, we understand that point. Here Lewis, F. 91, must, of course, be transcribed, *ipsissimis verbis:* 'At the distance of four miles further the road took us to the most distant fountain of the waters of the mighty Missouri in surch of which we have spent so many toilsome days and wristless nights. thus far I had accomplished one of those great objects on which my mind had been unalterably fixed for many years, judge then of the pleasure I felt in allying my thirst with this pure and ice-cold water which issues from the base of a low mountain or hill of a gentle ascent for ½ a mile. the mountains are high on either hand [but] leave this gap at the head of this rivulet through which the road passes. here I halted a few minutes and rested myself. two miles below Mc. Neal had exultingly stood with one foot on each side of this little rivulet and thanked his god that he had lived to bestride the mighty & heretofore deemed endless Missouri.' "—Coues' "Lewis and Clark," 1893, ii., text and note, p. 484.

---

[42]Sir Alexander Ross (1825) also entertained the same opinion as did Captain Lewis. His views follow:
"The spot on which we now encamped forms the extreme point of Flathead river, a distance of 345 miles from its entrance into the main Columbia, a little above the Kettle Falls; of which some 250 are navigable for craft of moderate size and the rest for loaded small canoes. On the top of the mountain before us, over which our road led, and not more than a mile from our camp, was a small circular spring of water issuing out of the ground. I stood over it for some time, smoking my pipe, with a foot on each side of it. Yet this spring is the source, as far as I can learn, of the great Missouri river, which, after meandering through the mountain, nearly parallel with our road, crossed the grand prairie, where, uniting with several other small streams, a river fifty feet broad and about two and a half deep is formed, which then flows in an easterly direction."—Ross's "Fur Hunters," 1855, vol. ii., p. 46.

We here leave Captains Lewis and Clark and their faithful followers on their successful expeditionary explorations to the coast and return, accomplished in the time from May 14, 1804, to Sept. 23, 1806, with the loss of but one man, Sergeant Charles Floyd, buried near Sioux City on the outward voyage.

Their discoveries and explorations broadened the republic to the Oregon coast.

On the first official map of Montana, by W. W. de Lacy, of date Jan. 1, 1865, the Lewis and Clark nomenclature is somewhat changed, the principal stream above the mouth of Horse Plain (Prairie) creek, appearing as "Red Butte Cr," later to be known as Red Rock river, the designation following the name of an immense red butte on the east bank of the stream below Lima, Mont., similarly following the adopted mode of naming Beaver Head county and a part of the same river channel after Beaver Head Rock.

On De Lacy's map no Red Rock lake appears, leading to the conclusion that at that time (1865) he had no knowledge of the lakes of that name.

VIEW OF UPPER RED ROCK LAKE, MONTANA.
Looking North; the Main Range of the Rocky Mountains in the Rear; the Centennial Valley in Front.

§IX LEWIS AND CLARKE—WESTERN STATEHOOD.

The charming and enchanting pen of Washington Irving, in volumes of history,[43] on statements of fact, has given to the world a permanent record of the wildest life and the most stirring scenes lived and enacted on the "Bison Plains," with "The Hunter Nations,"[44] on the branches of the Missouri, the river itself and the country beyond. The mountains and buttes, rivers and cañons, caves and plains, peaks and gulches, the whole broad bosom of the western wilds, for more than seventy years after Lewis and Clarke resounded with the results of the war-whoop of the savage, his dances and scalps; the trader's revenge; the trapper's wild life; the explorer's courage; the miner's color; the sportsman's luck; the marches of the armies, and the battles of the West; the graves of the dead, and the lives of the living; studies of the scientists; surveys of the government; ministers' missions; the inroads of slavery; political plots; Mormonism; stage lines and robberies; hold-ups and horse thieves; the waylaid emigrant, and the murderous onslaughts; the cannibal's hunger and haste; organized robbery, and the vigilantes' ways; trials without law, and executions with dispatch; stockades and forts for defense; expeditions; the lives of the ranchers; cowboys; early steamboating; buffalo hunts; the annihilation and disappearance of game; miscegenation of the races; industrial life; the founding of towns and the building of cities; Pacific railroads; that labyrinth of fame and famous men, brave wives and women, and the organized society which has gradually evolved from that massive domain west of the Mississippi twenty-three states and territories, nearly half of which are affected by the water-shed of the Missouri, require the pen of an Irving for an adequate description, and he would need a vast conception to adequately depict the historical facts.

Hardly can I expect here to mention one and ignore another, each being equal, in a desire to preserve and record some further unknown facts concerning the Missouri, and yet such names as Wilson Price Hunt and Ramsay Crooks; Manuel Lisa and Andrew Henry; John Colter and James Bridger; Jean N. Nicollet and George Catlin; General Bonneville[45] and Wm. Sublette; John Jacob Astor and General Fremont; those magnificent generals of the army, the dead and the living, who have

---

43Irving's "Astoria" and Irving's "Captain Bonneville," which see for remarkable descriptions of life on the Western plains, in the mountains and down to the coast.

44Henry W. Haynes' "Cabeza de Vaca."

45"A band of wild horsemen came dashing on at full leap into the camp (Bonneville's), yelling and whooping like so many maniacs. Their dresses and accoutrements, their mode of riding and their uncouth clamor, made them seem

SPOTTED HORSE.
A Crow Chief.
A Phrenological Study in Indian Character.
From a Photograph by D. F. Barry.

battled with the savages; the soldiers of the nation who
silently occupy the graves of the dead, unmarked on the western plains, inscribed only in unwritten letters, "Died in the
Cause, that Others May Live;" the wives and mothers of those
who never returned; the victims of massacres and the unfortunates of the ambush; the tortured prisoner, and the escape by suicide; all must be left to those magnificent societies
and those magnetic writers, whom to observe is the record
itself.   The explorer, the miner, the emigrant, the trapper and
hunter, the trader, the army and the Indian, the stage driver
and highwayman, the rancher and the traveler, the scientist
and scholar, historian and geographer, capitalist and tramp,
men, women, and children of all climes and colors and of all
nations and conditions, pleasure-seekers, artizans, farmers and
laborers, the devout and the criminal, the chaste and the fallen
have contributed to the pages of that grand history of the
West, that will live long after the waters of the Missouri were
reddened with blood from its source to its mouth, and from the
days of Marquette to the date of its states, when lawful order
emerged from the disturbances where chaos reigned.

---

a party of savages arrayed for war; but they proved to be principally half-
breeds and white men grown savage in the wilderness, who were employed as
trappers and hunters in the service of the Hudson's Bay Company."—Irving's
"Bonneville," 1837, vol. iii., p. 165.

It was believed, that at this time there were 25,000 trappers, traders, hunters, horsemen and squaw-men tramping and wandering in every part of the
West, engaged in the traffic and trade in furs.

"The consequence is, that the Rocky Mountains and the ulterior regions,
from the Russian possessions in the north down to the Spanish settlements of
California, have been traversed and ransacked in every direction by bands of
hunters and Indian traders; so that there is scarcely a mountain pass, or defile,
that is not known and threaded in their restless migrations, nor a nameless
stream that is not haunted by the lonely trapper."—Irving's "Captain Bonneville," 1837, vol. i., p. 29.

TZI-KAL-TZA.

A Chopunish Half-Breed, Born in the Rocky Mountains, March, 1807.

(Of Historic Interest.)

See photograph, presented to the Historical Society of Montana by Hon. Nathaniel Pitt Langford and identified by Hon. Granville Stuart.

SCENE AT THE BASE OF THE MAIN RANGE,
EFFECTS OF A SNOW SLIDE.

ROCKY MOUNTAIN VIEWS, MONTANA.

(80)

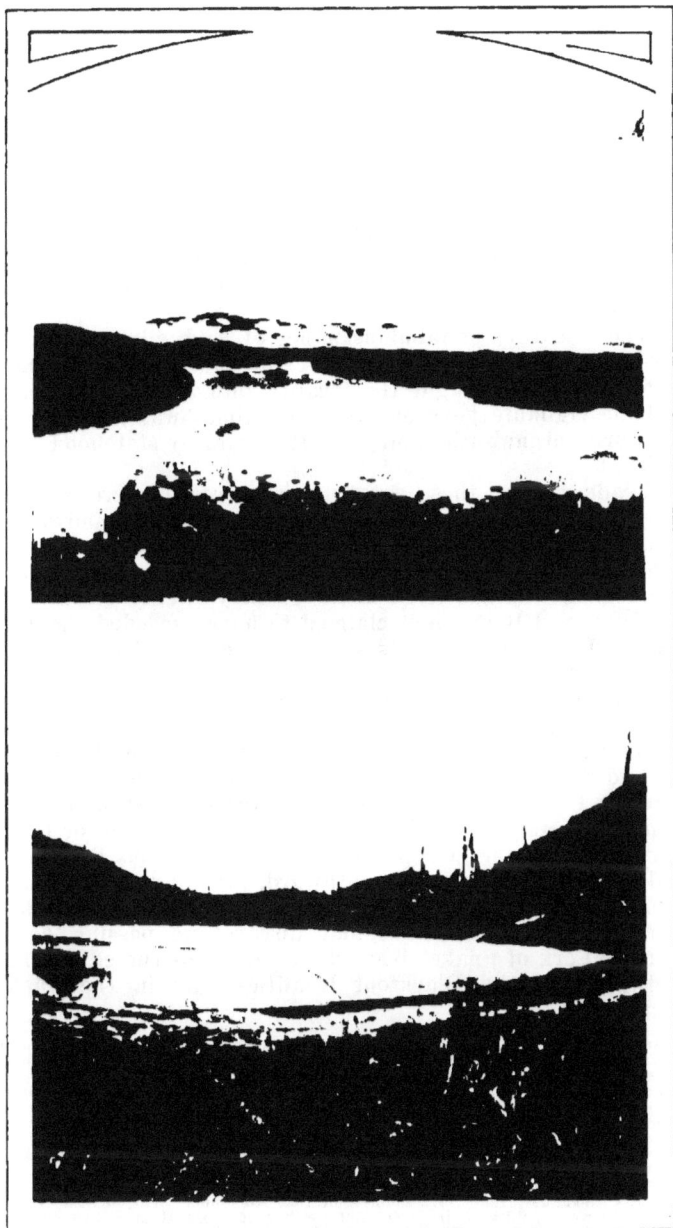

ON RED ROCK RIVER OR UPPER MISSOURI.

LILLIAN LAKE, SUMMIT OF THE MOUNTAINS.

SCENES IN MONTANA ON THE UPPER MISSOURI.

(84)

§ X. EARLY TRADERS AND MONTANA MINES.

It has come to be accepted as a fact, and correctly so, that the utmost source of the Missouri river is in the Rocky Mountains, above, and not far distant from, the Red Rock lakes, situated in the Centennial Valley, Madison county, Montana, in a southerly direction from Virginia, the county seat, and distant therefrom something more than sixty miles, rugged mountains and cañons intervening a considerable portion of the distance.

The discovery of fabulous mines of gold, silver, and copper in the mountainous Montana region on the upper branches of the Missouri brought the locality into great prominence, and the vigilante government of the times was followed by territorial organization, May 26, 1864, and by statehood Feb. 22, 1889.

Leading up to these dates, the occurrences were remarkable and historic, the Indian origin and Spanish advances being veiled in mystery, while the French discoveries are none too clear, for Verendrye himself says he heard of a Frenchman who had lived in the country twenty years prior to 1742,[46] and Bourgmont claimed to have ascended the Missouri 800 leagues and to its source still earlier than either of those dates.

After the remarkable escape of John Colter, in 1808, from the onslaughts of the Blackfeet Indians near the Three Forks,[47] Manuel Lisa and Andrew Henry were probably the next to appear after Lewis and Clark on the Jefferson and Madison Forks of the Missouri as representatives of the Missouri Fur Company, building a fort at the junction of those streams. This fort was pillaged by the murderous Blackfeet, and its occupants escaped southward, probably up the Madison, through Raynolds' Pass to Henry's lake, of which they were undoubtedly the original discoverers, passing down Henry's Fork of Snake river where they constructed another fort[48] beyond the Blackfoot localities and in the Snake country.

[46]"We can indulge with a reasonable degree of certainty in the presumption that Canadian, Spanish, and French hunters and trappers, and traders with Indians, and the employes of the Hudson Bay Company had seen before the nineteenth century the mountains, valleys and streams which are within Madison county. They constructed no buildings and left no monuments of their wanderings, but their footprints are upon the sands of tradition."—Judge Henry N. Blake, "Historical Contributions of Montana," 1896, II., p. 78.

[47]See Chittenden's "Yellowstone National Park," 1895, pp. 28--31, which gives a condensed account of Colter's escape after his companion was shot.

[48]It is commonly but erroneously supposed that the Henry who built this post was Alexander Henry, Jr., nephew of that Alexander Henry whose travels of 1761--76 were published in 1809. But neither of these Henrys was ever on the headwaters of Snake (Lewis) river. Alexander Henry, Sr., took part in the formation of the Northwest Company, 1784, retired 1796, and died at

Following Andrew Henry's escape southward from the Missouri, nothing was known of the Red Rock lake locality until the advent of the settlements, fifty years later, although it is noted on Captain Raynolds' chart; but his command did not go to it.

Fort Union on the Missouri was constructed, near the mouth of the Yellowstone in 1829; and the remarkable mountain adventurers under Captain Bonneville had almost encircled the head waters of the Missouri. But they did not visit the locality immediately west of Henry's lake, but passed farther to the southward on the other side of the mountains.

On June 25, 1860, Capt. W. F. Raynolds, U. S. A., under the guidance of James Bridger, passed with his command northward around the east shore of Lake Henry and through Raynolds' Pass[19] to and down the Madison river.

On the exhaustive chart[50] prepared by Capt. George M. Wheeler, U. S. A., it is shown that no government expedition has extended its explorations through the Alaska Basin and

Montreal 1824, aged eighty-seven. Alexander Henry, Jr., was drowned in the mouth of the Columbia, with Donald McTavish and others, in going from Fort George (Astoria) to board the ship Isaac Todd, May 22, 1814. He had reached Astoria the previous Nov. 15, 1813. A third Alexander Henry was killed at the Fort Nelson massacre, before Jan. 15, 1814. Robert Henry was a person of consequence in the old Northwest Company. He retired in 1817, settled in Coburg, and died there in 1859, aged eighty-one years. William Henry was a cousin of Alexander Henry, Jr. The two were associated on the Red River of the North and Saskatchewan, 1806 and later. About 1810–11, William had a post on the headwaters of the Athabasca; and in 1813–14 on Willamette river in present Oregon. And this William Henry, likewise in the service of the Northwest Company, starved to death at the fort on Mackenzie river the winter of 1810–11.

None of the foregoing has anything to do with the post on Snake river. The person here concerned was Andrew Henry of "Louisiana," associated March 7, 1809, in the Missouri Fur Company, with Manuel Lisa, William Clark, and others. [For details, see "Lewis and Clark," edition of 1893.] In 1808 Andrew Henry had a post at the forks of the Missouri (junction of Jefferson, Madison, and Gallatin rivers), which he was compelled to abandon by Indian hostilities. He fled across the mountains to build on some upper branch of Snake river, and his fate was unknown in St. Louis in the winter of 1810–11. On May 26, 1811, the overland Astorians, under W. P. Hunt, met Edward Robinson, John Hoback, and Jacob Rizner, who had been in the service of the old Missouri company under Mr. Andrew Henry, and were the survivors of a massacre which had caused, in the spring of 1811, the abandonment or destruction of the post on Henry's Fork, which Andrew Henry had established in 1809 or 1810. This is the Henry for whom were named the river and Henry lake, west of the Yellowstone and east of Red Rock lakes, and within that curious dip of the Rocky Mountains, through which four distinct mountain passes were found by the Indians, who maintained migratory trails through each of them.

"On the evening of the 8th October [1811], after a cold wintry day, with gusts of westerly wind and flurries of snow, they arrived at the sought-for post of Mr. Henry. Here he [Henry] had fixed himself, after being compelled by the hostilities of the Blackfeet to abandon the upper waters of the Missouri. The post, however, was deserted, for Mr. Henry had left it in the course of the preceding spring, and, as it afterwards appeared, had fallen in with Mr. Lisa at the Aricara village on the Missouri, some time after the separation of Mr. Hunt and his party. The weary travelers gladly took possession of the deserted log huts which had formed the post, and which stood on the bank of a stream of a hundred yards wide, on which they intended to embark." —Irving's "Astoria," ii., pp. 158, 159.

49"I named it Low Pass, and deem it to be one of the most remarkable and important features of the topography of the Rocky Mountains."—Report of General Raynolds, 1868, Senate Doc. 77, p. 98.

50Report upon United States Geographical Surveys west of the One-hundredth Meridian, 1889, p. 412.

the Centennial Valley of Madison county, Montana, to the Red Rock lakes, a locality around which is centering considerable interest as giving birth to the longest river channel in the world.

Following the discovery of gold in Montana by Francis Finlay, usually known as "Benetsee," a half-blood, interest soon awakened, and the remarkable history of mining life in Montana, from the times of James Stuart to the present day, followed. It is a book of wonderful facts, unwritten, except in the scattered lines of diaries and collections, volumes of adventures and personal reminiscences. Millions upon millions of the precious metals have been taken from the mines situated upon the upper branches of the Missouri, and untold fabulous wealth still remains beneath the surface in that locality.

Prof. George F. Becker has very kindly furnished for these pages a scientific description of the manner in which these ores were precipitated, and his communication is reproduced in full, without change, as requested, and as succinctly describing the origin of ore deposits of such economic value to the people of Montana:

DEPARTMENT OF THE INTERIOR,
UNITED STATES GEOLOGICAL SURVEY.
WASHINGTON, D. C., Dec. 2, 1895.

Sir: The ultimate origin of the ores of gold, silver, and copper is unknown, but it is certain, that, in some cases, the plutonic rocks, such as granite, contain these and other metals in small quantities. Gold, and the sulphides of copper, mercury, zinc, iron, arsenic, and antimony, are soluble in hot waters containing alkaline carbonates together with hydrogen sulphide. This composition corresponds to that of most hot sulphur springs in volcanic regions. The same liquid dissolves silica and some silicates. In many cases, at all events, the veins were deposited from such solutions flowing toward the surface from deeper sources. The causes of the precipitation of ores from solution are, in part, relief of pressure and the diminution of temperature near the surface of the earth, for the solvents are capable of retaining more ore in solution at high temperatures than at low ones. In some cases the precipitation has taken place through the chemical effect of the wall rock on the solutions. Thus, at Leadville, the limestones have thrown down the lead ores, as was shown by Mr. Emmons, and the same process has gone on at Eureka, in Nevada. Iron ores, too, have been precipitated in a similar manner.

The ore solvents are commonly of volcanic origin. Whether they have in general dissolved the ores from slightly metalliferous rocks, or have derived their metallic contents from the source whence the rocks also were charged, is uncertain. So, also, is the part played by gases in the solution and precipitation of ore.

You are at liberty to print the whole of the foregoing either in your text or in a footnote, but not to use a portion only of it.

Yours truly,
GEORGE F. BECKER,
U. S. Geologist.

Mr. J. V. Brower.

The Bannock Indians had, for an unknown length of time, maintained trails, on their hunting expeditions, from the headwaters of Big Hole river, eastward, to Red Rock lakes, past Henry lake to Tar-ghé pass and the Yellowstone locality. The surface of the country indicates its long occupancy by these Indians, and the abundance of buffalo, elk, mountain sheep, antelope, and some remarkable fisheries demonstrates that they then lived in plenty. The remaining evidences of these hunting expeditions are numerous and unmistakable, and it was undoubtedly upon these trails that white men first approached the Red Rock pass through the Rocky Mountains and to a discovery of the lakes of that name and the remarkable valley there situated. Whoever first made that discovery neglected to make known the importance of his explorations, accounting in a measure for the fact that it is so little known of and understood by the world at large. Probably prospectors as early as 1865 had traversed the region, but no mines have ever been opened there or found until very recently.

The Bannock Indians, at Fort Bridger, by treaty made July 3, 1868, for a pittance, relinquished to the United States their entire right to the locality, covering the southwestern portion of Montana,[51] and all that it contained. This treaty converted the claim and extinguished the right of the Indians to the whole of Red Rock river, so called, its numerous branches, and the adjacent mountain ranges and valleys.

§ XI. BANNOCK AND VIRGINIA.

The gold excitement in Montana centered around two of its earliest towns, Bannock and Virginia, ever to be remembered as mining towns and the "Vigilantes Days and Ways," when the sheriff of the county and his horde of highway robbers and horsethieves were summarily executed by an organization for the public safety. From these two towns numerous exploring expeditions penetrated to various parts of the mountain region for hundreds of miles, notable among which were those headed by James and Granville Stuart and Samuel T. Hauser (afterwards governor), to the Yellowstone; and one headed by Walter W. De Lacy which passed entirely around the Red Rock lakes in a circuit of several hundred miles, south to Snake river, up that stream to the Yellowstone

---

[51] Revision of Indian Treaties, § 2, p. 933. The names of the Bannocks signing the treaty are: Tag-géo, Tay-To-Ba, We-Rat-Ze-Won-A-Gen, Coo-Sha-Gan, Pan-Sook-A-Motse, and A-White-Etse. They call themselves Pan-i-tl.

locality, returning by way of Madison river, the time occupied being fifty-one days.[52] This party crossed the main divide not far from where the Utah Northern railroad enters Montana from the south, at the little station called Monida, a modern town of unpretentious size, which derives its name from a combination as follows:

Montana, Idaho;
Monida;

intended to commemorate, no doubt, the construction of the railroad from Pocatello to Butte City, where it crosses the state line between Montana and Idaho, from the Pacific to the Atlantic slope.

Other and numerous explorations took place in the early days of Montana, but unfortunately the events of but very few of them have been perpetuated by a permanent record, and none of them, so far as I can learn, penetrated the rugged and precipitous mountains at the point where the Missouri river assumes its utmost course at the summit of the continental divide.

There is perhaps an explanation of the causes why no exploration of the locality has been made, which is found in the enduring impenetrability of the wildest and most dangerous defiles found in Montana, where snow and landslides are liable to often occur, and where the snow falls about every month of the year, on account of excessive elevation, and is perpetual in many places, of which fact the snow-capped mountains are in constant evidence.

The thrilling history of Bannock and Virginia indelibly perpetuates the beginning of the record of a remarkable state, and volumes have since been filled in relating the causes and consequences.

52DeLacy's Map of Montana, made in 1865, is a valuable chart of that date, and contains much of historic interest which should be preserved by a reproduction of the map, now out of print, and that the memory of the first mapmaker of Montana, now deceased, may be revered.

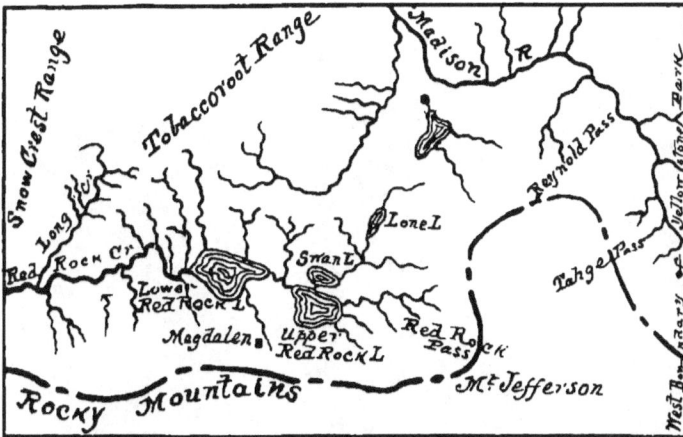

EXTRACT FROM THE GENERAL LAND OFFICE MAP OF MONTANA, 1894.

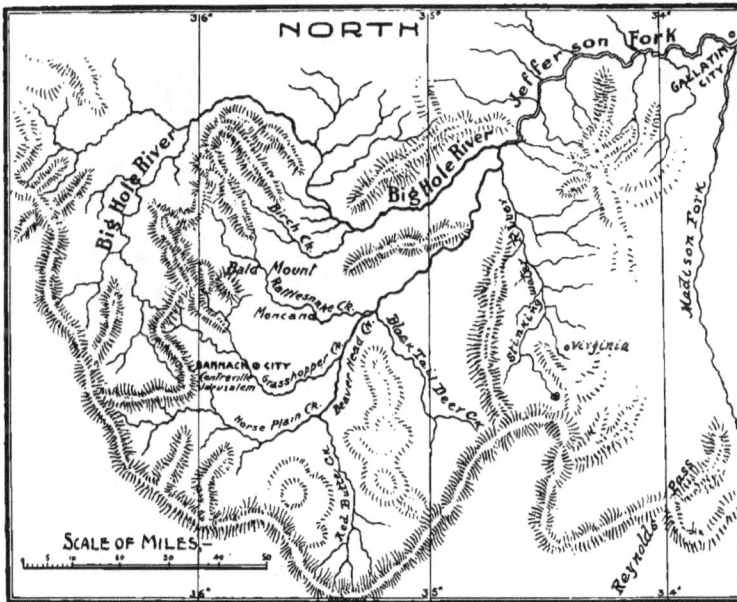

EXTRACT FROM WALTER W. DE LACY'S MAP OF MONTANA, 1865.

§ XII. GEOLOGICAL SURVEY BY THE AUTHORITIES OF THE UNITED STATES.

Immediately to the eastward of Madison county, Montana, the United States Geological Survey in 1872 completed a reconnoissance of Henry lake and its volcanic surroundings.

The opposite page map is an extract from "Sketch of Lake Henry, the Sources of West Fork of Snake River, including Tahgee, Madison and Red Rock Passes, after a reconnoissance by Gustavus R. Bechler, Chief Topographer, Snake River Division, U. S. Geological Survey of the Territories, F. V. Hayden in charge," found opposite p. 56, U. S. Geological Report of 1872. An annotation on the map indicates that the dotted line .... was the limit of explorations westward and that "the topography west of" the dotted line was made after descriptive information. The scale is slightly reduced from one-half inch to the mile. The latitude indicated for the base of the range on the south side of Alaska Basin ("Grassy Bottom") is N. 44° 35′, and the longitude west from Greenwich for the same base is stated at 111° 40′. It is stated in the interesting report referred to: "Henry's lake is a fine illustration of a remnant dating back probably to Pliocene times, when all these valleys were filled with water, perhaps connecting the drainage of the Missouri with that of the Columbia, and as the waters subsided, formed the vast chain of lake-basins along all the important streams on both the Atlantic and Pacific slopes, of which our present lakes are only insignificant remnants." (P. 57.)

HAYDEN'S REPORT.

"I have no doubt that the lowest strata of unchanged rocks about Henry's lake are silurian, probably of the Potsdam group, but I looked in vain for any traces of organic remains. The carboniferous limestones higher up were filled with characteristic fossils. I regard this as one of the most interesting geographical points in the West. Within a circle of about fifteen miles in diameter there are four most important passes in the Rocky Mountain divide, which may represent the four points of the compass. The East or Tahgee Pass connects the Yellowstone National Park, the sources of the Madison, and the Yellowstone, with the Pacific coast. It has an elevation of 7,063 feet. The second may be called the North or Raynolds Pass, and leads from the Snake Valley by way of Henry's lake, over a smooth, grassy lawn, into the lower Madison valley. The third is the Red Rock or West Pass, which opens into the valley of the Jefferson (Missouri) by way of Red Rock lake, and is as smooth and easily traveled as the Madison [Raynolds] Pass. The South or Henry's Pass completes the circle, and is lower than either of the other three. The ease with which railroads or wagon roads can be constructed across these great divides is almost incredible to one that has not made them a subject of study, and the great area of valuable territory which may be opened to settlement through them may entitle them to the appellation of the Great Gateways of the West."

These conclusions are from the pen of Prof. F. V. Hayden, the geologist in charge.

To the report of Prof. Frank II. Bradley, in the same volume, pp. 191, 271, the following extracts are credited, as constituting a special reference to the topographic and other features surrounding the ultimate basin of the Missouri river, immediately to the westward from Henry's lake, near the headwaters of Snake (Lewis) river:

BRADLEY'S REPORT.

"Passing a little to the northward, older rocks appear on the higher slopes of the mountain and soon form its entire face, the volcanic rocks disappearing beneath the valley.

"On the opposite side, these appear again in the high mountain lying directly south of Henry's lake, known to us as Sawtelle's Peak, whose lower spurs run down nearly to the lake shore. The rugged precipitous sides of the peak, without well-marked stratification, led to the suspicion that it might be of volcanic origin, and it was accordingly visited by Mr. Taggart and myself. It was found to constitute the eastern and northeastern wall of a great crater, some 1,200 or 1,500 feet deep, whose east and west diameter is about a mile and a half, with a transverse diameter of about a half mile. The sides are much washed down and the bottom filled up; but, from the position of the portions of what was apparently the original wall which are still standing, it is probable that the original crater had very nearly the dimensions above given. The walls consist of ragged, cellular, largely amygdaloidal porphyry, containing crystals of quartz, calcite, etc., partly weathering with a very rough surface, partly decomposing into a coarse, brittle sand, and making very treacherous footing. Lower down, the slopes consist of very dense, nearly black, basalt. The western and northwestern walls were not visited; but their style of weathering indicates much softer material than was found on the part visited. Considerable portions of the crater, as well as the outer slopes of the mountain, were well covered with tall pines and spruces; while the higher portions had only scattered and stunted trees and the crests were entirely bare, though enough dead stems of small pines or cedars were found even there to make a small signal fire. The small plants of the summit are mostly of alpine forms. Trails of mountain sheep were abundant, but the only vertebrate seen was a large gopher, (?) very distinct from any species of which I have been able to find a description, or figure, or mounted skin; unfortunately, he escaped my bullet. The elevation of the peak, as indicated by two readings of my aneroid barometer, is about 10,600 feet.

"No lines of outflow were traced down to the plain; but, from the size and position of the crater, and the character of the lava of its lower portion, it is evident that this was a prolific source of the basalt which so many times filled the great plain stretching off to the south and west. The isolated cluster of mountains, about half way between this peak and the Sand Hill Mountains, has apparently the same structure, and may have been another source of outflow. The lowest gap in the crater wall of Sawtelle's Peak faces northward; and the principal outflow of lava was probably from that point, escaping thence down the valley of Henry's Fork, though other portions may very probably have escaped through subterranean passages and cracks in other directions, as is frequently the case in those volcanoes whose modern eruptions have given opportunities for the observation of their phenomena. The portions of the lava next to the mountain and out of the center of the valley are all pretty solid basalt, while the farther side of the valley deposits, and those which form the slopes of the eastern mountain, consist of the older porphyries and volcanic sandstones.

"The peaks of the westward continuation of the range of which Sawtelle's Peak forms the eastern termination show such structure, as seen from a distance, as to indicate that they also are of volcanic origin, and may have been other sources of the basaltic outflow. It is not known to any of the present inhabitants of the region that any of these volcanoes have been active in modern times; but Irving, in his 'Astoria,' states that Mr. Robert Stuart, a partner of Mr. Astor in the Pacific Fur Company, when crossing the mountain range west of Pierre's Hole, in the fall of 1812, 'observed to the northwest, between Henry's Fort and the source of the Missouri, several very high peaks covered with snow, from two of which smoke ascended in considerable volumes, apparently from craters in a state of eruption.' The location indicated would apply well to peaks of the range now under consideration. It is hardly to be supposed that so experienced a mountaineer should have been deceived by timber-fires, or that such fires should occur near the summits of peaks covered with snow.

"The ranges on the north and south sides of Henry's lake are nearly parallel, while the cross range west of it is nearly at right angles with them, thus giving a quadrangular form to the plain, which here terminates the broad valley of Henry's Fork. From three points it has easy passages to the neighboring valleys and the region beyond. From our camp on the east side of the valley, Tyghee Pass, named for an old Shoshone chief who was wont to use it, gives a smooth road, with very gentle grades, into the valley of the Upper Madison. From the north end of the lake, a broad, grassy plain, with scarcely a perceptible rise to the divide, about four miles distant, shows a clear road to Virginia City and the lower Madison. This is called Raynolds Pass, from having been used by that officer in his expedition of 1859-'60, and described in his report. Tyghee Pass is also mentioned and mapped in that report as having been examined by Dr. Hayden. From the southwest angle of the valley, Red Rock Pass affords a broad, flat, grassy opening to Red Rock lake, one of the ultimate sources of Beaver Head Fork of the Jefferson. This was not visited by us, though seen from a distance. It was afterward examined by Messrs. Peale and Holmes, of Dr. Hayden's branch of the expedition. The levels, as decided by the observations of both parties are as follows: Henry's lake, 6,492 feet; Tyghee Pass, 7,063 feet; Raynolds Pass, 6,911 feet; Red Rock Pass, 7,271 feet. The most favorable route for a railroad from Montana to Corinne, which is now talked of, is apparently via Raynolds Pass and the valley of Henry's Fork. Down this valley the grades would be very easy, averaging only about twenty-five feet per mile from the pass to Taylor's bridge, on Snake river, and the cost of grading very slight, while the large valleys which open on the east, containing large areas of grazing and farming land, would be opened to settlement, and would very soon furnish considerable local business."

On the 27th of August, 1872, Dr. A. C. Peale, mineralogist, Mr. Henry Gannett, astronomer, Mr. W. H. Holmes, artist, and Mr. Joseph Savage, members of the same Geological Survey, made a reconnoissance through Raynolds Pass, across the divide to Henry lake, thence recrossing the divide to the westward, to the valley of Red Rock lake. Dr. Peale seems to have been very careful not to infringe upon the field of

examination and exploration occupied by Professor Bradley
and his party, for in his report only two references are made
to the reconnoissance of historic importance, which are found
upon pp. 16 and 185, Geological Report for 1872,[53] as follows:

DR. PEALE'S REPORT.

"On the 27th we camped just outside the cañon, and from this
point, in company with Messrs. Gannett, Holmes, and Savage, I made a
trip through Raynolds Pass to Henry's lake, and thence across the divide, again to the valley of Red Rock lake. The metamorphic strata still
continued dipping southwest. At Taghee Pass, east of Henry's lake,
I believe they are capped with carboniferous limestone. Reynolds Pass
is low, only 6,911 feet in height. The ascent is very gradual, and it is
difficult to determine exactly where the stream running into the Madison
ends and that running into Henry's lake begins. To the southwest of
Henry's lake I noticed in the distance a volcanic range. This section
of country, however, will probably be fully treated of by Professor Bradley, and I therefore pass it. The divide between Henry's lake and Red
Rock lake is 7,271 feet high, the distance between the lakes being about
eight miles. On the Red Rock side of the divide I found in the valley
of a small stream an excellent exposure of reddish quartz schists, the
thickness of which I estimated at about 2,000 feet. I am of the opinion
that they rest immediately on the granites. They dip southwest at an
angle of 20°. Viewed from a short distance the outcrop has the appearance of a huge staircase. Between Red Rock lake and the Madison valley the formations are mostly modern, mingled with igneous rocks, the
exact relations of which I had no time to determine carefully.

"CATALOGUE OF ROCKS COLLECTED.

No.	Name.	Locality.
248.	Talcose-schist	Near Red Rock lake, Montana.
249.	Quartz-schist	Near Red Rock lake, Montana."

[53]In a letter dated March 11, 1896, Dr. Peale further says: "Leaving the
Madison valley on the 28th of August, 1872, we crossed the 'Divide' to Henry's
lake. We first crossed the terrace of the Madison valley and followed up a valley which is about three miles in width, gradually narrowing to the 'Pass.' On
the left of this valley were the mountains through which the Madison river cuts
the cañon through which we had just passed (on the 27th). The range is apparently made of Archean or other metamorphic rocks, and as we approach
Henry's lake sedimentary beds appear, capping the older rocks. The latter show
also on the right (west) of the 'Pass,' with a dip to the southwest. Gneissic
schists seem to prevail, with numerous seams of quartz. About ten miles from
our camp we crossed the 'Divide,' the ascent to which is very gradual, apparently not more than about ninety feet to the mile. It would make a good route
for a railroad. We camped at Henry's lake until the morning of the 28th, when
we started for Red Rock lake. The mountains southwest of Henry's lake are
of volcanic origin, and as we passed towards the 'Divide' to Red Rock lake we
crossed basalt and other rocks of igneous age. Farther to the west, however,
the range is apparently of metamorphic rocks, capped with sedimentaries. We
camped near Red Rock lake on the evening of the 28th of August and the next
morning I made a short trip around the southern end of the lake. The drainage
into the lake from this side cuts cañons or gorges into reddish crystalline schists
mostly quartzitic. They dip to the southwest and the inclination is about twenty
degrees on an average. There is a very great thickness of these beds, probably
about 2,000 feet as estimated, and they rest apparently upon gneisses and granitic
rocks. Crossing from Red Rock lake to the Madison valley, August 29th, we
passed by Lone lake, which has steep walls. The rocks in the divide to the
Madison were largely quartzitic schists, with argelites, chloretic schists and
gneisses mingled, with volcanic rocks, the latter showing especially as we approached the Madison valley, where they cap the terraces in columnar masses.
The pass from Henry's lake to Red Rock lake, like the one to the Madison valley, is smooth and grassy and very easily crossed, the stream flowing into Red
Rock lake passing through a fine meadow-like bottom

Dr. Peale also furnishes an annotated description on the map, indicating his route of travel, which shows that his party, Aug. 29, 1872, proceeded direct through Red Rock Pass from Henry lake to Red Rock lake, camped on the north side of the river, near the latter lake, examined the locality around the south shore of the same, and the next day proceeded northeastwardly to the Madison river.

These full details are given in an endeavor to ascertain if the remotest source of the Missouri river was discovered and surveyed by either Professor Bradley's party or by Dr. Peale and his party. They make no mention whatever of that subject, and enter no description of the rise and course of the stream which flows into Upper Red Rock lake.

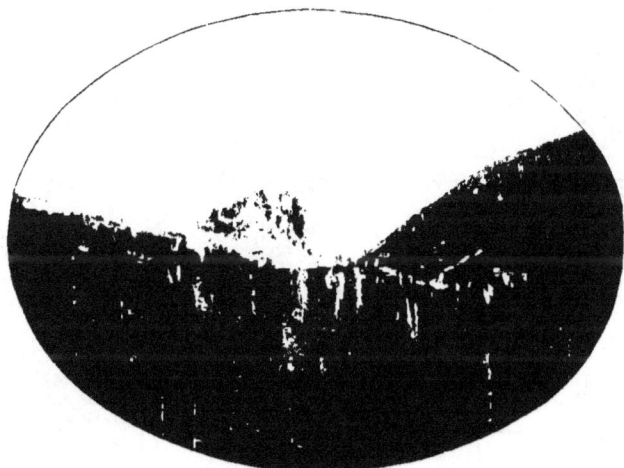

VIEW FROM NEAR THE SUMMIT OF THE ROCKY MOUNTAINS
On the utmost branch of the Missouri river.

(Hanson's Mountain in the distance.)

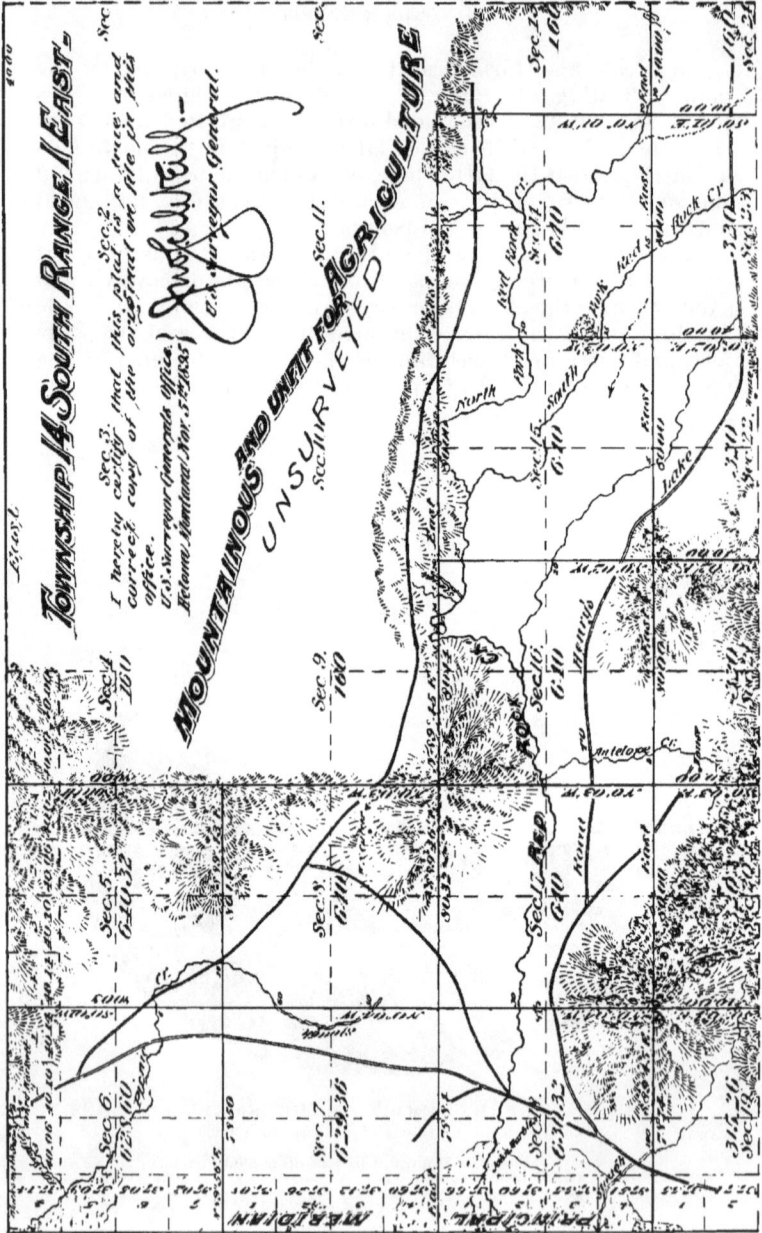

§ XIII. THE CENTENNIAL VALLEY.

By an examination of any correct map of the main range of the Rocky Mountains, immediately west of the Yellowstone National Park, it will be noticed, that, after the general dip of the mountains northward and around the Henry lake basin, thence southward to Red Rock Pass, the trend of the range is, with an occasional deflection, nearly west for about one hundred miles. Bordering the northern slope of the mountains and commencing at the western terminus of Red Rock Pass there extends a fertile and picturesque valley, fifty miles long and from two to six miles wide, bounded on the

FREDERICK I. HANSON.
Alaska Basin, Montana.

north by mountain uplifts, designated on the general land office map of Montana for 1894 as "Tobaccoroot" and "Snow Crest" ranges. This valley is drained down through its lowest depression by Red Rock river, so-called, which is supplied in its perennial flowage with the water discharged from about sixty-eight subsidiary branches, coming in on either side, above the Red Rock guide meridian, where the valley terminates in its western limit, while near its eastern extremity the uplifts intervene to such an extent that the river is bordered on either side by the mountain ranges, thereby practically dividing the valley into two basins, the lower and larger of which contains the Red Rock lakes, and is called "The Centennial Valley," its first settlement having been made by Messrs. Poindexter and Orr, for stock-raising purposes, in 1876, and the upper basin, being less than five miles long and two miles wide, has been named by Mr. S. B. Burnside, "The Alaska Basin," owing, it is said, to excessive depth of snow in the winter months, or for his relatives in some way,

MR. FREDERICK I. HANSON.
Sole occupant of the Alaska Basin.

who live in Alaska. The planimetric surveys of the government were extended to each of the localities described as
early as 1891, Mr. Harry Redfield of Montana officiating as
the contracting deputy surveyor. The usual rule of quick
work for a minimum price obtained, with the result that the
topography as shown on the government plats is inaccurate
and of little or no value for distinguishing correct topographic
features, and the mail-route map of the government for that
locality is no better, while the chart of the geological survey
of a portion of that country was reduced by Mr. Gustavus
R. Bechler, "after descriptive information;" Dr. A. C. Peale
contributing no chart of his explorations to the westward
from Red Rock Pass.

In the manner stated, one of the most important geographical localities in the world has remained unsurveyed and unexplored, so far as can be learned from all available data,
and it was toward an exploration of the longest and largest
of the streams in the Centennial Valley and Alaska Basin,
beyond the limits to which the several surveys mentioned
were prosecuted, that the present work was intended to
adequately extend for a better understanding of its geographic importance.

No map yet made has correctly delineated all the hydrographic and topographic features of that mountainous region,
nor can such a map be made except as a result of long and
painstaking examinations and surveys, for the volcanic uplifts
and terrific defiles have been designated as "Hell Roaring,"
a name which I have tried to eliminate.

Following the first advance of civilized life, scattering
settlements extended along the valley, until in 1889 a postoffice was established at Shambow Creek, now called Magdalen, and the only office on the triweekly stage line supplying
mails between Monida, on the Union Pacific, and Henry lake
in Idaho, covering a distance of about sixty miles. The settlements are principally ranches located on sparkling mountain streams where they emerge into the valley from the
heights above. The stage route is along the south side of the
valley, where the streams are very numerous on account of
the northern slope of the mountains holding the snow the entire season, thus gradually supplying a constant flowage,
which induces the growth of numerous groves of pine timber,
adding to its attractiveness and shielding the homes of the
settlers. Shambow Pass is an opening through the main
range, south to Idaho, opposite Lower Red Rock lake, from
which flows Odell creek. The numerous streams have been

STAGE DRIVER DELIVERING THE MAILS IN ROADSIDE BOXES.
The Centennial Valley, Montana, 1895.

HERD GRAZING.
ISAAC JACQUES AND TEAM.
LANDSCAPE SCENE.
IRRIGATING DITCH.   BURNSIDE'S STATION.
SCHOOL HOUSE.   GEORGE HUMPHREY'S HOUSE.

CENTENNIAL VALLEY VIEWS, MONTANA.

(99)

quite generally named after the settler occupying the locality with his herds, the principal industry; and the postoffice is scarcely needed by the ranchers of the south side, for each has a postoffice box located on the route opposite his ranch, into which the mails are delivered as the stage passes by. The custom is an excellent one, and the orderly but scattered community has a mail service, with "certainty, celerity, and security," more regular than many older localities in the distant East.

One little log schoolhouse at Shambow Creek serves the double purpose of an institution of learning and for religious worship, with occasionally a talented young schoolma'am, but no preacher. The people need no missionary, in fact, for it is the most orderly and lawful community on the remotest frontier that I have noticed in many years. I hid my purse, charged my Winchester and sheathed my hunting knife, on my first trip through the valley, expecting a possible hold-up that didn't occur, and the hospitality and hearty welcome extended by all I met strengthened the impression that the tales that are told are not all true. There are no Itasca thieves in the Centennial Valley.

Among the first settlers were Messrs. James Blair, Frederick I. Hanson, Henry Hackett, and Mr. and Mrs. William N. Culver; the first school teacher was Miss Millie Coffin, and the first postmaster, Mr. William Smith.

Here the Bannock Indians roamed on hunting and fishing expeditions for an unknown length of time, and the game and fish, then so plentiful, from all indications still exist in abundance throughout the region; however, the game is shy and hard to hunt in the mountain fastnesses.

These valleys were formerly lakes, now converted to mains and meadows by the lapse of eroding centuries, the Red Rock lakes remaining in low depressions but remnants, cast asunder by the gradual disappearance of the parent water, creating the meandering river of recent origin in a geological sequence of departing time, which, in not an unusual order, has channeled a stream-bed, connecting the Alaska Basin with the Centennial Valley, at section 16, township 14, S. range 1 E. of the principal meridian of Montana. Across the mountain Mr. Culver has his abode at a remarkable spring, out from which flows Picnic creek, and Mr. Frederick I. Hanson is the only claimant of any portion of the Alaska Basin, at which he has a stock range where succulent grasses grow in great abundance.

Fields of grain are unknown in that region, while the garden spots of the ranchers are results of the irrigating process, a constant and liberal supply of water being drawn from the mountain streams with little trouble and no expense, a necessity on account of the absence of rainfall, the elevation above the sea exceeding 7,000 feet.

Snow falls every month in the year, except July, and yet the heat of the summer is sometimes intense, while in winter the temperature seldom falls to —40° Fahrenheit.

The whole surroundings are grandly picturesque and interesting; the waters supply the anglers with superb fishing, mountain trout and grayling being abundant, and at Henry's lake, salmon fisheries have been maintained to some extent for the markets, the catch being transported to Monida in bull-boats made of frozen ox hides and hauled over the snow like toboggans.

MR. JAMES BLAIR.
Rocky Mountain guide and hunter.

The Alaska Basin is noted for its deep snows, and in winter the stage sets landmarks along its route by which to be guided in case of tempestuous storms, while passing to and from Lake postoffice, in Idaho, where, at or near Sawtell's ranch, Joseph Sherwood, postmaster, Ira Livermore, Gilman Sawtell and others established settlements at one of the grandest and most picturesque localities on the American continent, at Henry's lake, five or six miles eastwardly from the Alaska Basin, the Red Rock Pass affording an easy and excellent location for a roadway along the old Bannock trail leading from the Centennial Valley to Tar-ghé Pass (Beaver Cañon) and the Obsidian Cliff in the Yellowstone Park; Sawtell's Peak, an extinct volcano, and the Three Tetons with surrounding mountains and valleys, forming a southern landscape of surpassing beauty as seen from the mountain heights at Henry's lake.

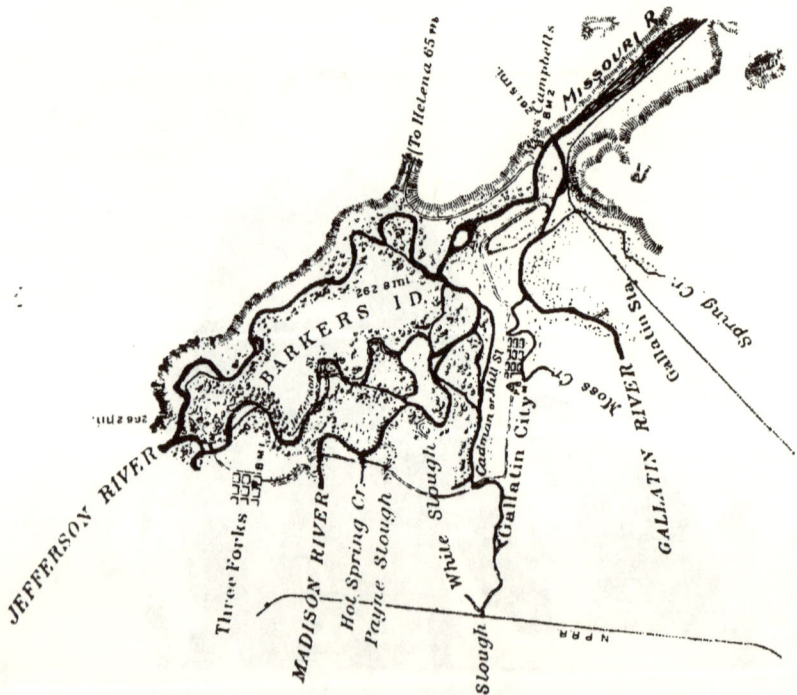

EXTRACT MODIFIED FROM CHART OF THREE FORKS.
(Missouri River Commission.)

MOUTH OF CULVER'S CAÑON.
SITE OF EXTINCT WATERFALL.

VIEWS AT CULVER'S CAÑON, MONTANA.

(103)

VIEWS AT CULVER'S CAÑON, MONTANA.

§ XIV. THE UTMOST SOURCE OF THE MISSOURI RIVER.

On the 28th day of July, 1895, and soon after my return from the source of the Mississippi, Bemidji, Cass, and Leech lakes, in an examination of the tumuli, relics and remains of prehistoric man found at those points, I departed on another expedition in search of the utmost source of the Missouri river.

UTMOST BRANCH OF THE MISSOURI RIVER
In the Rocky Mountains.

The time occupied traveling westward from St. Paul, Minn., to Helena, Mont., was very pleasantly enjoyed on the Northern Pacific railroad, which traverses the great wheat lands of the Red River of the North near Moorhead and Fargo, in the dry basin of the great Lake Agassiz,[54] across which the fields of golden grain could be seen in almost unlimited extent.

Passing w e s t w a r d out from the Red River Valley and into the James River Valley of North Dakota, tributary to the Missouri, the surface of the country gradually changes.

[54]The glacial Lake Agassiz, held in the basin of the Red River of the North and of Lake Winnipeg by the barrier of the receding continental ice-sheet in the closing or Champlain epoch of the Glacial period, was named by Warren Upham in the eighth annual report of the Minnesota Geological Survey, for the year 1879, in honor of Louis Agassiz, the first prominent advocate of the theory that the glacial drift was formed by land ice. Leveling along its highest beach shows that Lake Agassiz, in its earliest and highest stage, was nearly 200 feet deep above Moorhead and Fargo; a little more than 300 feet deep above Grand Forks and Crookston; about 450 feet above Pembina, St. Vincent, and Emerson; and about 500 and 600 feet, respectively, above lakes Manitoba and Winnipeg. The length of Lake Agassiz is estimated to have been nearly 700 miles, and its area not less than 110,000 square miles, exceeding the combined areas of the five great lakes tributary to the St. Lawrence. Thirty successive shore lines of the glacial lake are traced along the greater part or considerable portions of their course, showing gradual diminution of the area of the lake, due to the erosion of the deep Brown's Valley, which was its outlet southward, by the glacial River Warren (now the Minnesota river) to the Mississippi, due

It is in the Dakota states where the greatest pressure of artesian flowage is obtained; a remarkable system of deep wells having been located recently east of the Missouri.[55]

With one day's time at my disposal, I drove out from Bismarck to the Sibley rifle-pits on Apple creek, where thirty-five years before, I had, with the Sibley command, met the treacherous Sioux face to face,·when the only salutation was by carbines and cartridges, tomahawks and scalping knives.

The rifle-pits remain intact, on a terrace above the Missouri, and their appearance does not seemingly indicate the lapse of so many years since they were constructed.

Proceeding on my way, I noticed after passing through the Bad Lands, a village of prairie dogs, west of Medora and east of Andrew's Station, where were a vast number of burrows, probably as many as five thousand in all, and seemingly a dog for every burrow.

---

afterward to change of the place of outlet, then flowing northeastward, and due, in larger measure, during both of these stages, to the slow uplifting of the lake basin while the vast weight of the ice-sheet was being removed by its final melting. This glacial lake is described by Mr. Upham, in reports of the Minnesota Geological Survey, in the annual report of the Geological Survey of Canada, vol. iv., new series, for 1888-89, and most fully in Monograph XXV. of the United States Geological Survey, with many maps, sections, and views from photographs.

[55]The following notes of the remarkable artesian wells in the basin of the James river, tributary to the Missouri, are contributed by Mr. Upham, being chiefly based on an article upon this subject in the American Geologist, vol. vi., pp. 211-221, October, 1890: "Deep artesian wells of somewhat saline and alkaline water are obtained on a belt that extends across North and South Dakota from Devil's Lake to Yankton and Vermillion, including the greater part of the James river basin. Wherever borings along this belt have penetrated to the Dakota sandstones, the lowest Cretaceous formation in the Upper Missouri region, artesian water has been found. Probably as many as two hundred wells have been bored, their depths ranging from 900 to 1,550 feet, except in the southern part of the James and Vermillion valleys, where many wells are only 600 to 750 feet deep, and a few, the farthest southeast, are between 300 and 400 feet in depth. These wells are mostly five or six inches in diameter, and their strong pressure, commonly from 50 to 175 pounds per square inch at the surface, makes them valuable not only for fire hydrants, but also to furnish power for manufacturing purposes. Several wells have been bored at Aberdeen, and five years ago fifteen wells were in use in Yankton. The pressure of the wells in Yankton is sufficient to raise the water 129 feet, and in numerous places along the middle portion of the James river valley, as Huron, Redfield, and Aberdeen, the pressure corresponds to a rise of more than 400 feet above the surface. All the eastern outcrops of the Dakota sandstone are lower than the upper portions of the James river basin and the wells farther west at Highmore and Harold. These outcrops, therefore, cannot be the sources from which the sandstone receives its artesian water, but instead they are the avenues of its natural outflow. We must look to the much higher western outcrops of this formation, where it skirts the Black Hills and exposes its upturned edges along the base of the Rocky Mountain ranges, for the areas upon which the water (doubtless in part leaking directly from the channel of the Missouri river itself) is carried downward into the sandstone. Thence we know this stratum to be continuous beneath the plains to the James river valley, for there are no nearer nor other inlets from which the copious supply of the artesian wells can come. At a plane of similar or greater depth an artesian reservoir exists beneath much, if not all, of the country westward to the mountains. The gradients of the altitudes to which the water of wells is capable of rising along east-to-west lines in South Dakota, as at Huron, Miller, and Highmore, are approximately the same as the average westward ascent of the country, demonstrating this western origin of the water supply, and indicating that such wells may be obtained upon an extensive region of the arid plains."

The valley of the Yellowstone, with all its historic interest, is not disappointing in the varied scenes it presents, and the Crow Indian can be found, not murderous or thieving as in former years, but on a final reservation, through which the Northern Pacific winds its way to Billings, Livingston, and Bozeman, the latter situated in the remarkably fertile Gallatin Valley, extending to Three Forks, where the Jefferson, Madison, and Gallatin converge into the main Missourian stream-bed, the former being the larger and principal river, draining the chief and continuous valley, while the last two are lateral affluents, coming in at the side.

Visiting Helena,—a gem set in the side of the mountains,— for a thorough examination of all the official plats of the United States Surveyor General's office, so far as necessary, on the 2d of August I arrived at Lima, Mont. This little town is situated in the immediate valley of the Missouri, about ten miles above the red butte after which the river at this point takes its name.

Assuming that the present Jefferson Fork, Beaver Head, and Red Rock, as one continuous, unbroken, and direct principal channel, constituted the headwater branch of the Missouri, every precaution necessary was taken to determine the relative importance of all the larger upper branches of the Missouri system.

Engaging Mr. Isaac Jaques and a commodious conveyance, we left Lima August 3d, and proceeded up Red Rock river by team to the western extremity of the Centennial Valley, where an abortive attempt had been made to dam the river for irrigating purposes, about fourteen miles above Lima. The flood of water had swept everything away, cutting a new channel through the narrow pass in the mountains. At this point the indications are very distinct as determining the western limit of the ancient glacial lake which existed in this valley, covering an undetermined area of about 300 square miles, extending to the Alaska Basin and Red Rock Pass. Proceeding on our way along the north side of the valley as far as Long creek, upon which is situated an extensive bed of coal, we crossed the river to the south side, and proceeded up the valley to Blake's ranch, Magdalen, Shambow Pass, Lower and Upper Red Rock lakes to Culver's ranch at the head of Picnic creek, crossing, examining, and photographing numerous sparkling mountain streams flowing down into the Red Rock fork from the snow-capped summits of the Rocky Mountains above us.

The river channel down through the Centennial Valley is very crooked, and meanders through the meadows of grass, along the lowest depression of the ancient glacial lake bed, fully doubling the distance by land.

Lower Red Rock lake is a very shallow broadening of Odell and Shambow creeks, four or five feet deep and matted with innumerable shoals which were covered with a dense growth of rushes. This lake is situated to the southward of the main river, which does not flow through it, all charts and maps to the contrary notwithstanding, and at no distant geological date it will entirely disappear from the causes proceeding from stream erosion through the adjacent cañons and gulches to the southward. There is no timber growing on its shores.

The Upper Red Rock lake is a very different body of water, its general recess extending along the center of the upper portion of the valley, the main river forming its inlet and outlet. It is from ten to twenty feet in depth, bordered by a growth of pine timber on the south side immediately at the base of the main range of mountains.

It cannot be said of either or both of these lakes that they are of importance as hydrographic features of the locality, for no stream takes its rise in them, and they are but a broadening out of the streams, into the lowest depression of the upper end of the valley.

Swan lake is a small body of water on the north side of and almost a part of Upper Red Rock lake, divided by a narrow, wet marsh. Some enterprising gentlemen of Montana resort to these lakes in the hunting season for ducks, geese, swan, and other fowls which find here a brooding place each season.

After rest and refreshment at Mr. Culver's commodious mountain home, I extended to the Alaska Basin particular attention, exploring the entire locality.

With Mr. Jaques and his team, I left Mr. Culver's home on the 4th of August, crossed over to the Alaska Basin, and examined its entire surroundings. This basin is the eastern extremity of the ancient lake which formerly existed in what is now the Centennial Valley. There is no timber, except at the base or on the flanks of the mountains, and patches of undergrowth along the streams, so that from the summits a view of the entire locality can be had, which is easy of access and grandly picturesque in its mountain scenery. Skirting the basin at the base of the mountains I explored numerous little streamlets flowing in from the cañons and gulches, subsidiary to the North and South forks, as designated on the government plat.[56] The two forks mentioned were found to

[56] See the plat at p. 94.

flow out from Culver's Cañon on the south side of the basin, and after a meandering circuit of about three miles, they come together again lower down near the center of the depression below which another considerable stream comes in, from the base of Hanson Mountain, which is known as Horse Camp creek.

Culver's Cañon is not very far west of the center of the south side of the Alaska Basin, and discovering that the principal stream issued out from it, in four channels, cast asunder by an impetuous current plunging over a detrital mass to a quaternion division, a thorough exploration of the locality was deemed advisable and necessary.

On the 5th of August, after a needed rest, accompanied by Messrs. Culver and Jaques, I entered upon the exploration of Culver's Cañon, and an examination of the stream flowing out from it. We picketed our horses at the base of the lofty mountains, and proceeded on foot up over an immense accumulation of debris consisting of trees, detritus, and material that had been thrown down and out by the waters of the stream flowing from the summits above. We soon reached a gorge where the rock in place was nearly perpendicular, and a choice between proceeding up over the declivities or wading up the stream was necessary, and neither could be accomplished without some personal danger.

CULVER'S CAÑON.

At this point is located the site of a former cataract, now a rapids, where the mountain range has been practically severed in twain by the eroding action of unceasing and long continued flowage.

The perpendicular rock, especially on the eastern limit of Hanson Mountain, is a geologic calendar of time, the different deposits, somewhat faulted, indicating distinctly the colors and capping of their stratigraphic order of formation.

Proceeding up this remarkable mountain stream, in full view of the summit of the Rocky range beyond, observations for temperature and elevation were made, photographs taken, velocity and depth measured and field notes for topography reduced to writing for future use.

Without an exploration of this entire locality, we returned to our horses at the mouth of the cañon, that we might not be overtaken by the darkness of night in the wildest region of the Missouri Basin.

Beginning on the 6th of August and continuing until the 28th, I traversed numerous localities in Montana, examined the characteristics of Big Hole river, visited the Three Forks on two separate dates, and instituted a careful inquiry into the question of mileage distances and elevations; considering the effects of the system of irrigating ditches, very few of which were found on the Big Hole as compared with the number from Whitehall to the Red Rock lakes. It may be noted here that the question of irrigation is an important one as affecting the volume of water in these streams.

Returning to the Alaska Basin on the 28th of August, with Mr. Jaques, I was joined by Mr. Culver for a more extended exploration of Culver's Cañon, which we explored to the summit of the mountains and to the utmost source of the Missouri.

August 29th we left Mr. Jaques with the horses at the base of Hanson Mountain, on Horse Camp creek, and with one pack horse proceeded over the summit to Culver's Cañon to avoid the difficulties encountered during the former exploration.

There was little difference in the difficulties encountered, for climbing and descending was the necessary order of procedure, dead and down timber impeding our progress on every hand. Arriving at the cañon we passed along the slope of the mountain to a crossing of four small creeks, finally descending with difficulty into the bed of the main stream, where it was found unadvisable to proceed with the pack-horse on account of numerous ledges, windfalls, and declivities.

At this point we picketed our animal, deposited our provisions, and proceeded on foot up the winding course of the cañon, with no burden except my camera, barometer, and one small compass.

Following the bed of the stream as best we could and against an increasing rapidity of current, we finally arrived at a small flat and marshy locality, on the west end of which is located a little lake, which we called Lillian.

But a short distance beyond Lillian lake we suddenly came in full view of a hole in the summit of the Rocky Moun-

CALENDAR OF GEOLOGIC TIME, AT CULVER'S CAÑON.

VIEW ABOVE HORSE PICKET HOLE, MONTANA.

(111)

tains, immediately west of the crest of the main range, and circling around which were numerous peaks, apparently of volcanic origin.

From this Hole in the Rocky Mountains, the little rivulet, two feet wide and scarcely two inches in depth, drawing its utmost supply from the inner walls of the mighty and tower-ing uplifts sur-rounding it, takes its course out into, and down through Culver's Cañon to the valleys below, broadening, deep-ening, and strengthening its importance from the base of adja-cent and enor-mous ranges, on every hand, until its turbulent wa-ters, severing the mountains and channeling the valleys, open the gate to an issue

THE HOLE IN THE MOUNTAINS.

in the parent ocean, thousands of miles away, by the longest continuous and uninterrupted river channel known to the world.

The formation of this unique, most distant, and peculiar source of the Missouri was undoubtedly caused by volcanic action, similarly to the manner suggested by Captain Dutton concerning crateriform depressions in Hawaii.[57]

The rocks in some places are faulted and folded, and one massive solid rock shaft, nearly fifty feet in height, stands in plain view near the summit, east of the lower extremity of the Hole in the Mountains, which itself indicates, apparently, a former volcanic eruptive force.[58]

[57]Captain Dutton, U. S. A., considering volcanic eruptive action, states: "Numerous small crateriform depressions are found in many parts of Hawaii, which also seems to me to be homologous to Kilauea, some of which are only a few hundred feet in diameter, and none of them exhibit any signs of recent activity. Considered with reference to their origin, the evidence is conclusive that they were formed by the dropping of a block of the mountain crust, which once covered a reservoir of lava, this reservoir being tapped and drained by eruptions occurring at much lower levels."—United States Geological Survey, Fourth Annual Report.

[58]"The character of all this mountain region was decidedly volcanic; and to the northwest, between Henry's Fort and the source of the Missouri, Mr. Stuart observed several very high peaks, covered with snow, from two of which smoke ascended in considerable volumes, apparently from craters in a state of eruption."—Irving's "Astoria," iii., pp. 68-69.

The Sawtell crater is in this range, to the eastward, and the mountains, as suggested by Dr. Peale, show evidences of volcanic formation.

During past ages, previous to the existence of Culver's Cañon, at and above the base of Hanson Mountain, it would seem probable that a considerable lake existed in this mountainous depression, and that the waters of that lake formed the cataract which severed the range and the cañon, and its magnificent mountain stream followed as the results of erosion during the lapse of departing geologic eras.

During our brief examination at the source, readings for altitude were taken, and a faulted rock was marked with the letters "B & C," near which we deposited a copper plate with the date and name of the river engraved thereon.

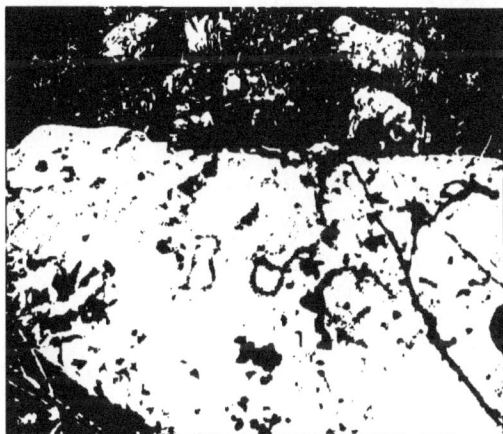

THE B. & C. ROCK.

After making about twenty exposures for photographs, we hastily descended from this elevated region, reaching Horse Camp creek as the shades of night approached, where we joined Mr. Jaques, who had prepared a bounteous repast of mountain trout, coffee, and toast.

Following these observations, I had the pleasure of examining forty-eight mountain streams which flow from the Rocky Mountains into the Centennial Valley, between Culver's Cañon and Monida.

It will be noticed, that the peculiarities of the region traversed are such that the utmost branch of the Missouri, from its source, flows in a westerly direction to Lima, while the head waters of Henry's Fork of Snake river flow eastwardly from Red Rock Pass. This feature is caused by the mountain range encircling around the Henry lake basin, west of which the Missouri takes its rise at the utmost limit of the Missouri Basin, so that, while the source is west from the mountain range at that point, it is on the eastern or Atlantic slope.

Few names have as yet been given, as I prefer, on the final chart, now in course of preparation, to attach such names as will be appropriate, and at the same time satisfactory to the people residing at the points most affected, and Mr. Culver, upon whose able and trustworthy assistance I have largely depended, has consented to prepare a corrected and accurate list of the names that different points in the Centennial Valley are to be known by.

Mr. James Blair having explored the mountains above Horse Camp creek, I deemed it very appropriate to name the little lake in that locality, and the creek, in his honor, but I do not know whether Blair creek flows out of Blair lake or not, as my party did not explore the locality in that direction, and Mr. Blair's explorations were prosecuted on snow-shoes in the winter season, so that no one yet knows the true conditions.

Lillian lake was at first called Gem lake, but subsequently Mrs. Lillian E. Culver organized an expedition to that locality, as will be shown, and I changed the name on that account.

Hanson Mountain, with a double summit, situated between Horse Camp creek and Culver's Cañon, has been named after Frederick I. Hanson, whose ranch has been located at its base in the Alaska Basin.

Horse Picket Hole is so called to identify the locality where we were obliged to picket our pack horse and proceed on foot.

Culver's Cañon has been very properly changed in name from "Hell-Roaring Cañon," in honor of my discovering companion, and without his consent.

The three mountain peaks adjacent to Culver's Cañon have no name. The largest of the three has an altitude of about 9,500 feet, and is plainly observable for thirty miles down the valley. It is this mountain which the waters have severed apart from Hanson Mountain as before described.

The Hole in the Mountains will be named in time for the final chart of the locality, as no really appropriate name has yet been determined upon by Mr. Culver and myself.

Evidences of the existence of elk, deer, bear, and wild sheep in Culver's Cañon were noticed in many places, and the only sign that man had ever visited the locality was an old Indian trail, and where they had hacked down a small tree with a hatchet, near Lillian lake, in characteristic Indian fashion. The Bannocks have occasionally resorted to the lower portion of the cañon, hunting sheep.

On the 9th of the following September J. B. Bishop, T. F. Bishop, and R. B. Wright found their way into this cañon and staked out a mine, marking the same as follows:

"Location of Quartz.
S. W. Corner of the Porcupine Location
Sept. 9th, 1895."

This quartz was noticed by Mr. Culver in August, but we made no location at that time.

The Messrs. Bishop and Wright reside in Idaho, on the other side of the range.

On the 26th of September Mrs. Lillian E. Culver and Mr. Allen made a visit to the Hole in the Mountains, at the utmost limit of the Missouri Basin, crossing over Hanson Mountain and to the left of Horse Picket Hole, by which route they were able to ride mounted to the farthest limit of the basin, where they marked the utmost spring of the Missouri upon the side of the mountain very near the Idaho state boundary. Mrs. Culver says:

"We decided to see just where the creek headed, so kept going for about three miles, and almost to the top of the divide. Suddenly the creek turned quite abruptly and headed in the north-east at quite a pretty spring, which came from under a large black rock on the side of the mountain near some balsam. It is a lonesome, wild place, and a dozen or more tiny springs higher up run into this one. Marking the spot with my name and the date on a tin plate, and depositing a shoe that my horse had cast upon the largest rock, we commenced to retrace our steps hurriedly. The rock is marked 'L. C., Sep., 1895.' We found two mounds that have the appearance of Indian graves below Bishop's mine, not far from where we crossed the Missouri coming out.

"Truly I have been to the head of the Missouri, which is said to be 4,100 miles long. I think you will soon find it longer. A snowstorm had occurred and the tracks of elk and grey wolves were noticed."

By this exploration, Mrs. Culver assumes a place in history similar to the lamented Mary Turnbull, the first white woman at the source of the Mississippi, for certainly no lady has preceded Mrs. Culver at the utmost source of the Missouri.

In order that no error or false claim may be set up, I will state here, that, while there does not appear any probability that these explorations to the summit of the Rocky Mountains were not the first discovery of the utmost limit of the channel of the Missouri river, if any legitimate and truthful record exists of a prior geographical exploration of the locality, Mr. Culver and myself will cheerfully yield the honor of a first discovery.

Mrs. Culver, who is an accomplished botanist, has also furnished a complete description of many of the floral plants of Montana, intended for insertion herein. Owing to a disappointment in securing colored plates of some of her most prominent displays, furnished for that purpose, only meager and unsatisfactory reference can be made at this time on the subject of plant life in the Centennial Valley.

Mrs. Culver writes as follows:

"* * * * We have nearly one thousand tabulated species of wild flowers, one hundred and four of native grasses, ten of ferns, forty of mosses, and fifty of algae. The Centennial Valley, the uppermost in the Missouri Basin, is a most beautiful and picturesque locality, and its flora is something magnificent. There are about three hundred varieties of wild flowers of every shade and color possible, from the dainty lilac-colored wind flower (*Anemone*), that blooms in the spring before the snow disappears, to the dashing, red-painted cup (*Castilleia*), which borders our groves of pine so richly, interwoven with dog-tooth violet, (*Erythronium*), and *fritillaria pudica*. The dignified purple larkspur (*Delphinium*), that holds its head so proudly for all to admire, is a wolf in disguise, as it is a deadly poison to the ranging herds. The yellow goldenrod (*Solidago Serotina*), is produced here in profusion, which, with some of 'God's smiles,' welcome us everywhere, and which, with the Montana state emblem, the bitter-root, (*Lewisia rediviva*) giving name to the Bitter Root Mountains, and growing to the very summits of the most barren peaks, literally 'stars on the earth,' extend to our mountain home many of nature's heavenly pleasures."

Mrs. Culver would have been astonished to have witnessed the flora at what is now the Centennial Valley, could she have seen the conditions existing at the time the coal deposits were thrown down at Long creek, probably during the carboniferous age.

The coal vein referred to was discovered recently, and is now being opened preparatory to an intended operation of the mine by its discoverer.

CHANNEL MILEAGE OF THE LONGEST STREAM-BED IN THE WORLD.

The longest river channel in the world, the mileage of which has been very carefully computed from all available sources of information obtainable, is the stream-bed from the mouth of the Mississippi to the mouth of Missouri, thence up the channel of the Missouri to the Three Forks; thence up the longest and principal branch to the summit of the Rocky Mountains, where it takes its rise. Never in the history of man has any portion of this wonderful river been known to be without perennial flowage from natural causes.

The supply has been drawn entirely from the effects of secular aërial precipitation seeking the sea-level in various ways, from surface flowage, melting ice and snow, springs, lakes, and even from the magnificent geyser basins of the Yellowstone National Park, and the glaciers of the Rocky Mountains; undiminished except from the effects of climatic influences or artificial interference.

The following tabulated mileage distances indicate the true length, now given for the first time, of the main and longest channel, from tide water at the Gulf of Mexico to the utmost Basin of the Missouri in the Rocky Mountains, above and beyond Upper Red Rock lake in the State of Montana.

Location.	Miles.
S. W. Pass at the delta of the Mississippi river	00
Thence to New Orleans	111
Thence to mouth of the Ohio	965
Thence to city of St. Louis	182
Thence to mouth of the Missouri	17
Total	1,276

From mouth of the Missouri river, thence:

To St. Charles bridge	28 miles
To Wild Horse creek	48 miles
To Port Royal	50 miles
To St. Albans	55 miles
To Washington	71 miles
To New Haven	86 miles
To Bridgeport	98 miles
To Hermann	103 miles
To Gasconade river	110 miles

To Bluffton	115 miles
To Portland	120 miles
To St. Aubert	130 miles
To Bonnot's Mill	138 miles
To Osage river	141 miles
To Jefferson City, Mo	151 miles
To Marion	167 miles
To Providence	179 miles
To Rocheport	194 miles
To Booneville	205 miles
To Lisbon	225 miles
To Bluffport	234 miles
To Cambridge	245 miles
To New Frankfort	252 miles
To Grand river	260 miles
To Miami	271 miles
To Laynesville	283 miles
To Mills' Point	310 miles
To Lexington	322 miles
To Wellington	328 miles
To Camden	336 miles
To Napoleon	342 miles
To Sibley Bridge	350 miles
To Missouri City	362 miles
To Kansas City, Mo	390 miles
To Kansas City, Kan	391 miles
To Kansas or Kaw river	392 miles
To Leavenworth	421 miles
To Fort Leavenworth bridge	424 miles
To St. Joseph bridge	479 miles
To Mount Vernon	509 miles
To Big Nemaha river	529 miles
To Nemaha City	570 miles
To Nebraska City bridge	607 miles
To Rock Bluff	626 miles
To Platte river	635 miles
To Omaha, Neb	659 miles
To Florence	670 miles
To Fort Calhoun	682 miles
To California Junction	688 miles
To Blair bridge	694 miles
To Black Bird Hill	753 miles
To Omaha Mission	764 miles
To Floyd river	806 miles
To Sioux City, Iowa	807 miles

To Big Sioux river	810	miles
To Elk Point	837	miles
To Yankton, S. D	897	miles
To Fort Mitchell	941	miles
To Fort Randall	978	miles
To Wheeler	995	miles
To Chamberlain bridge	1,067	miles
To Fort Thompson	1,087	miles
To Fort Pierre	1,172	miles
To Pierre, S. D	1,173	miles
To Fort Sully	1,204	miles
To Fort Bennett	1,211	miles
To Fairbank	1,239	miles
To Cheyenne Agency	1,266	miles
To Fort Yates	1,373	miles
To Fort Rice Landing	1,404	miles
To Apple Creek, N. D	1,437	miles
To Fort Abraham Lincoln	1,444	miles
To Bismarck bridge, N. D	1,450	miles
To Mandan	1,452	miles
To Fort Stevenson	1,538	miles
To Fort Berthold	1,557	miles
To Little Missouri river	1,582	miles
To Nesson	1,673	miles
To the Yellowstone river	1,760	miles
To Black Duck	1,834	miles
To Milk river	1,937	miles
To Fort Peck	1,957	miles
To Musselshell river	2,075	miles
To Carroll, Mont	2,113	miles
To Gallatin Rapids	2,187	miles
To Judith	2,196	miles
To Steamboat Rock	2,215	miles
To Hole in the Wall	2,220	miles
To Twenty-four Mile creek	2,249	miles
To Marias river	2,262	miles
To Fort Benton bridge	2,284	miles
To North Great Falls	2,329	miles
To Great Falls, Mont., at railroad bridge	2,333	miles
To Smith River, Mont	2,361	miles
To St. Clair	2,388	miles
To Mid Cañon	2,407	miles
To Ox Bow Bend	2,431	miles
To Bear Tooth Rapids	2,438	miles
To White Rock Rapids	2,441	miles

To Stubbs Ferry............................ 2,463 miles
To Canyon Ferry............................ 2,470 miles
To Pine Tree Rapids........................ 2,484 miles
To Canton .... 2,495 miles
To N. P. R. R. bridge...................... 2,504 miles
To Townsend .... 2,505 miles
To Toston .... 2,519 miles
To Painted Rock station.................... 2,528 miles
To Sixteen Mile creek...................... 2,530 miles
To Magpie station.......................... 2,535 miles
To Gallatin river.......................... 2,546 miles
To the confluence of the Madison and Jefferson. 2,547 miles

FIRST RECAPITULATION.

Distance on the Mississippi, as stated.......... 1,276 miles
Distance on the Missouri, as stated............. 2,547 miles

Total from Gulf to Three Forks.......... 3,823 miles

From Three Forks, Mont., up the main course of
the one continuous principal stream-bed along
the thread of the channel of the Jefferson Fork,
Beaver Head, and Red Rock branch of the Missouri, that constituting the principal river (but
designated by three additional names), to the
Upper Red Rock lake, and thence to and up
through the Alaska Basin to Culver's Cañon;
thence up through said cañon to Horse Picket
Hole; thence to the summit of the Rocky
Mountains, where the utmost branch of the
Missouri takes it rise; the length of the chan-
nel is................................... .... 398 miles

SECOND RECAPITULATION.

The length of the Mississippi from S. W. Pass to
the mouth of the Missouri................. 1,276 miles
The length of the Missouri from its mouth to
Three Forks............... .... 2,547 miles
The length of Jefferson, Beaver Head and Red
Rock branch......... .... 398 miles

Total from Gulf of Mexico to summit of
Rocky Mountains by the channel of the
river .... 4,221 miles

The channel mileage from the source of the Mississippi to the Gulf of Mexico is............. 2,553 miles
The channel mileage from Three Forks to the mouth of the Missouri is................... 2,547 miles

Difference .... 6 miles

Elevation of the Three Forks, Mont............. 4,045 feet
Elevation of utmost source of the Missouri....... 8,000 feet
Elevation of source of Mississippi (which is above Itasca lake)................................ 1,535 feet

The mean average descent of the flowage in the Mississippi is a fraction more than seven and one-quarter inches per mile. The mean average descent of the flowage in the Missouri from the summit of the Rocky Mountains to the Gulf is about nineteen inches per mile.

From New York and Maryland to Montana, and from the British possessions in the North to Louisiana, upwards of 100,000 creeks, streams, and rivers contribute surface flowage to the Mississippian-Missourian river system.

VIEW AT CULVER'S CAÑON.

CRITICAL CONSIDERATION OF THE SOURCES OF IN-FORMATION ON RIVER MILEAGE.

The Mississippi River Commission and the Missouri River Commission, separate boards, constituted by acts of congress with ample annual appropriations, each maintaining its headquarters at the city of St. Louis, are preëminently first in ascertaining the true length of each river so far as their separate surveys have been extended. The methods have been based upon scientific principles, and the unlimited use of all modern appliances for ascertaining positions, distances, and elevations secures to the charts and reports the official results which supersede all other surveys and estimates. A regret may be expressed that the entire work of both commissions is not in one continuous connected form, from the delta of the Mississippi to the utmost source of each river, in place of the separate boards of commissioners with distinct surveys, in some particulars detached and referable to the elevation of Lake Superior.

From the charts of each commission, separately and combined, the distances from the Gulf of Mexico to Three Forks, Mont., have been reduced to a continuous channel mileage with results as stated, ignoring decimals, which do not affect the final result.

From Three Forks, Mont., up the channel of the Jefferson, Beaver Head, Red Rock, and the mountain stream issuing from Culver's Cañon, a very careful and painstaking estimate has been made without any actual measurement of the thread of the channel, and all authorities available have been consulted in arriving at the conclusion stated, a curtailed partial list of which follows herewith:

Table of distances by Benton Transportation Company.

Estimates by Capt. William Braithwaite.

Estimates by Capt. Isaac P. Baker.

Important letters and information furnished by Gen. John S. McNeill, Surveyor General of Montana, and Mr. O. C. Dallas, Chief Clerk of the same office, which has charge of all official planimetric surveys in that state; and also an examination and inspection of the official plats of the office at Helena.

Letters from Capt. J. A. Ockerson, United States Assistant Engineer of the Mississippi River Commission.

Letters from Capt. Hiram M. Chittenden, U. S. A.

Letters from Hon. J. M. Page, State Land Agent for Montana, who resides at Twin Bridges, on the Jefferson Fork.

Letter of concise information from Gen. Richard B. Hughes, Surveyor General of South Dakota.

Letters and circular from Capt. J. C. Sanford, U. S. A.

A report from Mr. Harry Redfield of Twin Bridges, Mont., Deputy U. S. Surveyor on the upper waters of the Missouri.

An interesting communication from Capt. W. H. Gould of Bismarck, N. D., who says: "I will say further, that the length of the channel of the Missouri varies with the stage of water, being at least one-eighth longer in low stages, as compared with high water flowage."

All of the official plats of North Dakota and the excellent map of that state by Mr. E. F. Higby, Chief Clerk of the Surveyor General's office at Bismarck.

Communications from the late H. S. Wheeler of the Historical Society of Montana, inclosing information formulated by the late Col. Wm. F. Wheeler.

The Upper Missouri River, by Thomas P. Roberts, 1876, vol. i., p. 234, Montana Historical Contributions.

The Dillon Sheet, U. S. Geological Survey, Montana, 1888.

Surveys of the Union Pacific Railroad system, from Monida to Melrose and Divide, Montana, for elevations and distances.

Mileage distances and elevations on the Northern Pacific Railroad line from Three Forks to Whitehall, Mont., and the Parrott Smelter Spur.

All the official maps of Montana, the Lewis and Clark map, the Le Lacy map of Montana, and various and numerous maps, charts, and profiles.

An inspection of the irrigating ditches along the upper courses of the principal stream-bed in Montana, which changes and modifies the original and natural channel.

The following quotations from Coues' *Lewis and Clark,* 1893, descriptive of the ascent of the river, in 1805, from Three Forks to the Continental Divide:

"Here the country opens into a beautiful valley from six to eight miles in width. The river then becomes crooked and crowded with islands."—Vol. ii., p. 454.

"We were now completely satisfied that the middle branch was the most navigable and the true continuation of the Jefferson."—Vol. ii., p. 465.

"We made five miles by water along two islands and several bayous; but as the river formed seven different bends toward the left, the distance by land was only two miles south of our camp."—Vol. ii., p. 467.

"16 '☞ The courses from the entrance of Wisdom [Big Hole] river to the forks of Jefferson river are taken directly to the objects mentioned and the distance set don't [down] is that by land on a direct line between the points,' Lewis' F. 75—an important memorandum, as courses and distances have hitherto been river-miles, sometimes one and one-half, two, or even three times as far as straight land-miles from point to point."—Vol. ii., p. 467, note.

"The river in fact has become so very crooked, that, although by means of the pole, which we now use constantly, we make a considerable distance, yet, being obliged to follow its wanderings, at the end of the day we find ourselves very little advanced on our general course. It forms itself into small circular bends, which are so numerous that within the last fourteen miles we passed thirty-five of them, all inclining toward the right; it is, however, much more gentle and deep than below Wisdom [Big Hole] river, and its general width is from thirty-five to forty-five yards."—Vol. ii., p. 468.

"A map of part of the continent of North America, by M. Lewis, 1806." "The Rocky or Shining Mountains."

It is a significant fact that on the above described map the name "Missouri River" occurs as designating the Jefferson Fork and Beaver Head, neither of which names appear on the map.

The information described is coupled with field notes, and the results of a personal inspection of the river at various and numerous points from Three Forks to Dillon, Lima, Centennial Valley, Red Rock lakes, Alaska Basin, Culver's Cañon, Horse Picket Hole, the utmost source of the Missouri and the summit of the Rocky Mountains, observed during the months of July, August, and September, 1895.

Mr. Joseph H. Willsey of Buffalo, N. Y., compiler of *Harper's Book of Facts*, 1895, a valuable quarry of concise historical information, on p. 520 of his work, summarizes the importance of the Mississippi system as follows:

"Mississippi River (Ind. Miche-sepe (?), 'Father of Waters') the largest river in North America, and, in length of navigable tributaries and facilities afforded to commerce, the greatest river in the world, being the recipient of all waters flowing east of the Rocky Mountains and west from the Alleghanies. * * * After flowing about 1,330 miles, it unites with the Missouri (termed a tributary, but properly the main stream), which, rising in the remote Rocky Mountains, flows 3,000 miles before reaching the junction, after which their united waters enter the Gulf of Mexico, 1,286 miles below." * * *

Mean annual discharge of the Mississippi into the Gulf is computed at 20,000,000,000,000 of cubic feet, varying in dry seasons from 11,000,-000,000,000 to 27,000,000,000,000 in wet, this amount being about one-fourth of the rainfall on the area of its drainage. * * *

PRINCIPAL PRIMARY AND SECONDARY TRIBUTARIES OF THE MISSISSIPPI, THEIR LENGTH, AND AREA OF TERRITORY DRAINED.

Primary Tributaries.	Secondary Tributaries.	Length.	Area Drained.
Missouri (length 3,000 miles.)	Yellowstone	600 miles	518,000 sq. miles. * * *
	Platte	900 miles	
	Niobrara	450 miles	
	Kansas	250 miles	
	Osage	500 miles	
	Big Sioux	300 miles	

Other authorities state the combined length of this great river course as follows:

"Encyclopedia Britannica," xvi., 578, about.....	4,200 miles
Winsor's "Narrative and Crit. His. of America"	4,506 miles
Johnson's "Universal Encyclopedia," v., 476.....	4,194 miles
"New American Cyclopedia," xi., 592..........	4,506 miles
"Chamber's Encyclopedia," vi., 489............	4,350 miles
"McCulloch's Geographical Dictionary," ii., 354.	4,400 miles
Montana Historical Contributions, i., 237.......	4,600 miles
"The Century Cyclopedia of Names," p. 691.....	4,200 miles
"Harper's Book of Facts" (J. H. Willsey), p. 520.	4,286 miles

COMPARISON.

Length of the River Nile.....................	3,370 miles
Length of the River Amazon (nearly)..........	4,000 miles

(See Encyclopedia Britannica, i. and xvii.)

The completion of the final measurements of the channel of the Missouri, from Three Forks to the summit of the mountains, will, it is believed, but slightly change the re sults now arrived at, and the length of the river is confidently stated as above given, without an actual measurement of its longest upper branch.

COMMON SEA LEVELS.

Various elevations above the sea have been ascertained by numerous and different surveys by the officials of the government, railroad engineers, and by barometric hypsom- etry along the course of the Missouri river.

From numerous observations, principally by the Missouri River Commission and railroad surveys, a limited number of elevations at principal points along the channel of the river are stated.

Elevations by the commission are referable to the St. Louis directrix, which is 412.7 feet above the mean tide of the Gulf of Mexico.

Bulletin of the U. S. Geological Survey No. 72, 1891, by Warren Upham, entitled, "Altitudes Between Lake Superior and the Rocky Mountains," is apparently the best ready reference, many levels in which are credited to Gannett's "Dictionary of Altitudes," while the Mississippi River Com- mission has established a datum-plane at Cairo, to which all precise levels are referred as an assumed plane 300 feet be- low the 9.16 foot gauge mark at the latter point.

Low and high water elevations create a wide discrepancy from time to time, varrying with the seasons, and the detached surveys of the commissions named, part of which were referable to the elevation of Lake Superior at 602 feet above the sea, and extending over a period of many years, are complicated to such an extent that popular comparisons are available only by a reduction of levels to actual elevations.

	Low Water. Feet.	High Water. Feet.
Sea level at the Gulf of Mexico............	000	000
Mouth of the Missouri river................	395	435
St. Charles, Missouri......................	416	443
Washington. Missouri......................	458	474
Hermann. Missouri.........................	479	505
Fisher's Landing. Missouri.................	502	517
Jefferson City, Missouri...................	523	545
Providence, Missouri......................	545	561
Booneville, Missouri.......................	564	588
Glasgow, Missouri	590	615
New Frankfort, Missouri...................	602	615
De Witt, Missouri.........................	613	636
Miami, Missouri	622	640
Waverly, Missouri.........................	645	669
Lexington, Missouri.......................	664	689
Camden, Missouri	678	693
Missouri City, Missouri....................	694	712
Kansas City, Missouri.....................	716	743
Leavenworth, Kansas......................	741	765
Atchison, Kansas..........................	765	789
St. Joseph, Missouri.......................	790	816
White Cloud, Kansas......................	828	851
Brownsville, Nebraska.....................	875	894
Nebraska City, Nebraska...................	907	922
Mouth of Platte river, Nebraska...........	941	961
Omaha, Nebraska..........................	960	982
Blair, Nebraska	986	1,006
Decatur, Nebraska	1,032	1,051
Sioux City, Iowa..........................	1,076	1,099
Mouth of Big Sioux river..................	1,080	1,102
Butler's Landing, South Dakota............	1,125	1,136
Yankton, South Dakota....................	1,157	1.198
Fort Randall, South Dakota................	1,235	....
Chamberlain, South Dakota................	1,323	....
Pierre, South Dakota......................	1,426	1,445

Bismarck, North Dakota	1,618	1,646
Williston, North Dakota	1,825	1,848
Mouth of Yellowstone river	1,855	1,875
Mouth of Poplar river	1,935	1,952
Mouth of Milk river	2,020	2,040
Mouth of Marias river	2,545	2,560
Fort Benton, Montana	2,565	.....
Foot of Great Falls, Montana	2,783	.....
Head of Great Falls, Montana	3,295	3,302
Mouth of Sunrise river, Montana	3,299	3,306
Townsend, Montana	3,793	.....
Mouth of Madison river, Montana	4,045	.....
N. P. R. R. crossing of Jefferson Fork	4,172	.....
N. P. R. R. crossing near Whitehall	4,354	.....
Dillon, Beaver Head Co., Montana	5,077	.....
Barrett, Beaver Head Co., Montana	5,263	.....
Red Rock, Beaver Head Co., Montana	5,440	.....
Lima, Beaver Head Co., Montana	6,265	.....
Upper Red Rock lake	7,000	.....
Culver's Cañon	7,375	.....
Utmost source of Missouri river	8,000	.....

Adjacent mountains	8,500, 9,000, 9,500 and 10,000 feet
Red Rock Pass	7,271 feet
Henry Lake, Idaho	6,443 feet
Raynold's Pass	6,911 feet
Tar-ghé Pass	7,063 feet

The elevation of the surface of the water in the river above Three Forks is practically stationary, which is caused by the absence of copious rainfall, the gradual disappearance of snow in the spring season, and a system of irrigating dams and ditches which extend to and down through the Centennial Valley.

The Dillon sheet of the United States Geological Survey indicates clearly the difference in ditching, as between the valleys of the main stream and the remarkably mountainous region bordering the Big Hole river. At times there may be more water in the Big Hole than in the Beaver Head branch, on account of these ditches in which the water is drawn away to flood the numerous fields.

The last irrigating ditch I noticed on the outward exploration was situated above Upper Red Rock lake, yet within the limits of the Centennial Valley. There were none at the Alaska Basin, and every stream was flowing full and rapid.

OBSERVATIONS FOR TEMPERATURE IN THE ROCKY MOUNTAINS

LOCALITY.	DATE.	HOUR.	OBSERVATION.
Lima, Mont.,	Aug. 2, 1895,	6 a. m.,	46° Clear.
Lima, Mont.,	Aug. 2, 1895,	12 m.,	75° Clear.
Lima, Mont.,	Aug. 2, 1895,	6 p. m ,	70° Clear.
Lima, Mont.,	Aug. 2, 1895,	10 p. m.,	53° Clear.
Blake's Ranch, Mont.,	Aug. 3, 1895,	6 a. m.,	45° Clear.
Alaska Basin, Mont.,	Aug. 3, 1895,	11 a. m.,	90° Clear.
Alaska Basin, Mont.,	Aug. 3, 1895,	Water.,	49° *Stormy.
Red Rock Pass,	Aug. 3, 1895,	3 p. m.,	62° Cloudy.
Red Rock Pass,	Aug. 3, 1895,	3 p. m.,	Water. 43°; Cloudy.
Culver's Cañon,	Aug. 4, 1895,	6 a. m.,	48° Clear.
Culver's Cañon,	Aug. 4, 1895,	9 a. m.,	70° Clear.
Culver's Cañon,	Aug. 4, 1895,	10 a. m.,	66° Clear.
Culver's Ranch,	Aug. 5, 1895,	6 a. m.,	35° Clear.
Culver's Ranch,	Aug. 5, 1895,	12 m.,	72° Clear.
Blake's Ranch,	Aug. 5, 1895,	6 p. m.,	71° Clear.
Lima, Mont.,	Aug. 26, 1895,	Snow Storm.	
Lima, Mont.,	Aug. 26 1895,	9 p. m.,	38°
Lima, Mont.,	Aug. 26, 1895,	Midnight.	35°
Lima, Mont.,	Aug. 27, 1895,	4 a. m.,	34° Cloudy.
Lima, Mont.,	Aug. 27, 1895,	8 a m.,	39° Cloudy.
Lima, Mont.,	Aug. 27, 1895,	12 m.,	49° Cloudy.
Lima, Mont.,	Aug. 27, 1895,	4 p. m.,	53° Cloudy.
Lima, Mont.,	Aug. 27, 1895,	8 p. m.,	43° Cloudy.
Lima, Mont ,	Aug. 28, 1895,	6 a. m.,	44° Clear.
Lima, Mont.,	Aug. 28, 1895,	8 a. m.,	50° Clear.
Centennial Valley, Mont.,	Aug. 28, 1895,	12 m.,	56° Clear.
Culver's Cañon,	Aug. 29, 1895,	9 a. m.,	50° Clear.

* Terrific electric storm below the mountain summits. Temperature of water at Culver's Spring, 41°.
Water in spring at base of Hanson Mountain, 39°.
Water in river, 45°; temperature of the air, 65°.
Width of water in stream, 25 feet.
Depth of water in stream, 12 inches.
Velocity per minute, 200 feet.

This test was made below Horse Picket Hole.

Hail storm at 2 p. m.; sudden changes in temperature.

No observations for temperature above Horse Picket Hole, as all instruments, except barometers, camera, and compass, were discarded, and the party waded up the stream to the site of Bishop's mine, and thence proceeded on the left bank.

The length of the stream from the Hole in the Mountains to Upper Red Rock lake, in its longest course, is about twenty miles.

While the absence of rainfall was marked, sudden changes in temperature were frequent.

The low temperature of the water in practically all the streams, and notably in all the numerous springs, many of which are large enough thence to form considerable stream-beds, is a consequence resulting from perpetual snow on the mountains above, which, melting in the sunlight, copiously saturates the entire range, and numerous creeks constantly flow out from the cañons formed by the long continued erosion.

THE STEAMER ROSEBUD ON THE MISSOURI.

13

§ XV. CONCLUSION.

A sincere regret is expressed that this curtailed address is brought to a close without entering upon a more extended historical resumé of the brilliant and daring military, civil, and personal expeditions conducted toward, to, and beyond the Missouri river, from Coronado's march, in 1540, to the capture of Chief Joseph and his warriors, in 1877, by Gen. Nelson A. Miles. The military accomplishments of Gen. George A. Custer alone would fill one volume; pages upon pages would be necessary to succinctly describe the great struggle for free soil in Kansas, when that state was brought into the Union without the negro slave as a personal chattel; the initiation of a polygamous religion, its rise, progress, the departure of its disciples westward, and its downfall, which attracted the attention of the whole world; while the Sioux outbreak, resulting in the expeditions to and across the Missouri, under command of Generals Sully and Sibley—is material of historic interest which already fills volumes, and the facts are not half recorded. The geographical report of Capt. George M. Wheeler curtails to a title reference historic events west of the Mississippi, and yet his Volume I. fills 780 pages. The names of the states and territories, why and how selected, and the defined meaning, though of modern historic importance, is a matter not yet satisfactorily adjusted for permanent preservation. The states of Missouri, Kansas, and Iowa, named after and in honor of tribes of North American Indians respectively resident at the Missouri Basin, when first heard of, through their Historical Societies are unable to certainly define how and why the tribes mentioned were so designated, and on those questions some light is thrown, but not sufficient to be considered final, unless possibly concerning the name Missouri.

The great strides of the Christian religion, sublime in its influence as against the degrading tendency of a wild and hazardous life upon the Western plains, disintegrating all social and ennobling qualities in its earlier history, now resuscitated with a new life by such men as Rev. T. M. Shanafelt, D. D., and a thousand co-workers in a new field, many

of them explorers[59] in the mountains and among the wildest
tribes of the plains, traveling thousands of miles to and from
remote fields of labor, is material for history of the greatest
moment.

An hundred or more important historic explorations remain unmentioned, but not unremembered, for the Societies
of the respective states, in addition to a permanent National
History, are carefully preserving all the more important facts,
while ethnologic research has baffled the brightest minds in
an endeavor to distinguish the origin of the tribes of men
inhabiting the Basin of the Mississippi when first discovered
by the enlightened races of humanity.

The endeavors of ethnologic students in that direction, up
to this time, while of absorbing interest, utterly fail to determine any correct identification of the original stocks
whence the Indian nations of America came, and the best
evidence comes from the Indians themselves—"Spontaneous
Man, who sprang from the bosom of the earth."

The land of America has existed for a much greater time
than 500,000 centuries, originally producing plant and animal
life, if we are to so determine by paleontological science,
which has sought out the best evidence obtainable. Who
can truthfully assert that all nations of men sprang from one
original parentage, or that the Indians of America did not
proceed from the soil of the Western Hemisphere?

If America has the oldest land, why not the oldest races
of men?

Scholars will do well to avoid the officious and confident
assertions of those whose vaulting ambition forms the basis
for opinions which are promulgated as facts concerning nations of men inhabitating America, whose origin is prehistoric.

No one can yet correctly state facts sufficient to identify
the people who first inhabited the Great Mississippian-Missourian Basin, and those facts are too important to permit
prejudiced opinions to prevail, in preference to facts not yet
obtained, but which, in the course of events, may be obtainable, as results of archaeological research.

To conclude: The Spaniards under Soto discovered the
Mississippi in 1541, and under Coronado the Missouri Basin
in the same year. Radisson and Groseilliers discovered the
Upper Mississippi about 1660, and heard of the Missouri as the
"Forked River."

[59]Dr. Shanafelt, in company with Rev. S. Hall Young, visited the source of
the Mississippi and the Tascodlac Effigies in Northern Minnesota in August,
1894, and the heights of land below Dutch Fred's, on the Mississippi, north of
Itasca lake are called "Shanafelt Bluffs."

Joliet and Marquette discovered the mouth of the Missouri in 1673. The Chevalier de la Verendrye reached the eastern slope of the Rocky Mountains in 1742.

The Mississippi takes its rise in an ultimate reservoir above and beyond Itasca lake, Minn., 2,553 miles from the Gulf of Mexico, by the channel of the river.

The Missouri takes its rise in a volcanic vent or Hole in the Rocky Mountains, twenty miles above and beyond Upper Red Rock lake, Montana, 4,221 miles from the Gulf of Mexico by the channel of the river, assuming that the source is:

> *The ultimate limit of the drainage basin contituting the watershed of the Missouri river, farthest from the Gulf of Mexico by the main channel of the river.*

That ultimate limit is at the summit of the Rocky Mountains, in Madison county, State of Montana, where the waters are gathered into a miniature stream-bed, from melting snows, and springs; thence flow down through Culver's Cañon to the Alaska Basin, where the stream is divided into four separate channels, and thence, augmented by the flowage from numerous smaller creeks, as one channel it passes out from the Alaska Basin into the Centennial Valley, and thence into the Upper Red Rock lake and to the main river channel below, in its regular course to the Mississippi and to the sea.

JAMES BLAIR'S HERD OF ELK.
Upper Red Rock Lake, Montana.

PART SECOND.

A SCAFFOLD BURIAL OF THE SIOUX.

Reproduced by permission of Dr. E. S. Hart. From a photograph by Mr. D. F. Barry.

PART SECOND.

§ XVI. CONCISE NARRATION OF THE RESULTS
OF EXPLORATIONS AND SURVEYS OF 1896, RE-
LATING PARTICULARLY TO GEOGRAPHIC, HY-
DROGRAPHIC AND ARCHÆOLOGIC EXAMINATIONS
IN THE MISSOURI BASIN.

UTMOST WATERS OF THE MISSOURI.

MR. JAMES BLAIR,
Assistant on the 1896 Surveys.
Source of the Missouri.

As soon as the limited first edition of this volume was completed and published, in May, 1896, all needed preparations
were perfected for a more thorough exploration of the remote
streams constituting the utmost waters of the Missouri river.

The principal object of a more extended geographical
reconnoissance of the mountainous region surrounding the
Missourian *caldera,* whence flow those utmost waters, was to
procure sufficient data from which to prepare a detailed chart
of the region explored.

The accompanying colored chart has been very carefully drawn from voluminous field notes, often reduced under very trying if not dangerous circumstances, on account of the great depth of snow at and below the crest of the Rocky Mountains, above the Alaska Basin, during the summer months of 1896.

The material and supplies brought into use in this work was every available necessity for a protracted sojourn in the rugged and precipitous region surveyed, from a train of pack horses to all needed instruments, camera, camping outfit and the employment of assistants schooled in the ways and means of successful use, among snow-capped peaks, deep cañons and sharp declivities, where tremendous snowslides are of common occurrence, and the displacement of considerable land areas is not unusual.

The surveys for 1896 were initiated on the thirty-first day of May. The preliminary preparations were completed at St. Paul, Minn., and at Helena, Bozeman, Butte, and Monida, Mont.

The first procedure in the field was at the crest of the main range of the Rocky Mountains, near Monida, where, from a known elevation, on June 2d, by barometric hypsometry, some desirable corrections in the sea levels were initiated, and thence observed to the principal field of operations. These levels (as nearly correct as barometric pressure constitutes them) are noted on the chart, and need not now be unnecessarily referred to in detail. I do not claim for these levels that absolute accuracy usually demonstrated by actual lines of level reduced from field notes which are the result of observations by latitude and departure. They are, however, quite sufficiently correct for all ordinary purposes.

The results show that the Red Rock lakes do not stand at an elevation of 7,000 feet above the sea, but rather at about the same position occupied by the Centennial Valley, changeable by a high and low water surface elevation. Those lakes are simply the broadening of the main and subsidiary streams filling the deepest depressions in the hacienda and alluvial deposits made observable by the disappearance of the glacial lake which formerly inundated the entire valley.

On the seventh day of June, at which time the hills and mountains were quite covered with a mantle of snow, the observations at the utmost waters of the Missouri were commenced. Every stream was a rushing torrent, consequent upon the gradual melting of the winter's accumulation of ice and snow, and the effects of erosion, noticeable on every mountain side and in every cañon, charged the waters with mud and debris. From the utmost perimetric boundary, sécancy prevails, and the eroding waters annually reduce in size the mountains and lakes. Nature's order is to cut and fill, and it is wonderful to contemplate the probable results of the elapse of time and the uninterrupted continuance of active erosion.

My first examination was from the Division Summits, across Picnic Mountain to the heights to the northward. These uplifts constitute a natural division between the Alaska Basin and the Centennial Valley, through which the main stream has formed its channel around the base of Picnic Mountain. The detritus has accumulated on the surface of the Alaska Basin to such an extent that the inclination is toward the utmost northwestern limit of the Basin, caused by sécancy at Culver's Cañon, Hanson Mountain and Upham Peak. The precipitation of the currents abruptly to the base of Picnic Mountain has constantly charged that locality with water sufficiently to cause a perennial and unique flowage through Picnic Springs and creek, on the opposite side of the mountain, which never freezes, standing at a normal temperature of forty degrees.

At this time (June 8th) a casual examination of the Elk lake locality was projected, where a magnificent Sabbath day was spent at this beautiful lake and at Hackett Cañon, and the home of James Blair at Elk Springs, where the party dined, with antelope and grayling as abundant delicacies.

MR. HENRY HACKETT,
Assistant, 1896 Surveys.

To the able hands of Mr. Henry Hackett was committed the task of charting the Elk lake and Hackett Cañon localities, and that portion of the colored map is drawn from Mr. Hackett's field notes. Also, as soon as the high waters had subsided, Mr. Hackett constructed a boat, and charted the locality from Upper Red Rock and Swan lakes, down the main river to the outlet of Lower Red Rock lake, which places those localities upon the chart in a somewhat different aspect, hydrographically, than has heretofore been definitely known.

The examination of Shambow Pass by Mr. Hackett, and
his report thereof, reveal a curious state of facts, showing a
considerable dip southward in the crest of the main range,
but the lines within which the final chart is curtailed does
not permit the full facts to be shown concerning that locality,
nor of the remarkably rugged and extensive Humphrey Mountain, named after the man who lost his life, in 1895, at some
unascertained place within its extensive boundaries. Mr.
Humphrey was traced to the base of the mountain by his trail
in the snow, which was soon lost, and he was never heard of
again. It is presumed he died in a beartrap or was fatally
caught in a snowslide, and I have felt justified in extending
the name of the unfortunate man to the place where he per-
ished.

On Monday, June 8th, mounted, I ascended the Antelope
Creek Cañon, thence to the summit of Coral Mountain, and
thence to the base of Preacher Peaks, passed down Coral
creek, up Battle creek the entire length of Marble Mountain,
returning to the mouth of Antelope creek, and thence explored
the Division Summits to Horse Camp creek and return. The
features of the day were the immense snow drifts on the sides
of the mountains and a vicious attack by a large porcupine.
I avoided the snow drifts; also, the porcupine. Tuesday
morning a north and south line from Burnside Mountain to
Elk Mountain was charted. On Wednesday, in company with
Mr. James Blair, mounted on a pair of his best saddle horses,
we explored Teepee creek, the Sand Hills, and passed on to
the outlet of Lower Red Rock lake, by way of Murphy and
Metzel creeks. Spending the night at the Metzel ranch, with
Herman J. Fisher in charge, we returned the next day by way
of the plains bordering the north side of the Red Rock lakes
and river, passing near the point where Teepee creek spreads
and sinks on the plain, observing quantities of old buffalo
trails, wallows, and bleaching bones. Cavities in the buffalo
skulls, through which the brain is extracted, indicate that
Indians participated in what was presumably the last buffalo
hunt in the Centennial Valley. White swan and the curlew,
preparing to nest, were quite numerous in the neighborhood
of Swan lake. We rode all day, leisurely, on the flat plain, in
full view of Peale Mountain and Upham Peak, but I could not
approach the river, either mounted or on foot on account of
the overflowed condition of the meadows bordering the stream.
Occasionally a depression in the surface filled with water indicated the uncertain existence of small ponds, but as the
time of high water passes they dry up and disappear. These
small ponds are quite numerous in the month of June, but not
sufficiently permanent to note on the chart.

On Friday, in company with Frederick I. Hanson, I traversed the Alaska Basin to Red Rock Pass, and thence across the state line into Idaho, on the mail route road to Henry lake. The division of the waters at Red Rock Pass is on a gradually sloping surface, the waters running east passing to Snake river, and those running west finally reaching the Gulf of Mexico through the channels of the Missouri and Mississippi. We proceeded forward to

VIEW AT RED ROCK PASS.
Looking East Across the State Line Between Montana and Idaho.

Henry lake, not ignorant of the fact that we had crossed the main range without ascending or descending more than a fair sized hillock, and so gradual and easy is the sloping ground that we experienced no inconvenience during the entire day. At Henry lake I was invited to the game-preserve of Mr. Richard W. Rock for the night. This remarkable man and his estimable wife are surrounded at their cabin home by elk, buffalo, moose, bear, and other wild animals, captured by Mr. Rock and hauled in from the surrounding mountains with sledge-dogs, on toboggans fitted up for that purpose.

No man living can boast, truthfully, of more rugged scenes, exciting incidents, or real hairbreadth escapes in the Rocky Mountains than can Mr. Rock, and yet modesty has not given place to an epitome of his wild adventures, requested for this record, since he lives near the head waters of the Missouri; and I take the liberty of preserving his portrait, knowing that his wild and adventuresome life is justly entitled to a place in any volume describing that locality.

On our return the next day, we camped at the base of the serrated range surrounding the Bradley Crater, and I ascended Duck creek, which flows into Henry lake, far up toward the immense summits forming the northern walls of the extinct volcano described in Professor Bradley's report of the United States Geological Survey, quoted in the text.[60]

---

[60]See ante, p. 90.

For the purpose of a more convenient reference to this important geographical locality, the serrated peaks mentioned have been designated "The Coues Peaks," in honor of the historian and scientist who so ably edited his "Lewis and Clark," 1893, the most important work ever written concerning the Missouri river. The Coues Peaks are situated entirely in Idaho, and for that reason do not appear on the chart, which indicates only the Missourian *caldera*, situated entirely in Montana. These peaks form the crest of an impassable mountain north from Crater Peak and eastwardly from Shangle Peak, the whole, with Sawtell Peak, forming a circuitous serrated range several miles in circumference around the Bradley Crater. This remarkable crater cannot be seen except from a position at or near one of the peaks surrounding it.

Sunday, June 14th. After the arduous labors of the week, this was in fact a day of rest, but not of inaction. A party of residents made a tour of the Alaska Basin, and I rode with them. While they were in pursuit of pleasure and recreation, I ascended to the crest of Monida Peak, from which I looked down upon Henry lake and both the Red Rock lakes and all the intervening and grand topographic formations of nature. It was on this Sabbath day that I noticed the discharge of the water from the eastern slope of Monida Peak into the Duck creek tributary of Henry lake, which by law[61] places a part of that mountain in Idaho.

After lunching on mountain trout and grayling at the mouth of Culver's Cañon, the party returned to Picnic Springs by way of the Division Summits. The two following days were devoted to correspondence, field notes, and preparations for a tour of the snow-capped peaks constituting the crest of the main range along the state boundary line between Montana and Idaho, immediately east of Preacher Peaks.

The pack animals and saddle horses used were tendered by my faithful assistant, Mr. James Blair, and as gratefully accepted as they were cheerfully tendered.

With all needed instruments, camping material and provisions, and with Mr. Blair as an interested companion and assistant (very valuably so, as it afterward came to pass), we set out on Wednesday, June 17th, having in view, first, the ascent of Burnside Mountain. On the approach of a sudden

---

[61]The congress of the United States established the state boundary between Montana and Idaho in part along the crest of the Rocky Mountains as follows:

"Commencing at a point formed by the intersection of the twenty-seventh degree of longitude west from Washington with the forty-fifth degree of north latitude; thence due west, etc., * * * thence due west along said forty-fourth degree and thirty minutes of north latitude to a point formed by its intersection with the crest of the Rocky Mountains; thence following the crest of the Rocky Mountains northward till its intersection with the Bitter Root Mountains," etc.— United States Statutes at Large, 1863-65, pp. 85-86.

electric storm we went into a temporary camp under the spreading branches of the pine timber on Antelope creek, near its head. Little time was lost, however, as these mountain storms often pass over as suddenly as they gather, and an hour later we were "tacking" up the western slope of Burnside Mountain, near, sometimes upon, the old Bannock trail, until, approaching the summit, an impassable snow-bank impeded the way. Here we were compelled to follow an old sheep trail up over crumbling and sharp-edged rocks, where it sometimes seemed probable that the animals might fall backward down the mountain side.

All went well, however, and the party soon reached the summit at a tableland that resembled a small prairie, more than half covered by extensive snow-banks.

Upon reaching an impassable drift of

OUR TRAIL PASSED OVER THIS DETRITAL MASS ON THE SLOPE OF BURNSIDE MOUNTAIN.

snow at the head of Horse Camp creek, we picketed our horses and effected an encampment for the night. The summit of Burnside Mountain is a rolling tableland, devoid of any considerable quantity of timber, and, in area, covers about thirty acres.

Here were seen evidences of the former existence of buffalo, and the old Indian trail indicated the ancient activities of the chase, long since abandoned here by these children of nature.

The rarified atmosphere and a sudden change of climate had superinduced a loss of appetite, yet I felt perfectly well, and determined to proceed the next morning on foot, leaving the camp and picketed horses, to which we were to return for another night's rest.

Our course lay over immense piles of snow, to a point on the state boundary line to the southward, where we commenced the erection of stone monuments. One view in the illustrations indicates the appearance of tree-tops protruding through the snow, over which we passed in the morning with-

out difficulty, the surface having frozen solid the previous
night. The objective point sought was the summit of Blair
Mountain in the distance, to the eastward. Stone monuments
were erected at some of the more important localities, to mark
our progress along the crest of the mountains. The ice in
Blair lake below us, as we passed, remained apparently firm
and unaffected by the heat of a summer sun. Finding the
difficulties greater than had been anticipated, we descended
from the crest, in search of a shorter route to the summit of
Blair Mountain, passing a log cabin erected by Messrs. Bishop,
Bishop & Wright, owners of the gold lode near Lillian lake.
The depth of the snow at their cabin had caused them to
cut the timber twelve and fifteen feet above the ground.
After ascending Blair Mountain about two thousand feet, I
wisely decided to permit Mr. Blair to go forward alone, for
my rubber boots were gradually but surely disappearing, and
my appetite had already successfully disappeared. While exploring Bishop's Pass and erecting a stone monument there,
on the state boundary, I saw Mr. Blair at the summit of his
mountain, a mere black speck in the elevated distance, probably the first man to ascend it, and for that reason I decided
to name it in his honor. The principal portion cf that great
mountain stands in Idaho.

On my winding course up a small creek heading near Bishop's Pass, I passed the tremendous indications of a recent and
extensive snowslide. The snow filled the cañon in solid
blocks, almost as hard as ice, and standing timber had been
crushed down and the logs and tree tops thrown far up on
the side of the mountain next opposite. I estimated that the
slide, in its entirety, was about one mile in length and about
two hundred feet wide, and that the descent was at an angle
of about fifty degrees.

After monuments had been erected at the summit of Blair
Mountain and at Bishop's Pass, we both, though separated,
stood in full view of the peculiarities of the Missourian *caldera.*

By a previous understanding, the state line westward to
camp was to be the returning route of travel.

On ascending the peak southwardly from the Lillian lake
flats, I undertook to descend into Idaho, on account of overhanging snow drifts, and found myself not only unable to proceed downward, but likewise unable to retrace my steps upward; so, clinging to the overhanging rocks, I finally reached
a few shrubs where the flora held the detritus from sliding,
and, grasping the roots and stems, reached the base in safety,
minus the needed portion of my footwear, around which I tied

my handkerchief, a strap and the fastenings of my lunch box. The lunch had long since been thrown away in the absence of any inclination to dine, either on boiled eggs, bacon, or bread.

At the crest, near Blair lake, the party was again united, and I kindly remember my companion when I contemplate that it was necessary for me to be supported by his strong arm in order that I might be able to reach the camp before the shades of nightfall overtook us in the midst of snow-capped peaks in the Rocky Mountains.

A small flask of wine, some determination and James Blair made the day's work for me a most successful one. We left no portion of the state boundary unexplored between the Low Divide and the summit of Blair Mountain. Innumerable snow banks were traversed, which, yielding under the influences of a disintegrating nature, thence gave forth their melting substance, half to the Atlantic and half to the Pacific, through the delta of the Mississippi and the mouth of the Columbia.

What joy to reach that camp, and what comfort to gather the fagots for hot tea and a cold night!

On the 19th of June, by no means early in the morning, we passed down, out of and away from that snow-capped region for rest and a renewal of our energies.

All needed preparations having been completed, on Monday, the twenty-second day of June, with the same horses and camping outfit, Mr. Blair and myself started for Culver's Cañon, to continue our explorations to the utmost limit of the Missouri Basin.

Our way was along the Division Summits to Horse Camp creek; thence across Hanson Mountain to Culver's Cañon. On my trail (of 1895) we became involved in deep snows and fallen timber, in a swamp south of Hanson Mountain. Extricating our horses finally, we went into an encampment near the main stream, opposite Upham Peak. Here we met disappointment, in not being able to go forward with horses, on account of the deep snows. The weather had been hot in the valley, above eighty degrees, and it was presumed that the snows had yielded sufficiently to permit of passage with our horses; but such was not the case. The snows were deep, and the stream swollen to the maximum.

Early on the 23d, leaving our camp and picketed horses, we pressed forward on foot up the cañon by way of Little Wisdom and Bishop's mine to the Missourian *caldera*, crossing and recrossing the stream on bridges of concave ice, under which the rushing waters plunged with a roar. The effects of land and snow slides were noticed in numerous places, and, becoming careless by practice, I know we often passed over dangerous places without hesitancy, endeavoring to make progress before the heat of the sun softened the frozen snow.

In the small view presented, Mr. Blair stands over the creek, on an ice-bridge, and the course of the stream can be noticed by the depression to the left of the pine trees.

We ascended the escarpments of the cañon and then the inner flank or amphitheatrical radiation of the *caldera* to the state boundary at the crest of the southern wall of Bradley's Crater, climbing, tacking and ascending through deep snows and over detrital masses, until the elevation was so great that every physical feature of the locality could be plainly seen and easily understood. Here at the crest we erected another stone monument, and deposited a copper plate with suitable inscription at the edge of a snow-bank that had drifted up out from the *caldera* and into the crater, until the depth of the snow in that particular place was about nine hundred feet down the sharp and dangerous declivity formed by the inner portion of the crater wall. Mr. Blair walked out on a projecting ledge of trachyte, and complacently viewed the deeply interesting scenes at the Bradley Crater. I attempted to do so, with only partial success, on account of an empty stomach and a dizzy head. My inclination was to fall backwards, constantly, which had been increased by a continued loss of appetite.

We here stood in full view of Sawtell Peak and the Coues Peaks, which form opposite serrated portions of the crater walls, but the snow was too deep and the conditions too unfavorable to undertake any considerable survey to ascertain the exact dimensions of the Bradley Crater.

In passing down and away from these never-to-be-forgotten volcanic scenes, we traversed the uplift resembling a great land-slide, situated near the center of the Missourian *caldera*, witnessing on every hand the topographic features displayed on the chart, and taking extensive notes for future use.

JAMES BLAIR
In the Snow, Missourian Caldera,
June 23, 1896.

From every snowbank along the course of our exploration —and there were thousands of them—a small streamlet thence proceeded downward, under the rays of a summer sun, to the lowest depressions of Culver's Cañon, where, uniting, the consequences incident to the birth of a plunging mountain stream were witnessed on every hand. Every declivity and each crevice of the massive mountains gave forth a contribution to the waters of the swollen stream, over which we effected our crossings with considerable difficulty and some danger. There were numerous places where, had the snowy covering broken, precipitation into the raging torrent beneath would have been instant death. The permeability of the anticlinal and synclinal rocks and porous landslides demonstrate the existing causes why numerous springs and streamlets abound, maintaining the central river with a constant and perennial flowage. The mountains are literally soaked with melting snows and an occasional rainstorm, and from every base the water constantly seeks its level. I noticed four small lake beds along the course of the stream in Culver's Cañon, situated at the *caldera*, Lillian lake flats, Horse Picket Hole, and above Hanson Mountain, which, by sécant action, has been separated apart from Upham Peak, the detrital mass below causing four channels to be formed from the main river, at the mouth of the cañon. It is not impossible that formerly these lakes may have covered the greater portion of the cañon, frozen in winter and overflowing in summer. The escarpments and declivities indicate the final result.

We then returned to camp by way of Horse Picket Hole and Blair lake.

On the 24th camp was removed across Hanson Mountain to Picnic Springs, where we were joined by Mr. W. N. Culver.

On the 25th, with all necessary paraphernalia, and a train of pack and saddle horses, Messrs. Brower, Blair, and Culver, after an adventuresome ride over Hanson Mountain, numerous snowbanks and the swollen river, past landslides and across summits, effected an encampment near Little Wisdom, from which, on the 26th, we proceeded on foot up the main stream and to the *caldera*, examining the localities traversed, in detail. Finally it was determined to explore the serrated peaks at the western limit of the Bradley Crater.

Messrs. Blair and Culver made the ascent to Brower Peak, erecting a stone monument there; thence they traversed the crater wall to an impassable portion of Crater Peak; thence returning, they traversed Shangle Peak to Lode Peak, where Mr. Blair discovered a well-defined gold-bearing quartz lode;

14

thence they traversed some remarkable benches, filled with snow, along the south side of Upham Peak, and thence down the mountain to camp. Mr. Brower traversed the north slope of Crater Peak, thence to Bishop's mine, thence to Lillian lake, thence to Little Wisdom and to camp.

On the 27th of June the entire party ascended to Lode Peak and traced the quartz lode, collecting samples for an assay.

We found an immense wall of gold-bearing quartz, projecting upward, from the south side of Lode Peak, extending north and south as far as we traversed the lode. Explorations were continued in the Centennial Valley and elsewhere until, r e t u r n i n g, Messrs. Blair, Brower, and Culver effected an encampment, with a pack train, at Lode Peak, during the fourth week in July, 1896.

MESSRS. BLAIR AND CULVER
At the Central Wall of the Quartz Lode, at Lode Peak.

At this time the electric storms had commenced, and the first night after our arrival we were in the central force of a tremendous thunder storm, which turned to snow, spreading a white mantle over the peaks. In the morning we found our camp was enveloped in clouds. The elevation was 9,600 feet above the sea.

Later in the season all necessary proceedings were initiated preliminary to a location of the Crater Mine.

On the 24th of July a party of tourists ascended Brower Peak. Mrs. Clara Shangle of Flint, Iowa, one of the party, describes their tour as follows:

Our party left the camp at Picnic Springs, with saddle and pack horses, to accomplish the ascent of Brower Mountain. Our route lay through Alaska Basin, Culver's Cañon, and thence to Horse Picket Hole, where we camped for the night.

The following morning we were early in the saddle; our way was over a steep rocky ridge, thence across a narrow valley through which ran the main branch of the Missouri, here a mere rivulet, lashing itself into foam as it bounded along its rocky bed. Crossing the stream we entered a pine forest beyond which we could see the sharp and well-defined pinnacles of the mountain, gleaming brightly in the morning air. For a mile or more we journeyed over uneven ground, interspersed with marshy basins and banks of snow, when we reached the dividing line between Idaho and Montana. Here we partook of refreshments; and our route being no longer practicable for horses, we tethered our animals and proceeded on foot toward the top of the highest peak near the head of the Missouri. It was a weary journey, but after several hours' toil over jagged rocks our object was accomplished, and at our feet lay what was once the crater of a volcano.

Looking about us we could see Henry lake, the Red Rock lakes and the Missourian *caldera* or Hole-in-the-Mountains. As evidence of our visit we erected a monument of loose stones, wrote the names of our party on paper, which we wrapped in the remains of a worn-out rubber shoe, and placed the package in the pile we had erected, retracing our steps to the tethered animals and thence down, out and away from a grandly picturesque mountain region surrounding the source of the Missouri, feeling amply repaid for efforts expended and time well spent.

CLARA SHANGLE.

Mrs. Shangle, as the second lady tourist to visit the source of the Missouri, earns a name upon the pages of its history, and Shangle Peak has been named in her honor.

Thus closes the Missourian explorations of 1896, made necessary for an intelligent display upon the chart of the physical features surrounding those utmost waters.

DESCENDING BURNSIDE MOUNTAIN.

§ XVII. GEOGRAPHIC NAMES.

The following names have been selected, from time to time, and a brief explanation concerning them is appended:

Montana....................Mountainous country.
Tozabe-Shockup............The country of the mountains.
Centennial Valley.........First settled in the Centennial year.
Alaska Basin..............Name probably suggested by deep snows.
Red Rock Lakes............After a red butte in Beaver Head county, Montana, which constitutes a prominent landmark.
Red Rock River............Same as the lakes.
Red Rock Pass.............Same as the river.
Metzel Creek..............After W. O. Metzel.
Murphy Creek..............After a settler.
Tepee Creek...............Suggested by Bannock Indians.
Hackett Cañon.............In honor of Henry Hackett.
Hackett Mountain..........Same as Cañon.
Skeleton Creek............After a fatal tragedy at that point, when several persons were shot as horse thieves.
Horse Thief Butte.........Same as Skeleton Creek.
Monida Peak...............*Mont*ana and *Ida*ho.
Pass Peak.................At Red Rock Pass.
Humphrey Mountain.........After George Humphrey, who met death in its environs.
Shambow Pass..............After a prominent citizen.
Shambow Creek.............Same as Shambow Pass.
Odell Creek...............After an early settler.
Peale Mountain............In honor of Dr. A. C. Peale.
Preacher Peaks............From an unknown missionary who first ascended them, from necessity, having reached a point from which he could not descend the precipitous range.
Low Divide................A dip in the main range.
Corral Creek..............After a stock corral located there.
Corral Mountain...........Same as Corral Creek.
Marble Mountain...........After an old resident.
Burnside Mountain.........After Mr. and Mrs. S. B. Burnside, of Monida, Montana.
Division Summits..........A natural division between the Alaska Basin and the Centennial Valley.
Hanson Mountain...........After Frederick I. Hanson.
Culver's Cañon............After Wm. N. Culver.
Blair Lake................After James Blair.
Blair Creek...............Same as Blair Lake.
Blair Mountain............Same as Blair Creek.
Horse Camp Creek..........After a corral for horses.
Upham Peak................After Prof. Warren Upham.
Horse Picket Hole.........Here we picketed our pack horse in 1895 and proceeded up the bed of the stream.
Little Wisdom.............Named by the first lady tourist.
Lillian Lake..............After Mrs. Lillian E. Culver.

Bishop's Pass.............After J. B. and T. F. Bishop, who discovered gold in Culver's Cañon Sept. 9, 1895.
The Missourian *Caldera*.....After the amphitheatrical formation at the utmost source of the Missouri River.
Bradley's Crater...........After Prof. Frank H. Bradley.
The Coues Peaks..........After the historian of the Lewis and Clark expedition.
Crater Peak..............A great crater wall.
Brower Peak..............In honor of the writer, by Messrs. Blair and Culver, my companions.
Lode Peak... ....After a quartz lode.
Shangle Peak.............After a lady tourist.
Sawtell Peak.............Sometimes called Jefferson Peak; named after an early settler.

HYDROGRAPHIC CONDITIONS.

All the waters flowing in the numerous streams above Upper Red Rock lake are drawn from the effects of secular precipitation. Artesian pressure exists only where the permeability of the rock structure forms a conductor between melting snows at the summits and living springs at the base. The mountains are extremely rugged, elevated and formidable. Snow falls usually eleven months of the twelve, and from December until April prevailing winds pile up tremendous snowdrifts on every crest and in numerous cañons. Overhanging drifts menace the life of every living thing that passes beneath them. The effect of snowslides creasing the declivities and demolishing the standing timber is everywhere noticeable. Principally on the northern slope of the mountains, where the snows are perpetual, in many instances, caused by immunity from the effects of the sun's rays, the timber has become dense, fed by the gradual melting of the snows above. Two dense and considerable forests are thus situated, at Humphrey and Burnside mountains. In most instances the timber is sparse and scattered, the growth being uncertain for want of moisture and the sustaining influences of proper climatic conditions. The valleys are covered with grama grasses and artemisia, and are devoid of timber. Rain storms are unusual, and occur infrequently during the latter part of July and a portion of August, often turning to snow at the higher elevations. An area is usually covered with hailstones, precipitated by the passing storms. Two of these hail storms were encountered, one in July, 1895, and the other a year later.

Such climatic conditions in a mountainous region keep the immense ranges saturated with the moisture of melting snows and rainfall, which, sinking deep down into every mountain, causes the existence and perpetual continuance of numerous springs, and from every spring passes a surface flowage. from which the principal streams are sustained in a perennial existence.

Prof. James Reid of Bozeman, Mont., has called attention to hydrographic conditions existing in the Big Hole Basin. That question has received such attention as I could extend without an actual survey of that locality. The mountains there are heavily timbered in many places, and the deep snows, occurring annually, are held by the shaded localities, almost as a reservoir supply to the river below.

My assistant. Mr. Henry Hackett, describes that locality as follows:

THE BIG HOLE BASIN.

Mr. Brower requested me to state why the Big Hole river carried such a volume of water at times. Having traversed that locality extensively, especially at the head tributaries, I ascertained facts which explain that question.

The streams of that locality take their courses out from one of the most elevated and rugged mountain ranges in the State of Montana, and all of the foot-hills on the west side of the valley are covered with a dense growth of fir and pine timber which extends far up into the mountains where the snowfall is excessive, and nearly every creek heads far back in some deep cañon or gorge. The east side of the valley is somewhat different. The streams there rise earlier in the season and commence to go down before the streams on the west side commence to rise. The main stream, by this natural cause, has a considerable stage of water before the melting snows from the timbered region on the west side commence to pour in a vast volume of water through every tributary creek.

I crossed the Grasshopper Divide on the third day of May, 1894. Bull creek was then very high and from fifty to one hundred yards wide. and Warm Spring creek was practically impassable, and North Bloody Dick, which heads in three different forks in a heavily timbered range at the south extremity of the valley, was a raging torrent, both wide and swift. By August these streams were all low and jumpable.

The Mulkey drains a large timbered and mountainous region at the southwest extremity of the basin. This is the main Big Hole proper. On the west side there are numerous tributaries, the most important being Miner creek, eighteen miles long; Battle Lake creek, fifteen miles long; Little Swamp creek, sixteen miles long; Big Lake creek, twenty miles long; Big Swamp creek, twenty-one miles long; and the North Fork, forty miles long, with numerous tributaries. All these numerous streams head in rough timbered cañons, and pour a vast volume of water into the channel of the Big Hole. No such conditions exist on the Red Rock branch of the Missouri. The valley is very narrow and long, and the river crooked, the channel being over one hundred miles long down through the Centennial Valley alone.

HENRY HACKETT.

The waters of the Red Rock and Beaver Head are extensively used for purposes of irrigation, but to what extent, in cubic gallons, has not been ascertained.

These observations close my geographic surveys and examinations at the utmost Basin of the Missouri. Much remains unfinished, and undoubtedly errors of various kinds exist, but the intention to gain a better knowledge of the locality has been a constant incentive to careful and painstaking observation with no pecuniary aid from any society or person.

For that invaluable aid extended to me by all the individuals mentioned, I feel profoundly grateful, and I know of no case where I have intentionally detracted from the accomplishments of others.

It remains an undisputed fact that this survey effected an original discovery of the Missourian *caldera*, Aug. 29, 1895, at which time a photograph of the locality was secured. The following month, the 9th of September, 1895, Messrs. Bishop, Bishop, and Wright discovered gold in the cañon, and on the 26th of the same month Mrs. Culver and Mr. Allen visited the *caldera*.

During 1896 archæological researches and examinations have been carried forward, incidentally, and the very interesting results are given in the following pages.

While Mr. Blair and myself were prosecuting our investigations in Culver Cañon, we discovered fossils of various kinds, and trilobites were taken from the center of fractured rocks.

An illustration is reproduced from an original sedimentary deposit, selected from numerous specimens, near the crest of Brower Peak, by Messrs. Blair and Culver. For a more complete description of the nature and age of these paleontologic deposits, the reader is referred to Professor Farrington's paper in the appendix.

It is proper to determine that a correct geographic description should be formulated as follows:

"That the longest headwater branch of the Missouri river takes its rise in the Missourian *caldera*, at the upper extremity of Culver's Cañon, Montana, 4,221 miles from the Gulf of Mexico and 8,000 feet above the sea."

Respectfully submitted.

J. V. BROWER.

§ XVIII. ARCHÆOLOGICAL ADDENDUM.

NARRATIVE DESCRIPTION OF EXAMINATIONS AND
EXPLORATIONS IN THE FIELD OF ARCHÆ-
OLOGY, DURING THE YEAR. CHRON-
OLOGIC ORDER OF DISCOVERY
OBSERVED.

FIRST: AT THE HEADWATERS OF THE MISSOURI.
SECOND: FORT FLAT MOUTH.
THIRD: QUIVIRA; THE ELLIOTT INDIAN VILLAGE
SITE.

BY J. V. BROWER.

FIRST: AT THE HEADWATERS OF THE MISSOURI.

During the continuance of the geographic explorations described in the foregoing sections of this work, particular attention was directed toward archæologic questions.

At the headwaters of the Missouri the examinations and
explorations were continued in 1896, incidentally with the
exploration for hydrographic and topographic data.

The following named citizens are entitled to this recognition for their valuable assistance:

Mr. James Blair, at Upper Red Rock Lake, Montana.

Mrs. Mary J. Blake, at Magdalen, Montana.

Mr. Earle B. Wittich, at Livingston, Montana.

Mr. August Gottschalck, at Bozeman, Montana.

The mountainous region surrounding the utmost waters of
the Missouri was the home and hunting ground of prehistoric
man. Concerning his identity and the date of his appearance
at that locality, practically nothing is certainly known. His
village sites were located at Elk Springs, Picnic Springs,
Blake's Springs, and at other points in the Centennial Valley
and at Henry Lake, Idaho; and from thence east, west, north
and south indications are extant that he penetrated to and

occupied numerous localities in Montana and Idaho, subsisting principally upon game and fish, then, probably, very abundant. The implements used were of chipped stone, principally of obsidian, a fair representation of which will be found in the illustrations. Detrital masses, mould and debris now cover the village sites to an extent sufficient to make it difficult to discover and secure the chipped implements, all of which are below the present natural surface on the plain, which is covered with a considerable growth of artemisia. The spade or the plow is quite necessary in a discovery of the implements, although some of the finest illustrated were thrown up by the excavations of badgers. Nothing remains to indicate the character of the habitations occupied, leading to the supposition that skin covered lodges were probably in common use. Only slight indications of pottery fragments were found. Mr. James Blair excavated several pieces at Elk Springs, which do not show any of the well-known ornamental fabric or other markings characteristic of the pottery found on the lower course of the Missouri. In fact, the limited number of specimens found are unornamented, and are made of pounded stone, sand, and pulverized shell. The great Yellowstone obsidian quarry was drawn upon for a supply of material for chipped implements, and the fractured blocks and spalls are scattered about the surrounding country in profusion, indicating that the locality has no doubt been the home of man for many centuries. A stone knife and broken obsidian lance-head were found at the crest of the main range near Shangle Peak. At Henry lake Mr. Richard W. Rock excavated a grooved stone hammer while digging a cellar. The hammer was found about four feet below the surface. No burial mounds were noticed at the Centennial Valley or at Alaska Basin. Wolves and coyotes are numerous, and the habits of the Bannock Indians in historic times respecting the burial of the dead show that the remains were usually deposited in stone cairns far up in the mountains, to prevent despoilation.

It is probable that the ancestry of one or more of the North American tribes were the people who occupied the locality in early times.

The material at hand for an intelligent consideration of this question is quite sufficient; but I do not propose to assert that I know, exactly, all the particulars, antecedent and subsequent to this early prehistoric occupancy. No one can know beyond a study of that which is left, and the forms of the knives, scrapers, lance-heads, and arrow-points appear to be little different from the same class of articles found in the

Basin of the Mississippi, except that the predominating character of the material used was obsidian.

In many places springs of pure water exist. The Picnic Springs are ideal ones, flowing from the rocks at the base of the mountains, just above which circles a beautiful grove of pine timber. At the upper limit of the timber an immense snow-drift accumulates during the winter months, which saturates the side of the mountain with moisture during a greater portion of the summer season. This climatic action causes the timber to thrive, but at a point where the saturation ceases, an artemisia plain begins. Through this plain Picnic Springs sends forth a creek tewnty feet wide and a foot in depth. The water stands at 40° without appreciable change during the whole year, and therefore never freezes. At the edge of the timber around the springs and along the terrace on both sides of the creek, prehistoric man located his village. The site was well selected, and the accommodations afforded by timber, water, and a terrace formation, ample. The plain was a vast pasture for buffalo; elk and antelope grazed on every hillside; bands of wild sheep herded on every crest, and all the streams were stocked with fish. Here man lived and thrived in savage comfort. Later, he fought for possession and supremacy, for his implements of war, made of stone, seem unmistakable in characteristic forms. Periods and epochs have passed; the occupancy has changed. All that is left, of absorbing interest, fails to certainly disclose the identity of the earliest man.

The descriptive outline of the Picnic Village site can be applied to the other locations, for they are all quite similarly situated.

§ XIX. Second: FORT FLAT MOUTH.

Esh-ke-bug-e-coshe (Flat Mouth), an Ojibway Indian, born about 1772, became a famed chief of the Pillagers, at the headwater basin of the Mississippi. Hon. W. W. Warren, the historian of the Ojibway people, was a mixed-blood. During the last years of Flat Mouth's life, the two Indians became fast friends. From Flat Mouth's knowledge of the affairs of his people, Mr. Warren drew largely, through numerous visits and personal interviews, for the written history of the Ojibway people, which has come down to the present generation through Vol. V., Collections of the Minnesota Historical Society.

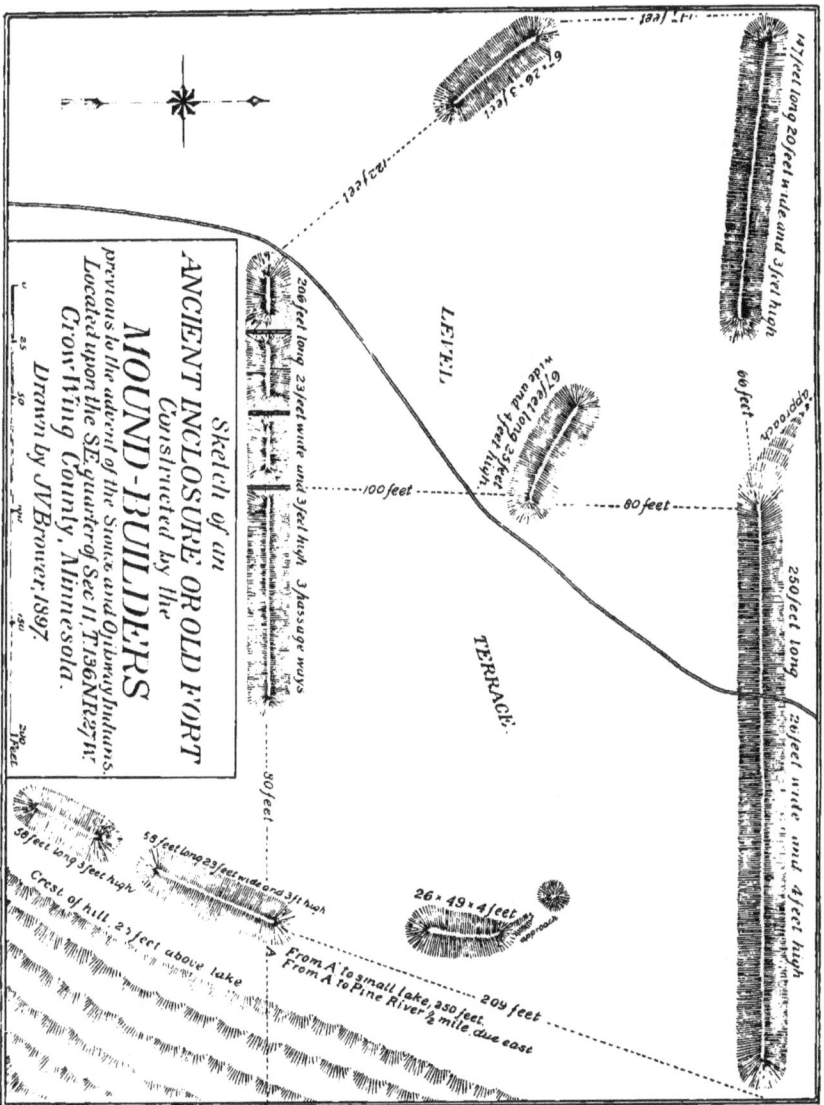

FORT FLAT MOUTH, CROW WING COUNTY, MINNESOTA.

Sketch of an

ANCIENT INCLOSURE OR OLD FORT

Constructed by the

MOUND-BUILDERS

previous to the advent of the Sioux and Ojibway Indians.

Located upon the S.E. quarter of Sec. 11. T.136 N.R. 27 W.

Crow Wing County, Minnesota.

Drawn by J.V.Brower, 1897.

147 feet long 20 feet wide and 3 feet high

117 feet

68 x 3 feet

122 feet

250 feet long 20 feet wide and 4 feet high

60 feet

80 feet

LEVEL

61 feet long 25 feet wide and 4 feet high

100 feet

206 feet long 23 feet wide and 3 feet high, 3 passage ways

TERRACE

26 x 49 x 4 feet

30 feet

55 feet long 23 feet wide and 3½ high

50 feet long 3 feet high

Crest of hill 25 feet above lake

204 feet

From A to small lake, 250 feet.

From A to Pine River ½ mile due east

The two Indians mentioned, both long since deceased, frequently discussed "the mounds which are everywhere to be met with throughout the entire region of country covered by [the] sources of the Mississippi."

Mr. Warren, writing in 1852, said:

Esh-ke-bug-e-coshe, whom I have already mentioned as the truth-telling and respected chief of the Pillagers, still living and now in his seventy-eighth year, informs me that in the course of his lifetime he has made numerous war parties and peace visits to different tribes who live on the banks of the Upper Missouri river. He states that a tribe who are known to the Ojibways by the name of Gi-aueth-in-in-e-wug, signifying "men of the olden time," and named by the French, Gros Ventres, claim to have been formerly possessors of the country from which the Mississippi takes its rise. Their old men relate they were forced or driven from this country by the powerful Dakotas, who have in turn given away to the Ojibways, now its present possessors.

The Gros Ventres further stated to the Pillager chief, that their fathers lived in earthen wigwams, and the small remnant who have escaped the scourge of the scalping knife and smallpox still live on the banks of the Missouri in these primitively constructed dwellings. This is an important fact in the early Indian history of Minnesota, and the writer has taken every pains to procure every account and circumstance which might conduce to prove its truth.

It will account at once for the numerous earthen mounds which are to be found at different points on the Upper Mississippi, as they may then be safely considered as the remains of the earthen lodges of these former occupants of this fair region.

So wrote Mr. Warren, as the result of his researches among his people, that the mounds in Northern Minnesota were of Gros Ventre origin, and Flat Mouth was his best authority.

Both were in error.

The history goes on to describe the location of numerous groups of mounds on all the principal lakes of the Upper Mississippi region, and that at the mouth of Pine river, now in Crow Wing county, Minnesota, there is a group of nineteen of these mounds in which the Ojibaws found bones.

These historic suggestions indicate how very ignorant the Ojibway Indians were of the fact that a Mound-Building race of men preceded them in the regions of the north.

Following the inquiry by Mr. Warren concerning these mounds, a few years later Mr. Alfred J. Hill commenced a scientific study of the mound question in Minnesota, gathering information, prosecuting surveys and drafting charts preparatory to a more thorough understanding of the numerous works constructed by prehistoric man in Minnesota, Wisconsin, and elsewhere. Unfortunately death, in 1895, put a stop to Mr. Hill's researches, and the work came to a sudden end, and the charts and papers are now in the hands of the authorities as an estate for administration.

Whether or not Mr. Hill continued his examinations and surveys to the group at the mouth of Pine river mentioned by Mr. Warren forty-five years ago, I do not know.

In October, 1896, while at the city of Brainerd on the Upper Mississippi, I engaged a conveyance and drove northwardly over an undulating region dotted with lakes, pine groves and small farms, to the mouth of Pine river, there to make examination of the mounds mentioned by Mr. Warren. At the Mission lakes, half a mile from the westerly bank of the Mississippi, the road passed directly over a prehistoric mound, one of a group of thirty-six. Continuing my drive to the mouth of Pine river and noticing that the whole vicinity was probably a rich archæologic field, I dismissed the team and engaged accommodations at the farm house of William Marcho, on the shore of the Mission lakes.

After making a sketch of the mounds and prehistoric village site at the Mission lakes, which I have named after the lakes, an examination of the Pine river locality was proceeded with.

Mounds were noticed a mile above the mouth of Pine river on section 24, and a prehistoric inclosure is situated on section 11, three miles north of the confluence of Pine river with the Mississippi and a half mile west from the mouth of the Little Pine. The approach of cold weather, followed soon after by a heavy snowfall, brought an end to those examinations. The intention was to return after the election in November and make a detailed survey of all these works, but on account of the deep snow and severe weather the project was abandoned.

A brief description of the earthworks examined follows herewith.

On the outward ride the first mound group noticed was on the creek uniting Lower Mission lake with the Mississippi river. There is also a village site there which probably extends to the terrace bordering the river on the west side. These mounds and the village site were not explored, for want of time. Miss Gertie Daniels presented a large greenstone celt from the locality. I counted sixteen mounds, and there are probably more than that in the group. The location is upon section 9, township 135, range 27, Crow Wing county, Minnesota.

The next location is the Mission Lake Mounds and prehistoric village site, situated upon section 4 of the same township and range. A beautiful terrace adjacent to the channel connecting the two lakes noted on the accompanying chart, was selected by the Mound-Builders as their village site at

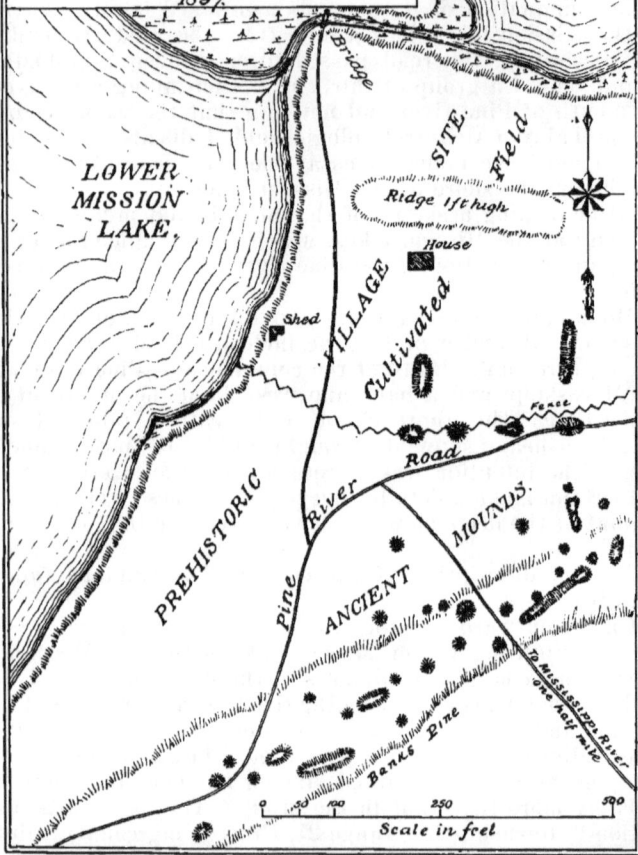

Sketch of the
MISSION LAKE MOUNDS AND VILLAGE SITE.
NE Quarter, Sec 4, Town 135, Range 27
Crow Wing County, Minnesota.
Drawn by
J. V. Brower.
1897.

UPPER
MISSION
LAKE

LOWER
MISSION
LAKE.

SITE.

Field

Ridge 1 ft high

House

VILLAGE

Cultivated

Shed

Fence

Bridge

Road

PREHISTORIC

River

Pine

ANCIENT

MOUNDS.

To MISSISSIPPI River
One half mile

Banks Pine

0   50   100   250   500
Scale in feet

that locality. The site extends along the shore of the lower lake, thence up the channel to the outlet of the upper lake. A small cultivated field inside of Mr. Marcho's inclosure yielded about one hundred specimens of pottery shards of many different kinds and varieties and a considerable number of chipped stone implements, not materially different from similar articles found in the Upper Mississippi Basin.

The terrace gradually rises into a low ridge about twenty feet above the surface of the water in the lakes, and on the inner flank of this ridge the mounds of different sizes and forms are situated, extending down to the terrace conformable to the contour limits of the lower lake. It would seem that the mounds and embankments were located at the outward limit of the village. Several of the mounds have been excavated and found to contain the remains of the dead, but no system was observed, and therefore no actual results can be stated by those who have heretofore opened the several earthworks unscientifically explored. The material of which the mounds are constructed is principally sand. No doubt nearly or quite two hundred Mound-Builders were interred within the mounds of this group, but the remains are so decomposed that it is difficult to determine the facts.

The next group examined is situated about one mile north of the mouth of Pine river, upon section 24. There are seven round mounds there, two of which are large and about twelve feet in height. The large one nearest the river was excavated by Gilbert M. Daniels in 1889. Two excavations were effected by Mr. Daniels, from both of which he removed human remains. Along the river slight indications of a village site were noticed. Mr. A. S. Kenna reports that still another group exists northwestwardly from the last mentioned mounds.

These explorations led up to an examination of the most interesting earthworks of the locality, an inclosure situated upon section 11, township 136, range 27, three miles north from the Mississippi and one-half of a mile west from Pine river.

It is believed that Flat Mouth, the old chief hereinbefore referred to, was the first person to call attention to the prehistoric works of this neighborhood. From that circumstance the dead chief should be remembered in archæologic history, notwithstanding the fact that he was entirely mistaken concerning the identity of these works, when he called them the earthen lodges of his predecessors, the Gi-aueth-in-in-e-wug, "men of the olden time." Circumstances of this character induce me to call the inclosure on section 11

FORT FLAT MOUTH.

This formidable work was visited and explored, and sufficient data reduced to writing to permit a fair sketch of the inclosure to be drawn and presented in the accompanying curtailed chart.

A small lake covers a considerable depression on the southeast corner of the section 11 mentioned. Pine river flows past this lake only a few feet to the eastward. At the west extremity of the lake a terrace is situated, at the crest of a hill, 250 feet distant from, and at an elevation twenty-five feet above, the lake. This level table land overlooking the lake and river bottoms is admirably situated for a work for defense, as no enemy could approach the inclosure without being detected and warded off by such appliances of warfare as may have been the means of defense, in times of conflict, during the prehistoric period when the Mound-Builders were occupants of the territory described.

The mounds described, and several other groups at Gull lake, on the Crow Wing river, at Sandy lake, and at other localities not far distant, indicate a considerable prehistoric population in the near and remote vicinity of Fort Flat Mouth. They were the builders of this inclosure. No legendary information comes down to us indicating the cause of its construction, and therefore the only consideration available is a study of the surroundings, indicating that it was an assembly ground for some purpose, and that purpose, probably, a question of defense against the approach and onslaughts of warring enemies.

The sketch map gives the dimensions and contour limits of the inclosure, over which a forest of timber has grown since its construction, which has disappeared from natural causes, leaving the embankments undisturbed and intact.

§ XX. Third: QUIVIRA; THE ELLIOTT INDIAN VILLAGE SITE.

Mr. L. R. Elliott of Manhattan, Kan., writing in 1895, submitted to me for examination some rude flint implements which were found in a cultivated field about fifteen miles, by the usually traveled road, south from Manhattan, accompanied with a request for information concerning their identity.

QUIVIRAN FLINT POINT.

The implements consisted of chipped spear-heads, tomahawks, scrapers, arrow-points, and knives, bearing upon their face unmistakable evidence that they were made and used by a warlike race of men who were a hunter nation, previous to the introduction of firearms. From time to time other like implements were sent by Mr. Elliott, from the same cultivated field, until, in October, 1896, four hundred of the flint implements, of many sizes and kinds, formed a collection, concerning which I was in some doubt, as a very few appeared to be similar to the implements taken from mounds in the Mississippi Basin, but the great majority of them were much different from the usual forms made by the mound-building people. The material difference was noticeable in the large number of flint tomahawks (they can hardly be called by any other name), the form of the knives, and the rude and rough chipping. I was firmly of the opinion that they were wrought and used by Indians, at about the period of time when civilization first advanced toward the American seaboard. Calcareous tufa was present to some extent, and saturation had removed fossiliferous elements from the chert formation, and not an iron or copper or pottery remnant was found in the entire collection.

It was finally decided to explore the locality, and the results, very interesting to all concerned, follow herewith.

The trip from St. Paul through Iowa and Missouri to the city of Manhattan was uneventful. At the latter place I was joined by Mr. Elliott and Mr. W. J. Griffing, and by team we proceeded up McDowall creek on Friday, Nov. 20, 1896, to a farming locality in Geary county, Kansas, called Briggs, seven miles due south from the Kansas river, fifteen miles from Man-

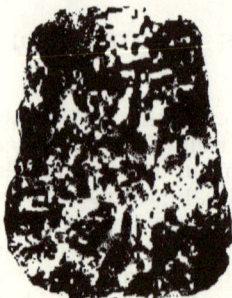

KNIFE.
One-half natural size.

NOTCHED BASE KNIFE.
One-half natural size.

POINT.
One-half natural size.

SCRAPER.
Natural size.

FLINT IMPLEMENTS FROM THE ELLIOTT SITE.
Geary County, Kansas.

hattan. During a past geological era a limestone formation accumulated at that point, and there is a very considerable deposit of blue chert, the whole bearing a fossiliferous element of an encrinal character, and no doubt there are other and numerous kinds of fossils in the rock formation of the neighborhood.

Since the deposition of the blue flint, erosion has taken place, and a picturesque valley has been formed, leaving the limestone and chert as an outcropping on the high bluffs. During the periods of erosion, terraces have been formed between the bluffs and the flood plain bordering the creek. Evidences of high water at various times are numerous, and the stream below the forks was formerly a considerable river, sufficient to permit the easy passage of canoes from the Kansas river to the point described. A narrow belt of timber borders the creek, and the character of the country above the valley, beyond the bluffs on either side, is a rolling table-land, devoid of timber, and may well be described as a buffalo plain. Nearly the entire valley has been acquired by farmers, and extensive corn fields indicate the character of the present industry.

By barometric hypsometry the elevation of the valley at Briggs was ascertained to be 1,130 feet above the sea, and the position, by dead reckoning, north latitude 39° and west longitude 96° 35′.

John Briggs, the oldest settler, acquired a portion of the land, Oct. 25, 1855, and has since resided there. During the forty-one years' occupancy of the premises, upon his and an adjoining farm, several hundred stone knives, spear and arrow points and other chipped implements have been found and disposed of by giving them away to the curious, or to collectors of such relics.

No attention appears to have been extended toward the locality by archaeologists in the past; at least, no publication describing the place has been found, although such may exist. Mr. Elliott, once before, drove to Briggs, examined both sides of the creek, noticing in several places the existence of chipped implements and flint spalls.

Such, briefly stated, was the situation at Briggs' when Mr. Elliott, Mr. Griffing and myself went into a temporary encampment near the creek, at that point, for the purpose of exploring the locality.

The second terrace above the creek, on the north side, was found to have been, at some unknown date, the site of an extensive Indian village. Two hundred and fifty chipped stone implements of different kinds, sizes, and varieties were picked up along the terrace, and placed in convenient piles. Flint blocks, rejects, finished and half-finished points and knives, broken implements, and a remarkable quantity of spalls, large and small, were scattered everywhere along the terrace. There are two cultivated fields there. Our cursory examination extended to but one of them on that side of the creek. At the point on the chart marked as the location of a workshop, we discovered about a hundred implements, and the spalls could be numbered by the thousand. Up to a late hour in the day no article of iron, copper, pottery, or lead was found. Finally two small pot-shards were picked up down nearer the creek, but away from the central locality of the village site. Crossing the creek on a fallen tree, with some difficulty, we were directed by Mr. Elliott to another spot where village debris was found, but in limited quantities. Returning to our team, the several piles of stone implements were gathered up and more were added. Wherever we searched, the surface was littered with flint spalls and chipped implements. Visiting the bluffs of the neighborhood, no mounds were found, and no graves or places of burial are distinguishable. Mr. Briggs pointed out the limits to which extended the scattered stone implements and debris, covering nearly one mile in length. The width of the village site is hardly ascertainable, for the terrace has been under a state of cultivation for so long a period, and the stone relics seem to be scattered so promiscuously from the flood plain to the base of the bluffs that it is difficult to determine the outward limits. The site is large enough to accommodate about one thousand ordinary sized lodges. Just how many there were will probably never be known. The little chart presented is a mere sketch, and the points of the compass are taken from the government surveys and the official map of the State of Kansas, while the extent of the village site is from information given by Mr. Briggs. Therefore the chart is simply preliminary in character and form. A sufficient number of the flint implements are reproduced as illustrations, to demonstrate the character, form, and size of the weapons of war, and the articles for domestic use and the chase.

Mr. Elliott has asked the question:

To what race of men can the establishment of this village be ascribed?

The answer, upon the meager information I have at hand, is not only a difficult but a delicate one. I have no set theory to inflict upon anyone. My opinion, based upon the facts as they appear at this writing, is probably not more reliable than is Mr. Elliott's. That they were not of the mound-building race of men is practically certain. That they were probably Quiviran Indians, whomsoever they may have been, is possible, and I shall entertain that opinion until better evidence to the contrary than I now possess is produced.

My reasons for entertaining such an opinion are stated as briefly as may be.

While searching for the facts in this interesting case, I addressed a letter to Dr. Elliott Coues, the accomplished editor of "Zebulon Montgomery Pike," concerning the Kansa Indians. Dr. Coues made reply by forwarding the following letter from the Bureau of Ethnology, with permission to publish:

SMITHSONIAN INSTITUTION,
BUREAU OF AMERICAN ETHNOLOGY,
WASHINGTON, Dec. 3, 1896.

DEAR DR. COUES: So far as can be determined, the name of Kansa (the plural form of which was applied to the state) refers to "winds," but the full definition is unknown.

In prehistoric times the Kansa(s) or "Kaw(s)" were with the Omaha, Osage, and Ponka Indians, after the separation from the Kwapa (Quapaw), going up the Mississippi, thence up the Missouri to the mouth of the Osage, where final separation was made, the Kansa continuing up the Missouri river about as far north as the northeast corner of the present State of Kansas, where they met the Cheyennes, who drove them south. This must have been after 1723, at which date Bourgmont speaks of the large village of the "Quans" on a small river flowing northward, thirty leagues above the "Quans River," and near the Missouri.

If the "Escansaques" or "Excanjaques" are identical with the Kansa, and there is every reason for believing them to be the same, then the first mention of the tribe was made in 1599, by Juan de Oñate, who encountered them on an expedition to find the "Quivira" of Coronado in the region of the great plains.

The name Kansa (pronounced Kon-za) was early used in various forms, as follows:

CANCHEZ. Le Page du Pratz, Hist. Louisiana, vol. ii., 251, 1758.
CANSA. Harris, Coll. of Voys. and Travels (map), 1705.
CANSE. Iberville (1702) in Margry's Découvertes, iv., 601, 1880.
CANSEZ. Del' Isle's map of 1701.
CANZE. Bienville (1722) in Margry, vi., 387.
KAH. Lewis and Clark, Discoveries, p. 13, 1806.
KAMSE. N. Y. Col. Docs. ix., p. 1057. (Doc. of 1736.)
KANCAS. La Potherie, Hist. Amerique, ii., 271, 1753.
KANS. Pike Expedition, 123, 1810.
KANSA. Ex. Doc. 56, 18 Cong. 1st sess. p. 9, 1824.
KANSAE. Coxe. Carolana, 11, 1741.
KANSAS. Schermerhorn in 2d Mass. Hist. Coll. ii., 32. 1814.
KANSE. Las Harpe (1722) in Margry, op. cit. vi., 365, 1886.
KANSES. Iberville (1702) in Margry, iv., 599, 1880.
KANSAS. N. Y. Col. Docs. ix., 621, 1855. (Doc. of 1695.)
KAUS. Johnson and Winter. Route across Rocky Mountains, p. 13, 1846.
KAW. Gregg, Commerce of the Prairies, p. 41, 1850.
KONZO. Long's Expedition (James ed.), i., 111, 1823.
QUANS. Bourgmont (1723) in Margry, vi., 393, 1886.

Many more forms of the tribal name occur in literature, but these will doubtless suffice.   Yours very truly.

F. W. HODGE.

The interpretation I place upon the letter of Professor Hodge precludes the possibility that the Kansa Indians were in the neighborhood of the Elliott Indian village site at the time the flint deposits there were wrought into stone implements by human hands.

The next document is an important communication from Mr. W. J. Griffing, who was in charge of an examination for the authorities of the State of Kansas when the prehistoric mounds of the vicinity of Manhattan were opened and examined.

Following is Mr. Griffing's letter:

MANHATTAN. KAN., Dec. 7, 1896.

Hon. J. V. Brower. St. Paul, Minn.,

DEAR SIR: Your favor of December 1st received, in which you request information regarding the prehistoric occupancy of this immediate vicinity. The evidence is quite strong that this section was at one time the home of a numerous race of people skilled in the art of making pottery and in manufacturing arrow-points, spear-points, knives, scrapers, etc., of flint; stone axes and hammers of flint and granite, pipes of red pipe stone and numerous instruments and ornaments of bone and shell.

The village sites are all located on bottom land near the margin of the creeks and rivers, obviously for the purpose of better securing food and water; game and fish being abundant and the rich soil of the low lands furnishing the best of ground for farming purposes.

The relics commonly found on these village sites are knives, arrow and spear-heads, scrapers, whetstones, rubbing stones, axes, flint awls, fragments of pipe stone, and an occasional pipe bowl, fragments of pottery, etc.

The arrow-points are of three different types: First—Plain triangular shape without notches. Second—Similar to first, with one, sometimes two, notches on the side near the base. Third—Are barbed, the barbs projecting backward, often having a serrated edge; *i. e.,* war arrow-points.

The scrapers are of flint, flat or curved on one side and rounding on the other.

The knives are of flint, of such a shape as to give four cutting edges.

The whetstones are of brown sandstone, generally grooved; were probably used to sharpen bone instruments.

Flint awls are from one and one-half to four inches in length, with an enlargement at the base.

Only two or three whole specimens of pottery ware have been found, though fragments are common. At least two places have been found where it was manufactured.

The rims of the pots were often ornamented. Sometimes ears or handles were attached to the rim, much like the handle of a jug. All were of a rounding kettle shape, with a capacity of from less than a pint to a few gallons.

The mounds are, with hardly an exception, located on the tops of the bluffs overlooking the streams, and were all used for burial purposes. They are composed usually of stone and common alluvial soil, the stones varying in size from gravel to rocks weighing one hundred pounds or more, and have been transported from neighboring ledges of limestone rock, found on the brows of nearly all the bluffs here.

KNIFE, BEADS, POINTS, AND SHELL ORNAMENT.
From the Griffing collection at Manhattan.
Photo by Swem, St. Paul.

No earthworks of any other description have yet been found, except slight elevations on the village sites, which are only the debris of former dwellings of some kind.

I have opened or assisted in opening some thirty or more of these mounds. The majority are about one to one and one-half feet in height and twenty-five feet in diameter at the base, and contain little else than fragments of burned human bones. The larger ones, however, ranging in height from one and one-half to four feet and twenty-five to thirty-five feet or more in diameter, besides the ever-present burned bones, teeth, etc., also yield other more interesting relics. The following is a list of some of them: Barbed or war arrow-points, spear-points, bone and flint awls, beads of bird bone (often ornamented with grooves), and also of shell and white stone, fragments of bone daggers and other bone implements and ornaments, and one bone fish hook, made from the side of a bone, without a barb; a few thin pieces of copper and fragments of pottery similar to that found on the village sites.

Nearly all the largest mounds show that more than one burial has taken place, and that cremation was commonly practiced.

In one, however, in section 19, near the mouth of Cedar creek, Pottawatomie county, an entire skeleton was found in a sitting posture, much decayed. It was an intrusive burial. Other bones and relics found were in every respect similar to those found in other mounds.

Another interesting mound opened is in section 34, near the mouth of Carnahan creek, Pottawatomie county. This was similar to the others in size, and contained burned bones, arrow-points, etc., and also some old-fashioned glass beads, blue and white in color, and a short coil of brass wire, showing contact with the whites.

These mounds and village sites are to be found up and down the Kansas and Blue rivers and their tributaries for long distances. There are undoubtedly many mounds that have never been opened.

The Kaw or Kansas Indians were located in a village near the junction of the Blue and Kansas on the first advent of the whites, at the beginning of this century. The village, of about 120 lodges built of poles covered with earth, is accurately described by Dr. Thomas Say, the eminent naturalist, a member of Major Long's exploring party sent out in 1819-20. The Indians were in possession of flint-lock guns, knives, axes, and other iron utensils, obtained from the whites. Their dead were buried in unmarked graves on the bottom land near the villages.

Yours truly,

W. J. GRIFFING.

It is very important to note that Mr. Griffing found glass beads of an old-fashioned character in one of the mounds excavated by him, for it is a historical fact that Coronado, the Spanish general, distributed glass beads and bells on his march from Culiacan to Quivira, in 1541, as will be shown hereafter.

A number of the Griffing beads were submitted for my inspection, and they were found to be an old style glass bead, but their identity is by no means an easy matter to solve.

The brass wire is also important, for every question on this subject should be intelligently considered and conscientiously criticised.

At this period, and at 2 o'clock A. M., December 19th, 1896, my entire personal belongings, library, charts, field books, scientific instruments, archæologic and ethnologic collection, manuscripts, letter files, photographs and negatives, all maps and drawings, and all and singular every article contained in my study and office, were destroyed by fire.

The plates appearing in this publication were, fortunately, in the press rooms of my publisher.

The valuable accumulation described was the result of researches and explorations in the Northwest commenced in 1860 and continued from time to time until the closing month of the current year.

Dated this 19th day of December, 1896.

Signed,

J. V. BROWER.

AN IRREPARABLE MISFORTUNE.
(See Appendix.)

CONTINUATION.

Under the most distressing and unfortunate circumstances, this descriptive article must now be briefly brought to a close,

without the aid of elaborate notes, specially prepared for
careful presentation herewith.

An ash heap, flooded, then congealed, and a fairly good
memory and some illustrations, are all that is left of painstaking preparations.

When Mr. Elliott, Mr. Grifling, and myself departed from
the village site near Briggs, a careful examination and study
of the country to the northward was commenced, and Mr.
Grifling's extensive notes and archæologic map were made
available for a very good general understanding of the prehistoric occupancy of Manhattan and its vicinity.

We found no mounds and no ancient burial places on our
returning route of travel until we reached the bluffs overlooking the Kansas river, and from thence, on both sides of the
stream mentioned, old village sites and mounds are extant,
and they continue up both sides of the Blue river, which forms
a confluence with the Kansas at Manhattan.

East of the confluence of the two rivers mentioned and on
the north bank of the Kansas river, the historic village site
of the Kansa Indians is situated.

On the east side of the Blue river, several miles up the
stream, we explored the Disney prehistoric village site, so
called after the young lad who, in 1895, discovered numerous
flint implements, spalls, and pieces of pottery, along a hand-
somely situated terrace, with three open landscape views in
as many different directions. This village site is twenty
miles northeastward from the Elliott site, and they differ
widely, in that, at the Disney site, broken pottery is of common occurrence on every hand, and the chipped implements
are somewhat different in size, form and character. One important fact, however, presented itself. While the absence of
broken pottery at the Elliott site was strikingly convincing,
a few of the chipped implements of flint at both sites were
quite similar. Dozens of broken war arrow-points were secured at the Disney site by Mr. Elliott, and the inference is
drawn that at least one prehistoric conflict for supremacy occurred there. The terrace occupied was admirably situated
for a natural defense, which strengthens that opinion.

It now came to pass that a careful comparison of the Griffing collection from the vicinity of Manhattan, with the Elliott
collection from the vicinity of Briggs, demonstrated that they
were not made by the same people. The first constructed
mounds and the latter did not. One made pottery and the
other made tomahawks. Domestic tranquility seems to have
prevailed with the former, and the latter were a savage hunter

nation, and from all that is left the inference is drawn that they ate their meat raw, wore raiment of skins, and lived in lodges.

This is all that I certainly infer up to this time, and the regret is expressed that the names of several gentlemen who have heretofore worthily participated in archæologic explorations at Manhattan and a description of their work went down to ashes when my records were destroyed, and at this writing it is too late to be resupplied, for credit herewith.

All that is now convenient is a few brief references to trace the earliest advance of civilized man toward, to, or beyond the site of these interesting villages, situated in the interior of the State of Kansas.

Several authorities, all peculiarly reliable, are now consulted for information to partially resupply that which was lost, descriptive of the Spanish march to the cities of Cibola, and to Quivira, as follows:

Mr. Justin Winsor, in *Mississippi Basin*, 1895.

Mr. Henry W. Haynes, in *Narrative and Critical History of America*, ii., 473-98, appended to which is a "*Critical Essay on the Sources of Information*." See, also, Mr. Justin Winsor's Editorial Note, pp. 503-4.

Captain Geo. M. Wheeler, in *United States Geographical Surveys, West of the One-hundredth Meridian*, 1889, Vol. I., and his *Memoir upon the Voyages, Discoveries, Explorations, and Surveys,*—1500 to 1800, pp. 481-512. Also, the work of Buckingham Smith, of John Gilmary Shea, and others, available at St. Paul.

All the maps in the works quoted are referred to, and I acknowledge my great obligations in extending this credit.

Quivira is shown, not as a village, but as a province, containing several villages.

The vicinity of Manhattan is about one hundred miles southwestwardly from the Missouri river.

The Spaniards under Coronado spent twenty-five days exploring the province of Quivira, in all directions, before they retired in the direction from whence they came.

The Spanish explorations referred to are now concisely described.

Antonio Nuñez Cabeza de Vaca with two companions and a negro were the sole survivors of the unfortunate expedition of Pamphilo de Narvaez. They had sailed from the coast of Florida, in 1527, under embarrassing circumstances, westward to a point where fresh water was taken from the sea at the mouth of a large river, undoubtedly the delta of the Mississippi. The rude boats gave only standing room, and corn, the only sustenance, was eaten unparched. All were cast away at sea, and Vaca and his companions, thrown northward to the gulf coast, wandered to the interior. This party of unfortunates were the first Europeans to come in contact with the wildest hunter tribes of the Western plains. In 1536 they arrived at the Spanish settlements in Mexico, the first to report from the North the existence of the buffalo, and of riches in gold.

Describing what they had witnessed among the different nations, Fray Marcos de Nizza, a monk, was dispatched, with the negro as a guide and one companion, to investigate and report concerning these new discoveries. They crossed a desert, came in sight of the Seven Cities of Cibola, built a mound of stone, and, erecting a cross thereon, proclaimed a new Spanish acquisition. Returning with flattering reports, much overdrawn, a Spanish provincial governor, Francisco Vasquez de Coronado, was commissioned to command an army, which marched northward from Culiacan, Mexico, April 22, 1540, to take possession of the "New Kingdom of St. Francis," with its reputed riches in gold and precious stones. Coronado had pushed forward in advance of his army of 800 men, and by August 3d was enabled to report, not riches and priceless gems, but hostiles and disappointments. Natives to the eastward, from Cicuyé, some seventy leagues distant, came forward with bison skins, which were exchanged for glass beads and bells, and a detachment marched forward to visit their country, where a fortified town with 500 warriors was discovered. Here the Spaniards were met by a character whom they named "The Turk," from a place called Quivira, many days' march far to the eastward. The wonderful stories of gold and riches told by "The Turk," made Quivira, to Coronado and his followers, a famed city, and to some extent it has remained so ever since, and its position unknown and undiscovered.

Coronado and his army, having passed the Grand Cañon of the Colorado, wintered where the ice remained for four months. In April, 1541, Xabe, a native Quiviran, was made the guide to direct the Spaniards in their lawless conquest of the Quiviran possessions. They marched through mountains, crossed a large river and emerged upon the Western plains. Here the route of travel was northeastwardly, and discovering herds of buffalo, which they soon encountered in countless numbers, they were guided to a band of Indians, who were hunters, possessing lodges and dogs, seventeen days' march from the winter quarters. Hearing of a large river and of people upon its banks, they were told at a native town called Cona, that Quivira was many leagues to the northward, probably more than 500 miles, and "The Turk" was looked upon with suspicion and anger. At this point in Coronado's search for the reputed riches of Quivira, a detachment pressed forward to the north, under the commander-in-chief, and at the end of a month they came to a large river, when, crossing, they followed its course *northeast* to several villages, one of which was called Quivira. The huts were of straw and the people the wildest barbarians of the plains. The valleys were fruitful and productive, but the gold was missing, and instead a chief wore a copper plate, undoubtedly the richest gem of the fiercest Indians they had met in a march of 900 leagues. Here exploring parties were sent out in all directions, and "The Turk" was summarily strangled as a punishment for his misrepresentations.

It would seem that more than one people was visited in the vicinity of Quivira, for the languages differed and the tribes seemed not identical.

After the fruitless search for gold had terminated, Coronado and his followers departed from Quivira, never to return, and their subsequent adventures and wanderings do not concern the present inquiry.

At this time, map makers, historians, geographers and public writers are unable to agree concerning the identity of the locality of Quivira· Its importance in history emanates from the circumstances surrounding the most remarkable expedition of early times in America; yet nothing whatever has been discovered, up to this time, certainly identifiable in connection with the long-lost site of the Quiviran settlements, to pillage which the Spaniards, 356 years ago, marched several thousands of miles to and from an unknown and an unexplored country, which was inhabited by many of the wildest tribes of the new world.

There are numerous reasons to support a belief that the present state of Kansas encompasses the historic site of the long lost Quivira. Its greatest glory is in the interest surrounding the earliest and most remarkable exploration, by an armed Spanish mob, called an army, seeking to rob the possessors of wealth on the Western plains, with force and arms, murdering whomsoever might resist.

Thus came the first intelligence concerning the wildest savages in the Missouri basin.

The Spaniards who made this remarkable dash across the plains, were not fortunate enough to have in their company a Thompson or a Nicollet, hence their geographic position at

Quivira is not certainly known, although Coronado placed it at 40° north latitude, and to this day geographers and historians have been searching, on the maps, to solve this enigma of the earliest historic times concerning a settlement of savages who ate their meat raw, wore raiment of skins, were without cotton, and chipped their flint for implements of defense and for the arms of the chase.

Something tangible now presents itself.

Was the Elliott site a village of the Quiviran locality?

Possibly and probably.

Some brief considerations are now pertinent:

First: The archæology of Manhattan, Kansas, shows that several prehistoric villages existed there, east, west, north and south from the mouth of Blue river. The Elliott and the Disney sites are two of them, and the Griffing survey and map has brought to our knowledge several others.

Coronado discovered several villages at the Quiviran locality.

Second: These village sites are on both sides of the Kansas river, a large stream, flowing northeastwardly to the Missouri.

Coronado crossed a large river, followed it in a northeast direction to several villages, one of which was Quivira.

Third: Mound-builders near Manhattan, and Indians at the Elliott and Disney sites, formerly occupied the territory in the vicinity of the present city of Manhattan. The chipped stone implements differ, materially, in form, size and character. One used pottery, the other did not, at the Elliott site. These differing races of men were not identical.

Coronado found savages, near Quivira, differing in linguistic accomplishments.

Fourth: The Griffing excavations brought to light old-fashioned glass beads, taken from a mound near Manhattan.

Coronado distributed glass beads to natives in 1541.

Fifth: North latitude 40° has been considered as a limit to which the Spaniards penetrated in their march to Quivira.

All of the old village sites near Manhattan are situated between 39° and 40° north latitude.

Sixth: A circuitous route from Mexican possessions, northerly and eastwardly, 900 leagues to Quivira, is comparable with an identical route of travel terminating on the lower waters of the Kansas river.

This provisional consideration initiates an inquiry concerning the identity of the Manhattan prehistoric village sites, from the Elliott locality at Briggs to the Griffing explorations, the Disney discovery, and to Stockton and other places in that vicinity, where the early tribes and bands maintained their habitat long before and probably after Coronado's search for an opportunity to precipitate a conquest at Quivira, for the height of a Spaniard's ambition—gold and glory; peaceably if convenient, by force if necessary.

The many able gentlemen who have heretofore interested themselves in the archæology of Manhattan, whose names are partly lost to me by force of circumstances over which I had no control, should give to the world a better record than I could possibly hope to prepare, saving to their locality the honor of historical antecedents emanating from the earliest Quiviran settlements, if Kansas and Manhattan were actually the arena of those earliest historic times in the Missouri Basin.

In answer to the question asked by Mr. Elliott, respecting the identity of the savages who established the Elliott Indian village at the locality now known as Briggs, Geary county, Kansas, I can only say that I have not been able to satisfactorily determine to what linguistic stock they belonged.

There are, however, many reasons to support an opinion that they were possibly a race of men who established one of the settlements of the Quiviran Province, which was discovered in 1541 by Coronado and his followers, the identity of which has ever since been, and now is, in doubt.

The citizens of Manhattan owe it as a duty to themselves, to Kansas and to the world, to carefully and intelligently observe all available evidence obtainable, which is necessary to fathom the present impenetrability of their archæologic history.

Every place of interment should be most thoroughly and scientifically explored, that the contents intrusively historic may be carefully separated from the prehistoric deposits. Every stone implement, ornament, vessel and remnant from the several village sites should be compared with the statements of Coronado and his chroniclers. A study of the origin and early movements of the Kansa Indians is advisable; likewise the explorations of Juan de Oñate and the records of all the earlier Spanish and French travelers and traders.

In that manner some evidence may be found to more fully support an opinion that the Manhattan locality is the unidentified Province of Quivira.

It may not be out of place to state at this time that word has been received by me direct from the oldest and most intelligent Kansa Indians, now living at the Kaw reservation, Oklahoma. They know nothing whatsoever concerning the meaning of their name, its origination, or of their tribal identity. In this connection I acknowledge the courteous aid of their resident agent, Col. Henry B. Freeman, and regret the loss of the translated statement intended for publication herewith.

In closing this descriptive narration of the results of the deeply instructive and interesting surveys, I shall rejoice if Quivira has been found; and if not, no intentional harm has been selfishly perpetrated against the stability of history, or the indulgence of colleagues.

Disheartening and unfortunate circumstances beckon me away from the field of scientific literature, at a time when the value of equipment was immeasurably enhanced by the advice of scholarly friends.

Their good will and the pencil now wielded is all that remains. The rest is ashes.

QUIVIRAN FLINT KNIFE.
One-half natural size

APPENDIX.

16

MONTANA, IOWA, NEBRASKA, AND KANSAS.

HISTORICAL LETTERS DEFINING THE TRUE MEANING AND DERIVATION OF THE NAMES OF SEVERAL WESTERN STATES.

During the progress of the work described in this little volume, many letters of historic importance have been received, among which are the following, well worthy a permanent preservation.

The authors of these letters are able gentlemen, and the results of their researches are placed over their several names, intending thereby to award to them, severally, the full credit due to each writer:

HISTORICAL SOCIETY OF MONTANA,
HELENA, MONT., April 23, 1896.

J. V. Brower, Esq., St. Paul, Minn.,

Dear Sir: In reply to the questions contained in your favor of the 17th inst., I take pleasure in forwarding the following information. Before beginning I will state, that I had written a letter before this one, which was unsatisfactory, and so was not sent, for the reason that I desired to be certain as to the derivation of the name of this state, and have since been looking more closely into the matter, which will explain the delay. Notwithstanding the assertion contained in "the late issue of the ponderous nothingness" by a Chicago firm, and called "History of Montana," that the name "Montana" is a purely classic word, it is certain that such is true only in part. There is little doubt but that the word is originally derived from the Latin root *mont*, of *mons* (singular), meaning mountain; plural, *montes.* The work spoken of by you, on its first page, quotes the following passages to prove the purely classic nature of the name: "*Sunt loca montana, seu regivant pars regionis inter montes sita,*" Liv., 21, 34; "*Percentum inde ad frequentem cultoribus alium ut inter montana, populum,*" Pliny, 6, 22, 7; and *Ib.*, 6: "*Prasiorum gens, quorum in montanis Pygmæi tradunter.*" Here, however, the word is pronounced with the long sound of the *a*, as follows—*mon-tay-na*, or *mon-tay-nis*, while the correct and proper pronunciation of the word gives the Spanish sound of the *a*; not the long, as in fate, nor yet the flat, as in bat, but more nearly that of *a* in far, as *mon-tah-nah*, not too broadly given. So you will see that the word could not have been taken directly from the Latin. It is evident, as it is a fact, that it came directly from some other language founded upon the older tongue, and this language is that of Spain. The name comes directly from the feminine form of the adjective *montáno* meaning mountainous; from the noun *montáña*, a mountain or mount, and pronounced *mon-tan-nyah.* The feminine form of the adjective *montáno* is *montána*, which is pronounced *mon-tah-nah*, the signification of which is "a mountainous country." Hon. James M. Ashley, now of Toledo, Ohio. and once a governor of Montana, was in the house of representatives, United States congress, at the time the Territory of Idaho was organized and named, in 1863, and at that time attempted to give the name "Montana" to the new division. This was bitterly opposed by some Eastern congressmen, who insisted that Montana was no word, and meant nothing, and would never do for a name to be given to a territory. His idea carried, and I believe his selection of a name was given to Idaho. The next year

Montana was set apart, in 1864, and at this time Mr. Ashley was able
to carry the name through for the new territory, and so Montana it is.
It is a short, sightly, and simple name, and one of much euphonic beauty;
one which the people of this state would not care to part with for any
possible combination of letters. For any other points in reference to
the name I would advise you to correspond with Governor Ashley. As
to the signification of the word, no other one would so well describe
the topographical characteristics of the state, for with the ranges and
spurs and isolated groups of mountains the State of Montana is indeed
a mountainous country. First and foremost, of course, the main range
of the "Rockies,"—the backbone of the continent"—reaches from north
to south across the state, a magnificent mountain wall. Radiating from
it in many directions run spurs and lesser ranges as the Coeur d'Alene,
Bitter Root, Kootenai, Cabinet, Gallatin, Madison, Snowies, Highland,
Basin, and many more or less isolated groups and ranges, as the To-
bacco, Snow Crest, Crazy, Ruby, Milk River, Bridger, Pryor, Bull,
Little Belt, Big Belt, Bear Paw, Big Snow, Sweet Grass, Little Rockies,
Highwood, Wolf or Cheetish, Big Horn, and Rose Bud, some of which
reach eastward nearly to the the eastern boundary of the state.

As to "Tozabe-Shock-up" or "Tay-a-be-shock-up," I simply am informed that it means "The country of the mountains," but to what
tribe of Indians the word belongs I do not know, except that it does
not belong to the language of the Crows nor to the Flatheads, nor does
it, I am well nigh certain, belong to that of the Blackfeet. Hon. Granville Stuart, who was one of the earliest settlers of this region, and
as well able to advise on such matters as anyone I know, would be
pleased to give you any information in his power, and if you can
spare the time to write to him, it would be to your advantage to do
so. He is now residing at the legation, in Montevideo, Uruguay, as
the United States minister to Uruguay and Paraguay, South America.
I was pleased to receive your word of commendation with reference to
our Volume II. of the "Contributions" to this society. It has been well
received. The mechanical part of the work leaves much to be desired,
but it is something to have gotten out the work, so that we can afford
to overlook such an item as that. Hoping the above information is
satisfactory, I am,   Very truly yours,
                                              W. F. SANDERS,
                                                  Librarian.

HISTORICAL DEPARTMENT OF IOWA.
                              DES MOINES, April 10, 1896.
My dear Sir: It is a very difficult matter to define the precise
meaning of the word "Iowa." I have always supposed its signification to be "The Beautiful Land," and I am sure that this has been,
and is, the popular belief. Reference to our best authorities shows
that there is great diversity of opinion as to its origin and meaning.

A valuable book was published in this city in 1882, by the late
Hon. A. R. Fulton, entitled "The Red Men of Iowa." In that he
grouped together, in three or four pages, statements made by various
parties in regard to its origin and signification. One legend had it that
a noted Indian chief, upon surmounting a high bluff overlooking the
valley of the Iowa river, exclaimed, "Iowa! Iowa!" or, "Beautiful!
Beautiful!" The late Antoine Le Claire, a brainy man of French and
Indian descent, who was familiar with the language and history of
many of the Western tribes, asserted that its signification was, "This

is the place!"—as of one expressing satisfaction with a newly-found locality. Hon. Theodore S. Parvin, the Nestor of Iowa historical writers, as long ago as 1864, quoted this statement, in substance (from a letter by Mr. Le Claire), in one of his articles in "The Annals of Iowa." Rev. S. S. Howe, a former editor of "The Annals," also accepted the explanation of Mr. Le Claire. But Judge Fulton, after giving the statements and opinions of others, says that the word is of Dacotah origin, and that it signifies, "Something to write or paint with," as a pen or pencil. This name, he adds, with slight changes from time to time, was applied to a tribe belonging to the Dacotah race, and he remarks: "Why the name was given to the tribe we may never know, but we do know it became the name of our territory and state, because it was the name of the tribe who occupied the soil, and because it commended itself to the whites as euphonious and appropriate."

Dr. J. L. Pickard, a former president of our state university, who is one of our best informed students of Iowa and Indian history, writes me "that the meaning of the word is among the things yet to be determined. The French seem to have known of the existence of the word, and to have spelled it *Aiouez*—in the French language pronounced I-o-way."

Other writers might be quoted, but the theories of all seem to be more or less fanciful. We really have no basis of absolute, ascertained fact upon which to rest. I regret that I am unable to answer your question. It is one which has been often mooted, but left unanswered for more than fifty years.   Very sincerely yours,
                                                        CHARLES ALDRICH.

Hon. J. V. Brower, St. Paul, Minn.

                          NEBRASKA STATE HISTORICAL SOCIETY,
                                LINCOLN, Neb., April 15, 1896.
J. V. Brower, Esq., St. Paul, Minn.,
    Dear Sir: In reply to yours of the 13th April, I take pleasure in stating that "Nebraska" is from the Omaha Indian word *ne-brath-kae*, which, William Hamilton says, not being pronounced correctly by the interpreter, was pronounced *ne-bras-ka*. Hence our present name. It was the Indian name, meaning broad, or broad and shallow,—flat water, flat river,—and was given by the Indians to the Platte river, the word *platte* being a French translation of the same. (Nebr. State His. Soc. Pub., i., 73, 74, 76.)

    "Wyoming," says Malcolm Townsend, in "United States" (Boston. D. Lathrop & Co., p. 65), was carried to the West by Wyoming Valley, Pa., emigrants. It is a Delaware word, meaning "great plains," from *m'chenomi* or *m'chinwamis*.   Very cordially,
                                                        JAY AMOS BARRETT,
                                                                 Librarian.

                          STATE OF KANSAS. HISTORICAL SOCIETY.
                                TOPEKA, KAN., May 4, 1896.
J. V. BROWER, ESQ.,
    Dear Sir: Replying to your inquiry, for the Hydrography of the Mississippi Basin and allied examinations, as to the true meaning of the name Kansas, I am obliged to say to you that our Kansas State

Historical Society has never in any way authoritatively decided the question, about which, as you say, there are many different authorities. I refer you to a paper by Rev. J. Owen Dorsey, published in the "American Naturalist" for July, 1895, vol. xix, No. 7, p. 671, on the subect of the "Mourning and War Customs of the Kansas." Explanatory of a diagram in the article is this item:

"5. A Kanze (Kansas wind) man."

This seems to imply that the name Kansas means "wind." This, perhaps, is the highest authority on the subject.

In the volume by A. D. Richardson, entitled "Beyond the Mississippi," published in 1867, he gives the name Kansas as signifying "smoky." Several other writers seem to follow Richardson.

In John Fiske's "History of the United States," 1895, p. 441, he gives the name as meaning "South Wind People."

I regret that I cannot give you more exact information.

In behalf of our historical society I beg to request of you to give the society the benefit of the result of your inquiries.

Yours truly,
F. G. ADAMS.
Secretary.

FIRST OF LIFE ON EARTH.

BY OLIVER C. FARRINGTON, CURATOR FIELD COLUMBIAN MUSEUM.

Ages ago this world had a very different appearance from that which it has to-day. Instead of being covered with grass, flowers and trees, its seas swarming with fish, its air with birds and insects and its fields and forests with four-footed and creeping things, it was a cold, hard, lifeless ball revolving through space seemingly to no purpose. We may imagine that world a battlefield of the elements, a theatre for the strife of physical forces, but one into whose domain that mysterious, undiscoverable force called life had not yet entered. Into the arena where matter and physical forces wrought one upon the other, forming and transforming the lifeless substance of the world, God brought a new force, feeble in its beginning, yet destined to rule the world and to show the meaning and purpose of all that had gone before. This was the force called life, first visible perhaps as the feeble pulsing of a bit of jelly, which yet possessed powers of growth, of waste and repair and of reproduction. Or life may have first appeared as several distinct types of animal or vegetable life. At any rate it was a force which has greatly enlarged and expanded itself since its introduction, and it is the development of this force which the paleontologist seeks to trace. The study of living things is the province of the zoologist and botanist, but the paleontologist studies ancient life. The materials for this study are the fossils found in rocks. But one who expects to find in rocks "petrified" specimens of the animals or plants which lived at different periods of the world's history will be much disappointed. True petrifaction or turning to stone of the substance of a once living thing is extremely rare, and can take place only under unusual conditions. It is from remains of a different kind that the paleontologist must chiefly obtain his knowledge of ancient life. These are, first, the mineral parts or hard parts, the shell or skeleton of an animal or plant, and second, casts or molds showing the form of an organism, usually made from the fine sand or mud in which the parts were imbedded. Such relics of ancient life are preserved because they are rock themselves, and so may pass through exposure, hardening, and pressure without destruction. Even these, however, are rarely preserved entire, and may need to be looked at a long while before they indicate much as to the nature of the animal or plant to which they belong. A single tooth of an animal or the imprint of one leaf of a plant may be the only source of knowledge regarding a species. Yet to such a high degree of perfection has the study of comparative anatomy been carried that it is frequently possible from a single bone to reconstruct the entire animal. A reconstruction of the Megalosaur was made by Professor Dawkins of England from a fragment of the lower jaw of the animal, with which skeletons of the animal found later agreed in almost every detail. A single bone or leaf, too, may establish as well as a whole skeleton the fact of the existence of such an animal or plant at the time the rocks containing the bone or leaf were formed. This, for purposes of tracing the earth's history, is as important as the structure of the organism. In hall 35 of the Field Columbian Museum, may be seen a slab of red sandstone from Canyon City, Colo., containing shelly fragments which apparently have as little structure as so much sawdust. Yet from a study of remains like these, which are really plates and scales of ganoid fishes, Professor Walcott was enabled to establish the important fact of the existence of fishes in the Lower Silurian rocks.

To facilitate the study of this ancient life it has been found convenient to divide its history into periods just as human history is divided into periods, such as that of the Babylonian empire, the Roman empire, and so on. To these periods are given names from the rocks by which these periods are best represented. Thus we have the Silurian age, named from the rocks found in the region once inhabited by the British tribe of Silures; Devonian, from North and South Devon; Jurassic from the rocks of the Juras, and so on. These terms have now a wholly chronological significance, and refer simply to a certain period in the earth's history. Thus the limestone formation underlying Chicago and spreading over northwestern Illinois is called the Niagara limestone, because it is shown by its fossils to be of the same age as the rocks at Niagara Falls, where the fossils were first described. Such a nomenclature gives a convenient and positive standard of time.

We may now ask the question, How did life begin? With the primordial germ, from which all other forms of life have developed, as the evolutionists would have us believe, or were the great types of life outlined at the start? So far as the evidence from the rocks goes, the latter seems to have been the case. The nearest approach to the primordial germ found in the rocks is the so-called Eözoon Canadense, or dawn animal of Canada. Specimens of this animal are believed by some geologists to represent the remains of a gigantic foraminifer, an animal consisting simply of a jelly-like substance with a nucleus, and secreting a calcareous shell. The specimens show alternate layers of calcite and serpentine, the former of which are supposed to represent the shell of the animal, the latter, the space once occupied by its jelly-like substance. The fossil is found in the Laurentian gneisses or oldest of the stratified rocks, and if it can truly be regarded as representing the life of that period it indicates a very simple and humble beginning.

But most geologists hesitate to regard these structures as positively of animal origin, thinking that they are quite as probably wholly inorganic and have been produced by the separation of the mineral pyroxene into calcite and serpentine.

Aside from this no remains which can be positively regarded those of simple animals have been found, and when one passes in his study of the earth's history from that period which gives at best but doubtful evidences of life to that in which the existence of living things is unmistakable, he finds the new force in nature already firmly inaugurated, and the lines along which its energies are to be exerted indicated as the start. There can be little doubt, however, that this inability to trace back the diverging lines of life to their starting point is due to the imperfection of the geological record. The early animals probably secreted little mineral matter, and so left no trace of their existence. The wider study of pre-Cambrian rocks will undoubtedly bring to light more facts regarding early life, but its history, like that of the beginning of human history, is as yet involved in much obscurity. It is probably, therefore, a long time after the real beginning of life before the curtain rises upon a world in which lived representatives of six animal sub-kingdoms and of one class of plants, with nothing to indicate that one group of organisms had been longer in existence than another. These among plants include sea-weeds, and among animals sponges, corals, hydrozoans, echinoderms, brachiopods, mollusks, worms and crustaceans. There are delicate, moss-like markings called Oldhamia, which are remains of sea-weeds, rock tubes named Scolithus, which are borings made by worms forty millions of years ago, when the rock was mud. There are little blue shells found which are those of a brachiopod, Lingulepsis, and the outlines of pronged, jointed, segmented, sprawled, articulate creatures, varying in length from a fraction of an inch to two feet, which represent the deserted shelters of once gay and festive trilobites.

It may be well, at this point, to become acquainted with the trilobite, for it is one of the most distinctive types of early animal life and its remains occur in great abundance in Paleozoic rocks. It was an animal in some respects allied to the sowbug (that repulsive little crustacean which usually greets one who turns over a stone in a pasture), and in other respects to the king, or horseshoe crab. It derives its name of trilobite from the two furrows running lengthwise of the body, which divide it into three parts. In a direction at right angles to this, three divisions are also observable—the head, the thorax and the abdomen. The head was protected by a calcareous shield, parts of which were movable, and bore mouth parts and compound eyes. The eyes of some species are believed to have had as many as fifteen thousand facets. The thorax was made up of from two to twenty-six segments, usually movable one upon another, and enabling the animal to roll itself up like a hedgehog. On the under side were jointed legs and spiral gills. The segments of the abdomen, from two to twenty-eight in number, were fused together to form the tail, or pygidium, and probably bore appendages like the thorax.

The animal lived in mud flats or in shallow waters, much as modern crabs do, and crawled about on its jointed legs. Large slabs of sandstone occasionally found show trails left, probably by some of these animals as they crawled over the sand forty millions of years ago. They little knew how enduring would be the record of their wanderings.

The fossils from these early times indicate the existence of marine life only. It was a strange life, too, the forms in general differing widely from any which inhabit modern seas. There were grap-tolites—compound animals forming long stems with saw-toothed edges—whose remains look loke delicate quills and hence are called grap-tolites or writing stones. There were corals, not branching as do modern forms, but consisting of masses of parallel columns. These took principally the forms expressed by the names cup, chain, and honeycomb corals, by which they are commonly known. There were crinoids, remains of whose pear-shaped bodies, jointed stems and feathery arms are often found. There were brachiopods, animals having structures much like worms, but covered by bivalve shells. The shells are found in immense numbers in the rocks, and show how abundant the animals must have been in the early seas. There were mollusks, much like the modern snail and mussel, one genus of which, Pleurotomaria, has sent its descendants through the storms and cataclysms of many millions of years without being destroyed. If length of pedigree entitles to distinction, then this little sea snail surely outranks by many eras the proudest families of Europe.

The largest, and perhaps the strangest, of these early animals was the orthoceras, or straight shell. Its long, tapering shell, containing from ten to fifty chambers, sometimes reached a length of fifteen feet. As the animal occupied only the outer compartment, it is hard to see of what use its clumsy appendage could have been.

In all those early times there were no creatures with backbones. If they moved at all it was by crawling and squirming and carrying their houses about with them. The framework to which muscles could be attached was external, and hence little internal development of the body was possible. Such creatures were constantly hampered by their means of defense. It was a great improvement in life, therefore, when vertebrates were introduced. Their solid framework was within them, giving internal support and allowing alteration or enlargement as the demands of life might require. Hence the vertebrates after their introduction developed rapidly.

The next age, or Devonian, is known as the age of fishes, because of the abundance of these vertebrates. They were constructed on the old plan of external defense, and could not have been fitted for the quick, darting movements of modern fishes. Specimens of Bothriolepis, for instance, show mail-clad forelimbs extending backward from near the head. Others of these fishes had huge spines and teeth.

The lower forms of life of this age did not differ much from those of the Silurian. The introduction of the starfish is notable; also that of the first land plants.

Passing to the next age, the records which have been left in the rocks show it to have been an age of coal plants. The land has scarcely been inhabited before, but now it becomes clothed with dense forests and supports vast areas of vegetable life. As illustrated by specimens, the trees of these forests were the majectic prototypes of what are now some of our lowest and humblest plants. There were tree-ferns fifty or sixty feet in height, club-mosses or "ground-pines" four or five feet in diameter, and from sixty to ninety feet high; "horse-tails" or Equisetae, whose reed-like, hollow stems were thirty or forty feet high. There were also conifers, like the yews, the nuts called *trigono-carpum*, or three-angled fruit, representing their fruit. There were no flowering plants as yet, nor trees like those of modern forests. The wood of those days would have made poor fires, for it was soft and vascular. Yet by the accumulation of generation after generation of living forests, the carbon of their tissue was packed away in layers of considerable thickness in the form of coal. Thus Providence was preparing, ages before his advent, for the man that was to come. No stronger evidence of design in creation and of the preparation of the earth for man, rather than of man for the earth, can be presented, than that seen in the interpolation into the earth's history at this time of a period in which nine-tenths of all the workable coal of the earth was laid down.

The animal life of this period differed but little from that of previous ages. It was marked in the sea by the abundance of crinoids in bud-like plume-like forms, by columnar cup-corals such as Lithostrotion and by the introduction of echinoids like the modern sea urchin. The chain and honey-comb corals had become extinct and the trilobite and orthoceras nearly so. Animal life upon the land, too, was assuming considerable importance. Land shells were abundant, and there are found remains of insects. Tracks of a four-footed reptile, Sauropus, prove the existence of air-breathing vertebrates at this time. This one was probably an amphibian, living partly in the water and partly in the air. The air-breathing vertebrates had begun their career.

Thus briefly, have been traced the features of the Paleozoic era of the history of life. It was life of the character expressed by the term "Paleozoic"—ancient life. Few specimens of all these ancient forms survive at the present day, and so completely have most even of the types been obliterated from among the assemblage of living forms that it is hard to trace any resemblance between the one and the other. Hence by an acquaintance gained with the characteristic Paleozoic forms one may be able, by their very strangeness, to recognize at a glance the age of rocks which contain them. In regard to length of time, it should be noted that the Paleozoic era was four times as long as all the succeeding ages since the Archean. Atmospheric and physical conditions probably hindered rapid development of life, so that the ages which had passed had seen comparatively little progress. But as the air became purer and drier and the climatic conditions more equable, life, especially upon the land, diversified and advanced rapidly, and soon gave promise of the myriad forms which were later to inhabit the earth.

PAUL D'ENJOY'S MISSING LINK.

Recently there was an illustrated article published extensively in Europe and America, describing the discovery and capture of the missing link between man and the monkey, an Asiatic Moi, in the forests of India. An illustration accompanying the American condensation portrayed a perfect man, with a lengthy caudal formation and full beard. To the Marquis de Nadaillac, I am indebted for a further and remarkably different explanation than that contained either in the article as published in France or the American summarization. Through the politeness of Col. W. P. Clough, a translated extract of the French article, as published, and its refutation, remotely significant to the appearance of man upon the earth, is appended:

BULLETIN OF THE GEOGRAPHICAL SOCIETY, PARIS, 1895.

A VISIT TO THE MOIS BY PAUL D'ENJOY, PROCURER OF THE FRENCH REPUBLIC AT BAC-LIEU, COCHIN-CHINA.

Extract.

At last, we reached a Moi village, standing in an opening (in the forest). A long tunnel, made of stakes joined at the tops, as the legs the letter A, thatched with dried leaves, formed the solitary dwelling of the village. The tunnel was easily fifty meters long, one meter high, and two meters broad at the base of the triangle. The entrance was at one end, and the exit at the other. At the sight of us, great shouts went up from children who were capering in the grass. A multitude of strange creatures, naked, grinning, disheveled, rushed out of the tunnel and fled into the woods, bounding like a band of apes. Upon a big tree, at whose foot we had halted in surprise, a Moi was gathering honey. At the sound of the cries uttered by his companions, the savage climbed down swiftly, putting his feet upon wooden pins that he had driven into the tree to enable him more easily to ascend it. At five meters from the ground he jumped down like a cat, and precipitated himself upon us, head down, hoping to break our circle. But the effort was vain. We held the captive. At once, upon the flight of the Moi, we installed ourselves in the abandoned village. I visited the tunnel. It was deserted. Some polished stones, bamboo pipes, copper bracelets, pearl necklaces, lay upon the ground. I returned to our captive and caused him to be questioned. He remained dumb. We made advances, but he answered not. It occurred to me to give him a little liberty, keeping him under close watch. At once he began to talk. In a calm tone, he explained to us, that the village occupied by us belonged to the Leos, a brave and warlike tribe. He added, that though his companions had flown at our appearance, it had not been from cowardice, but because they had believed themselves to have seen, in my person, the moon-bodied demon who carries people off into the recesses of the swamps. My colonial costume of white cloth had caused all the fright of those invincible warriors. Like the Mois imprisoned at Bien-Hoa, our captive had enormous ankle bones, pointed as the spurs of a cock. His skin was brown, but rather tanned than black; his voice harsh;

his face oval; his nose prolonged; his hair straight. Thin; tall; his
limbs strongly knit; head carried high—he appeared a bronze statue.
But he had a tail, like a monkey. The discovery stupified me. I drew
near to him, and in order to be sure that I was not the sport of an illu-
sion, I felt the savage's caudal appendix. In this way I ascertained
that the vertebral column of the Moi extended beyond the body, with
three or four vertebræ, so as to form a small deer tail.

"That proves my purity of race," said he. "The Mois born from
unions contracted with strangers no longer have the tail. Also, with
each generation the tail becomes more infrequent; the pride less im-
movable. Our decadence dates from the day when our king, whose
tail was three cubits long, was chased from the rich plains, bathed with
rivers of gold, that our ancestors tilled. The forests are untilled; but
they are free." As he proceeded, he warmed up. Suddenly he gave a
savage cry, which echoed in the woods: "O-e-o!" Afterwards, he began
to weep; and finally, with a monotonous voice, broken with sobs, he re-
cited a long poem. That cry, the burning tears, which preceded the recitation, as also the sighs which went up from him, were, without any
doubt, an integral part of the poem. In the midst of those woods
which the winds caused to resound as an organ, at the foot of the
abandoned village, in the center of the squatting Annamites, the Moi
was truly imposing. His voice, sonorous and grave, his grand, frightened gestures, his handsome black eyes lifted toward heaven, and
moistened with tears, gave to his strange recitation an accent extra-
ordinarily attractive. Unluckily, the Annamite who served me as interpreter was not up to his task. I regretted this, but had to be content.

The poem, so vigorously spoken and gestured by the Moi, narrated,
it seems, about a king, agile as a monkey, whose retainers struck down
their enemies with their powerful tails. Demons, with faces round like
the moon (were they the Annamite invaders?)' had one day descended
upon their country, and, armed with thunder, driven the Mois before
them. Defeated, hunted, exterminated, the inhabitants fled to the forests of the East, preferring misery to slavery. This is all my inex-
perienced interpreter could translate.

Invited to drink, after his recital, our prisoner declined.

"Water distills the fever," said he.

In vain we asserted the excellence of our water, that we had carefully brought from our own country, to avoid the need of drinking the
waters flowing in the forest. The Moi persisted, and sucked the juice of
a plant.

Neither wine, liqueur, nor rice spirits tempted him.

"What do you understand the fever to be?" I asked.

"It is the plague of which they die who invade our forests," he
answered.

"Do you never suffer from it yourselves?"

"Sometimes, but we have a remedy that cuts it instantly."

"And what is that remedy?"

"A plant, like that which I have; but of a different species."

"Could you point it out to me?"

"To-morrow," said the Moi, laughing.

I remarked that laugh, which I took for a gratification of pride. I
was deceived; the next morning the Moi had disappeared; his guard
had delirium and fever, and vomited copiously. In a rational interval,
he related that the prisoner had invited him to taste the sap of a plant
that had fallen from a neighboring tree. "This gives strength," the
savage had said; and the simpleton took the captive's word. "The
Moi are too stupid to know how to lie," say the Annamites. Overcome
by sleep, immediately after having sucked the juice, the guard became
stupified, and when aroused fell into complete prostration. I tried to

give him a dose of quinine, but the sick man was unable to retain it. Frightened at his condition, I immediately decided to return to Bien-Hoa, where we arrived four days later. I have decided to return to those regions for an exploration of several weeks, but circumstances have not yet permitted me to carry out my plans.

PARIS, 18 Rue Duphot, 21 January, 1896.

Dear Sir: I delayed a few days answering your letter of December 27th to get accurate information on the article published in the "Bulletin of the Société de Geographie," which I forward per this same mail. I inclose under this letter one from M de Bizemont, secretary of the society, and another from M. Lefevre Dantalie, who has been secretary of our legation in Siam and has traveled long in the country of the Mois. These letters tell their own story. I will only add that the tailed man did not make any sensation here. It was never communicated to any of our learned societies, and the editor of the "Bulletin" I send you is much blamed for having published it without more information. M. de'Enjoy may have met a tailed man, a *lusus naturæ* [a pronounced monstrosity], as a hunchback, for instance, but the finding of a Moi with a tail (if the fact even is true) cannot bring the conclusion that all his countrymen possess this appendix. When I was prefect Basses Pyrenees, I presided at the military conscription. A man came before us with a caudal appendix two inches long. It was noted by the scientists as a case of malformation. It would be very strange, in the theories of evolution, that the Simians of the old continent, who never have a prehensile tail, should beget men with one!

I am sure your account of your explorations in the Rocky Mountains will be of the same interest as your preceding writings. All the vast past of America, so oddly called the "New Continent," when it is probably the oldest in existence, is most important for the history of man.

I am always at your disposal for any inquiries in this part of the world, and beg to subscribe myself,   Faithfully,

NADAILLAC.

PARIS, 17 January, 1896.

MONSIEUR LE MARQUIS:

Since I have received it, I have been much busied with the subject, so entertaining, of your letter of 13th January, and have spoken about it with several of my colleagues of the Geographical Society; Mannois, Grandidier, Dr. Hamy, De Laffrent.

The result of their opinions, quite concordant, in substance is, that the instance cited by M. D'Enjoy may be real; but that it constitutes a personal anomaly, and not a trait common to a tribe or race. Dr. Hamy, in particular, has said to me, that frequent similar cases have been observed, here and there, which have been mentioned in the works of Geoffrey Saint-Hilaire. It is more than possible that the valiant M. D'Enjoy has concluded a little too hastily from the particular to the general, and has allowed himself to be led into error, either by the native individual with the caudal appendix or by his interpreter. However that may be, for the purpose of clearing the matter up, M. Mannois proposes writing to M. D'Enjoy, to invite him to complete his observations and inquire in a way to bring the subject to a certainty. He also wrote Dr. Yasin, who, for four years has dwelt with the different tribes of Mois in the north part of Cochin-China, to study them; and called his attention to this subject. This is as much as I can say upon the affair

—quite wearisome, on the whole, because it has attracted the attention of foreign societies to an article in our bulletin, that might be taken seriously.

Please give my respectful homage, and the best remembrance of my wife, to Madame de Nadaillac, and believe me,

Your much devoted,

CTE. DE BIZEMONT.

3 RUE MONTALIVET, 13 January, 1896.

Monsieur: I should have been happy, not with reference to defense of dogma, but for amusement, to have met, beyond the seas, some one of those strange creatures, furnished with caudal appendix, from which it is so strenuously sought to make us descend. Unfortunately, I have never done so; and the Mois that I have often met in my journeys have not, from this special point of view, anything to offer us. I know that the Chinese and Annamites, who despise every other race than their own, have written or told singular tales concerning those they view as savages; but these stories merit no more credence than those most extravagant things that we relate about the Chinese themselves. The magistrate who has constituted himself the reporter of these fancies has merely copied the statement of some native. I cannot attach any credit to the pretended commission of the Geographic Society. Perhaps he has met, at Boc Lieu, some specimen of those monsters sometimes seen at shows. Did not the Siamese twins come out of Indo-China? All I can say is, that the picture, all imaginary, that Madame de Nadaillac has obligingly shown me to-day, has nothing whatever in common with photographs of Mois and Khas that I, myself, have given her. No resemblance can be found between these Asiatics and the type, essentially European, reproduced in the engraving. The forest hut that is made to appear his shelter, scarcely resembles the habitations, built on piles, common among the inhabitants of the interior; which I have permitted myself, with much indiscretion, to describe at length to-day, in Duphat street.

Please excuse me, with Madame Nadaillac, for her precious time that I have consumed in this matter, and accept the expression of my most respectful and devoted sentiments.

PIERRE LEFEVRE DAUTALIE.

WILLIAM MORRISON

At Itasca Lake, 1803.

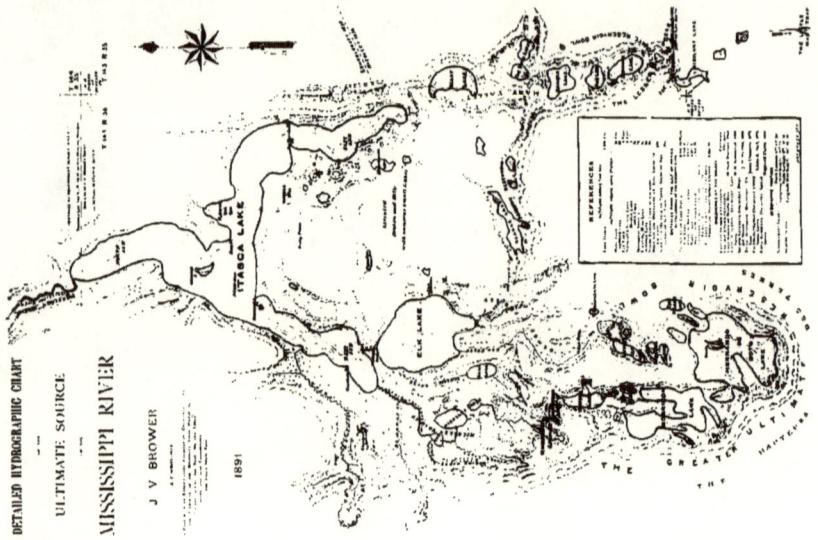

DETAILED HYDROGRAPHIC CHART

ULTIMATE SOURCE

MISSISSIPPI RIVER

J V BROWER

1891

THE SOURCE OF THE MISSISSIPPI. 1.

STATE OF MINNESOTA, ITASCA STATE PARK,
COMMISSIONER'S OFFICE,
ST. PAUL, MINN., Aug. 13, 1891.

His Excellency, William R. Merriam, Governor of Minnesota,

SIR: I have the honor to acknowledge the receipt of your favor of the third instant, requesting me to report to your department any facts in my possession, as commissioner of the Itasca State Park, or otherwise, descriptive of the hydographic and other features of the Itasca Basin, authorized by law to be set apart as a public park, to the end that facts regarding the ultimate source of the Mississippi river may be established and published.

During the year 1880, as a special commissioner of the Minnesota Historical society, a coördinate branch of the state government, I made a detailed hydrographic survey of the source of our great river, and formulated an exhaustive report thereon, which has not as yet been published.[2]

From the field notes then taken, the correspondence, and all examinations and researches made, I have the honor to report the following facts for the use of the executive department of Minnesota.

The drainage basin of the Mississippi river extends from the Gulf of Mexico, at the mouth of the river, to an ultimate limit above and beyond Itasca lake in this state. This great basin, more than 1,000,000 square miles in extent, is bordered on the east by the Alleghany and other ranges, and on the west by the Rocky Mountains, and contains about 100,000 rivers and streams, which flow toward and finally discharge their waters into the Mississippi, principally through the mouths of the larger and more important confluent and affluent tributary rivers. These waters are entirely supplied by the copious precipitation characteristic of the fertile basin drained from north to south by the Mississippi, as its principal and most important river.

To follow the proper rule in ascertaining, under commission, the true and actual source of this principal river, for geographic purposes, I consulted European and American geographers, scientists, and authorities, gaining the following varied information as to what constituted the source of a river:

"That the main stream of a river is that which flows along the lowest depression of the basin, and that a tributary which descends into it from a higher elevation, even if longer, is not to be considered the main stream."

"A river cannot have a source, but many sources."

"All our rivers have their sources in the clouds."

(This authority does not say that the clouds emanate from the oceans of the earth, or whence came the oceans.)

"The head of the longest continuous channel."

---

[1] Reprint from official reports.
[2] Published by the State of Minnesota in 1893.

"The sources of a river which are in a right line with its mouth, particularly when they issue from a cardinal point and flow to the one directly opposite."

Other authorities, some remote, and but a few reliable, suggest that the source must be a lake; must be the largest lake; should be the inner flanks of the heights of the land surrounding it; should be the source, because it was next to the historic pass, by which one river had, from ancient times, been left to reach another; because it was farthest from the mouth of the system; because it led down to the axis of the general valley of the basin; because it was at the head of the stream of largest volume; because it was geologically oldest, etc.

This widespread variance of authorities, good, bad, and indifferent, gave me but little comfort in an interesting geographic and historic research, the source of no two principal rivers of the world being alike, and I arbitrarily adopted a reliable rule of no uncertainty—a rule of nature—in ascertaining where the waters were gathered which form the ultimate source of the Mississippi, and for that purpose the length of the main river in statute miles up through the valley of the basin, was ascertained from the official records of the United States government and otherwise, with the following result:

	Miles.
From Gulf of Mexico, at the southwest pass, up the channel of the river to city of New Orleans	111.00
From city of New Orleans to mouth of Ohio river	965.50
From mouth of Ohio river to city of St. Louis	182.00
From city of St. Louis to city of St. Paul	728.75
From city of St. Paul to Falls of St. Anthony	13.00
From Falls of St. Anthony to Winnibigoshish lake	432.50
From Winnibigoshish to range 36 west of fifth principal meridian*	96.50
From range 36 west of fifth principal meridan to foot of Itasca lake	17.27
Total	2,546.52

Thus it appeared that the main river of the Mississippi Basin extends from the Gulf of Mexico to the Itasca Basin, a limited, permanent depression upon the surface of the earth at the ultimate source of the river.

The geologic and natural features predicating this conclusion are so well known and established that no reference to them seems necessary in this communication, excepting the possibility that the Missouri river, remotely suggested by occasional inquirers, might be called the main river; but inasmuch as it is a confluent branch of the main stream coming in at one side, similar to the Ohio and Red rivers, I see no good reason for discussing that question at this time, nor do I deem it necessary to follow the historic data, however interesting, which has brought to our notice and knowledge the existence of the main river extending from the Gulf to the Itasca Basin, where it takes its rise, for there can be no well-founded disagreement as to that fact, because the discovery of the Mississippi, by piecemeal, is co-extensive with the discovery of the coast line of North America, and the facts are indisputable, in consequence of which I must base my reply to your executive communication upon the facts as they have been found to exist at and above Itasca lake, which has been for so many years recognized as the true source. To definitely determine those facts it became my official duty to ascertain whence came the waters of Itasca lake. This required a line of levels in the field with the following results, to ascertain elevations above the sea:

---

*(The official surveys of the United States extend, upon the main river, only to the point where range 36 west of the fifth principal meridian intersects the channel of the river to and beyond Itasca lake. The fractional miles are taken from the record as it exists.)

	Feet.
Gulf of Mexico	0.0
City of St. Louis, above the sea	384.8
City of St. Paul	680.5
Above Falls of St. Anthony (Minneapolis)	782.0
Below Pokegama Falls	1,248.0
Winnibigoshish lake	1,292.8
Cass Lake	1,302.8
Itasca lake	1,457.0

The official reports of the United States government give the elevations to and including Cass lake, and an actual line of levels across the country from the railroad system of this state to Itasca lake, run by me in 1889, demonstrated its actual elevation above the sea at its outlet. The railway levels connect with the government levels.

With the distances and elevations thus ascertained, my survey of the ultimate source of the Mississippi river commenced in March, 1889, upon the frozen surface of Itasca lake, at the center of the channel of the river, at its *debouchure* from the extreme north end of the lake.

At a remote age the Itasca Basin was the bed of one lake, now extinct, which I deem it a privilege to designate as Lake Upham, and from this one lake of unknown ages, by erosion, the waters, probably having been increased by copious precipitation, cut their way through the ice formation and alluvial stratum to a natural condition of the river bed as it now exists, immediately below Itasca lake. This process of nature (the waters passing to lower levels) has given us nearly one hundred lakes and lakelets within the Itasca Basin, systematically divided apart, each of a different elevation, up the inner flanks of the Hauteur de Terre, surrounding the whole, from the summits of which the waters are returned to the oceans, through Hudson's bay and the Gulf of Mexico, the Itasca Basin itself being about seven miles long and five in width, and subsidiary to the main Basin of the Mississippi.

The formation of Itasca lake is a small body of water at and around Schoolcraft island, and three long, narrow arms projecting,—one to the southeast; one to the southwest, and one to the north,—from the last of which the Mississippi passes out from the lake. From the southeast and southwest extremities of the lake picturesque valleys extend, denominated Mary Valley and Nicollet Valley, respectively, and up these valleys numerous lakes exist, each at a higher elevation, as you pass up the respective valleys, than the one below, and each valley is drained by a running stream of perennial flowage, while at the side of the west arm Elk lake is situated, connected with Itasca by Chambers creek.

Lines of measurements and of levels were run to and up through each of these localities.

The distances are as follows:

	Feet.
From the outlet of Itasca to the extreme southeast point at the mouth of Mary creek	22,639
Up the channel of Mary creek to Mary lake	3,658
Total	26,297

From the outlet of Itasca to the extreme southwest point at the mouth of Nicollet's Infant Mississippi	17,926
Thence up the channel to Nicollet's Middle lake	8,513
Total	26,439

From the outlet of Itasca to the mouth of Boutwell creek	13,627
Length of Boutwell creek	8,700
Total	22,327

17

MOUTH OF NICOLLET'S INFANT MISSISSIPPI. ITASCA LAKE IN THE DISTANCE.

MOUTH OF CHAMBERS CREEK. ELK TO ITASCA LAKE.

From the outlet of Itasca to the mouth of Elk creek...................... 16,727
Up the channel of Chambers creek to Elk lake........ .... 1.100

Total 17,827

These are the only streams entering Itasca lake worthy of any consideration. The volume of water, width, depth, and flowage of these several streams was carefully ascertained, and the largest and most important one, at all times they have been examined by me, in 1888, 1889, and 1891. Nicollet's Infant Mississippi river, has been found to be the largest in volume of water and the larger and more important in every particular, with several perennial branches augmenting its prominence above the southwest limit of Itasca lake, where it discharges its waters into the lowest in point of elevation of the several lakes there situated.

Selecting Mary Valley and Nicollet Valley as the two most remote water sheds within the Mississippi Basin, the ordinary rules of hydrography were applied, and it was found that Mary Valley contained the Lesser Ultimate Reservoir and Nicollet Valley the Greater Ultimate Reservoir of the Mississippi system, each separate and distinct, drained by natural surface flowage. Then came the application of nature's common rule as to whence came the waters supplying the streams draining these two ultimate water systems at the source of the Mississippi.

It having been found that Nicollet Valley contained the more important reservoir, supplying to Itasca lake the larger and the longer volume of surface flowage, I beg your indulgence in a minute description of this most remote ultimate system in the great Mississippi Basin, situated within the state park.

The perennial stream flowing down the inner flanks of the Hauteur de Terre to Itasca through Nicollet Valley was discovered by Jean N. Nicollet in 1836. At the point where its waters flow into Itasca lake it was forty feet in width and two feet in depth at the date of my survey. Narrowing as you ascend the stream, it becomes three feet in depth a short distance from Itasca lake, with an increased current.

Passing up this interesting stream the explorer is impressed with its importance by its sharply defined banks, with its winding, meandering channel, deeply cut down into the stratum to a sandy, gravelly bed, with every appearance and characteristic of the Mississippi below Itasca lake. It has sandbars, sharp angles in its channel, deep and shallowing currents, and all the more striking features of a larger river. Large trees found near its banks incline toward the stream; a variety of fish, large and small, were found in its waters; the mink, otter, and muskrat abounded, and wild ducks of many Northern varieties were from time to time noticed in its channel. Trees have been felled in several places across its banks to permit of passage on foot. Upon the removal of these trees, canoes might be propelled nearly two miles up this principal channel from Itasca lake.

These are a portion of the characteristics of the stream, indicating its permanency and importance, and, what is true of no other stream within the state park, it has three affluent branches flowing in from the heights of land to the westward, which augment its importance and permanency above any other stream found there.

These are Demaray creek, over one mile in length, Howard creek, nearly one mile in length, and Spring Ridge creek, each fed by numerous springs, sharply indicating artesian pressure from the lakes higher up the flank of the Itasca moraine. At Nicollet's Middle lake is found the northern limit of the Greater Ultimate Reservoir, with the Mississippi flowing out from it toward Itasca lake.

My lines of levels and measurements were continued from this point up through the trough of the reservoir to Nicollet's Upper lake of doubtful existence, to the Mississippi Springs, Floating Moss lake, Whipple lake, the Triplet lakes, Morrison lake, and Hernando De Soto lake, the last named being the most elevated and distant water from the Gulf of Mexico within the Mississippi Basin, exclusive of waters emanating from the summit of the Rocky Mountains at the source of the Missouri.

Elevations above the sea at the Greater Ultimate Reservoir are as follows:*

	Feet.
Nicollet's Lower lake	1,473
Nicollet's Middle lake	1,474
Nicollet's Upper lake	1,500
Mississippi Springs	1,548
Floating Moss lake	1,561
Whipple lake	1,564
The Triplet lakes	1,568
Morrison lake	1,571
Hernando De Soto Lake	1,571
Summits of Hauteur de Terre	1,670

The summits of Hauteur de Terre (heights of land), immediately west of Hernando De Soto lake, divide the ultimate waters of the Mississippi from those of the Red River of the North.

The first surface flowage in the Greater Ultimate Reservoir is a tiny brook connecting Whipple lake with Floating Moss lake. Down the incline from Floating Moss lake the Mississippi Springs sends forth a surface channel to Nicollet's Upper lake, while 300 feet west and twenty feet lower the channel again appears in a continuous surface flowage to Itasca lake, which is 9,200 feet to the north. It might be well to mention the fact that the head of Howard creek, a small picturesque little stream, with several miniature waterfalls, in connection with the Infant Mississippi, constitutes the longest surface channel shown as follows:

	Feet.	Miles.
Gulf of Mexico to Itasca lake		2,546.52
Thence to the mouth of Nicollet's Infant Mississippi	17,926	
Thence to head of Howard creek	11,126	
	29,052	5.50
From Gulf to head of Howard creek		2,552.02

Other channel distances are:

From Gulf to head of Mary creek	2,551.50
From Gulf to head of Boutwell creek	2,550.74
From Gulf to Elk lake	2,549.90
From Gulf to extreme limit of the Greater Ultimate Reservoir it is	2,555.25
From Gulf to the extreme limit of the Lesser Ultimate Reservoir it is	2,553.47

The great river having now been actually measured in its entire channel length by connecting surveys, the distances given, for the first time, are certainly more accurate than mere guess work.

Since the Greater Ultimate Reservoir is the extreme limit of the Mississippi Basin, and the largest, longest, and most important stream above Itasca lake takes its rise therein as a perennial surface drainage, I have reported the same to the Historical Society as the ultimate source of the Mississippi.

ELK LAKE AND ITS DISCOVERY.

In 1836 the scientist and astronomer, Nicollet, laid down Elk lake as an estuary of Itasca, but since that time the alluvial stratum at the

*Corrected by a supplemental line of levels in December, 1891.

outlet of Itasca has been diminished by the constant flow of the water current until the latter lake has receded from the former to a lower level, and the two lakes are now connected by a short creek. The original discovery of this creek and of Elk lake must be awarded to Julius Chambers, who on the 9th of June, 1872, while encamped on Schoolcraft island, explored the shores of Itasca, passed up the channel of Chambers creek in his canoe to Elk lake, crossed to the southern shore of the lake, and, making a map of the lake, wrote: "Here, then, is the source of the longest river in the world,—in a small lake, scarcely a quarter of a mile in diameter, in the midst of a floating bog, the fountains which give birth to the Mississippi." He found the lake much larger than he at first supposed. The world was notified by Mr. Chambers of his discovery in the columns of the New York *Herald*, page 8, July 6, 1872.

Mr. Chambers then passed down the Mississippi, from Schoolcraft island to the Gulf of Mexico, in his canoe.

The next explorer to declare Elk lake the source was A. H. Siegfried, who, on the thirteenth day of July, 1879, reached the lake, and, taking a photograph of the same, declared it to be the "highest tributary to the Mississippi," in the columns of the Louisville *Courier Journal*, August, 1879.

The lake and creek were also visited in 1875 by Edwin S. Hall, in 1880 by O. E. Garrison, and in 1881 by Rev. J. A. Gilfillan. Whatever significance may attach to Elk lake as the source, Mr. Chambers must be awarded the honor of a first and original discovery, to the exclusion of all others, except Indians, known in our history, and the name "Elk," officially promulgated by the authorities of the United States, is the proper and legitimate name for this body of water, acquiesced in by legislative enactment, and Chambers creek takes its name from its discoverer. No one of the several brooks flowing into Elk lake are of any great importance, and all of them were completely closed with ice in March, 1889, and all of them were dry in August of the same year.

Geographic discoveries at and above Itasca lake prior to my survey in 1889, of authentic record, worthy of consideration and belief, are as follows:

ELK LAKE AND ITS DISCOVERY.

William Morrison, first of white men..................................... 1803
H. R. Schoolcraft, Itasca lake... 1832
Jean N. Nicollet, five inlets.. 1836
Julius Chambers, *Elk lake and creek..................................... 1872
E. S. Hall, government survey.. 1875
Hopewell Clark, special survey... 1886

Itasca lake is at the lowest depression of the basin, and Hernando de Soto, Morrison, and numerous other lakes, are at the summit of the basin, and the water pressure from the lakes above Itasca (the whole being exclusively supplied by precipitation) causes a contributory inflow into Itasca lake, which is increased or decreased from time to time, according to the quantity of rainfall or duration of drought, as either may prevail.

One peculiar significance is demonstrated by the fact that Itasca lake has a flood plain of but little more than three feet in elevation above the natural surface of the lake. The flood plains of the lakes

(*Elk lake and creek, discovered by Mr. Chambers in 1872, are constituted of waters erroneously claimed to have been discovered in 1881 by the person referred to in your communication.)

higher up are ten, fifteen, and twenty feet. Thus, while Itasca lake is always supplied and sometimes rises during dry weather, the lakes at the summit dry down rapidly to a lesser surface area, depending upon rainfall to resupply them. During the summer of 1890 copious rainfall caused Lake Itasca to rise a foot or more above Elk lake, and Chambers creek flowed into, instead of out from, Elk lake. The outflow of Lake Pepin, through which the Mississippi takes its course, is controlled by the inflow, and Lake Itasca presents a striking similarity.

Infinitesimal deductions are necessarily drawn, however, from ascertained facts in order to discover the location of the ultimate source. Itasca lake lies at the pit of the basin and receives the waters discharged into it from summits surrounding it, which in return pass out into the channel below, forming the main water course of our country to the Gulf. Consequent inferences may, therefore, be drawn by those who still believe that Itasca lake is the source of the river, it being situated at the pit of the lowest depression of the limited Itasca Basin, but I know it to be a fact that there is a Greater Ultimate Reservoir there at the summit, and it constitutes the ultimate source.

To prevent unauthorized, erroneous, and deceptive changes in our state map, I suggest that a *resumé* of the historical and geographical facts which led up to the final determination to locate the state park at the source of our great river be included in my forthcoming report, and then, by legislative enactment, prohibit, within our own state, the illicit changes in the state map so assiduously persisted in from mercenary motives.

The law requires me to report a detailed chart of the park, and topographic field notes for that purpose will be completed in due time.

Very respectfully, your obedient servant,

J. V. BROWER.
Commissioner.

MOST NORTHERN ISLAND IN THE MISSISSIPPI RIVER.

DESTRUCTION OF THE BROWER COLLECTION.

(Morning after the fire.)

Photo by Dickey, St. Paul.

CONDENSED MEMORANDUM.

List of maps, MSS, photographs, archæologic material, and effects, belonging to the author of this work, which, with the library and furnishings, were destroyed by fire, Dec. 19, 1896:

Number.

Maps, charts, drawings, sketches, and all notations............. 1,300
Charts prepared for this book; omitted....................... 500
Books, pamphlets, atlases, reports, magazines and public documents 2,600
Ethnologic, geographic, scenic, and personal photographs........ 1,100
All negatives preserved....................................... 850
Archæologic chipped stone implements, about.................. 5,200
New catalogue of same, was under preparation................. 1
All field books, of every kind and nature, about.............. 80
Entire set of field instruments and paraphernalia.............. 25
Grips filled with a complete camping outfit................... 6
Telescope cases filled with all manner of accumulations......... 36
Engraving and drafting material, complete set................. 100

Various and miscellaneous manuscripts, of all kinds.

Every letter, document, communication, clipping, report, and memorandum relating to the Source of the Mississippi, and the Utmost Waters of the Missouri, from which two volumes had been prepared; voluminous and numerous.

A package containing manuscripts, charts, notes, photographs, letters, clippings, engravings and material for a history of the Sibley Expedition against the Sioux Indians in Dakota, in 1863, from Fort Ridgely to the Missouri river.

Library and office furniture, effects, and cases.

Personal belongings, material and effects.

Honorable discharge papers from the Volunteer Army, and United States Navy, 1862-65.

Various official commissions, expired, state and national.

An interior civil warrant on the treasurer of the United States, for seven cents, in settlement of my accounts with the Interior Department, and preserved as a souvenir.

The value of the articles and material destroyed was inestimable and unascertainable, either from a personal or historical standpoint.

The greater portion of the articles lost cannot be replaced

SCHOOLCRAFT ISLAND, ITASCA LAKE.

INDEX.

www.ingramcontent.com/pod-product-compliance
Lightning Source LLC
Chambersburg PA
CBHW030357270326
41926CB00009B/1141